Conceptual Drawing

Joseph A. Koncelik & Kevin Reeder

Conceptual Drawing

Joseph A. Koncelik & Kevin Reeder

Freehand Drawing & Design Visualization for Design Professions

DELMAR
CENGAGE Learning

Australia • Brazil • Japan • Korea • Mexico • Singapore • Spain • United Kingdom • United States

Conceptual Drawing: Free-Hand Drawing & Design Visualization for Design Professions
by Joseph A. Koncelik & Kevin Reeder

Vice President, Technology and Trades ABU: David Garza

Director of Learning Solutions: Sandy Clark

Managing Editor: Larry Main

Senior Acquisitions Editor: James Gish

Product Manager: Nicole Calisi

Editorial Assistant: Sarah Timm

Marketing Director: Deborah Yarnell

Marketing Manager: Jonathan Sheehan

Marketing Specialist: Victoria Ortiz

Production Manager: Stacy Masucci

Content Project Manager: Andrea Majot

Technology Project Manager: Chris Catalina

Cover Image: Brian Lawrence

For product information and technology assistance, contact us at
Cengage Learning Customer & Sales Support, 1-800-354-9706
For permission to use material from this text or product, submit all requests online at
www.cengage.com/permissions Further permissions questions can be emailed to
permissionrequest@cengage.com

ExamView® and ExamView Pro® are registered trademarks of FSCreations, Inc. Windows is a registered trademark of the Microsoft Corporation used herein under license. Macintosh and Power Macintosh are registered trademarks of Apple Computer, Inc. Used herein under license.

© 2008 Cengage Learning. All Rights Reserved. Cengage Learning WebTutor™ is a trademark of Cengage Learning.

Library of Congress Control Number: 2007942015

ISBN-13: 9781418080976

ISBN-10: 1418080977

Delmar Cengage Learning
5 Maxwell Drive
Clifton Park, NY 12065-2919
USA

Cengage Learning products are represented in Canada by Nelson Education, Ltd.

For your lifelong learning solutions, visit **delmar.cengage.com**

Visit our corporate website at **cengage.com**

Notice to the Reader
Publisher does not warrant or guarantee any of the products described herein or perform any independent analysis in connection with any of the product information contained herein. Publisher does not assume, and expressly disclaims, any obligation to obtain and include information other than that provided to it by the manufacturer. The reader is expressly warned to consider and adopt all safety precautions that might be indicated by the activities described herein and to avoid all potential hazards. By following the instructions contained herein, the reader willingly assumes all risks in connection with such instructions. The publisher makes no representations or warranties of any kind, including but not limited to, the warranties of fitness for particular purpose or merchantability, nor are any such representations implied with respect to the material set forth herein, and the publisher takes no responsibility with respect to such material. The publisher shall not be liable for any special, consequential, or exemplary damages resulting, in whole or part, from the readers' use of, or reliance upon, this material.

Printed in Canada
1 2 3 XX 09 08 07

Contents

Chapter 1
**The Fundamentals of Conceptual
  Drawing 1**

Chapter 2
**Using Perspective in Conceptual
  Drawing 52**

Chapter 3
Developing Three-Dimensional Form 72

Chapter 4
**Conventions for Lighting and Surface
  Delineation 96**

Chapter 5
Human Scale and Context 129

Chapter 6
Interior Conceptual Drawing 159

Chapter 7
Presentation and Communication 190

Chapter 8
Hybrid Conceptual Drawings 238

Introduction

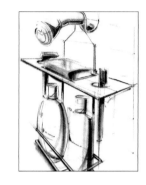

T he premise of this text is that educating designers in the skill set of conceptual drawing in specific and design visualization in general derives from the visual arts as a method for visual thinking. However, this critical aspect of design process has become, in the contemporary environment of design professions, an essential communication skill.

Second, the educational environment has changed regarding where the largest number of academic design programs is developing in the twenty-first century. The largest programs are flourishing in major universities such as: Arizona State University, The Ohio State University, North Carolina State University, Georgia Institute of Technology, Auburn University, and the University of Illinois, among several others. Third, the student profile—the characteristics of students matriculating in design—is different from their predecessors, who came through highly selective college-arts programs. The contemporary design student is far more broadly educated and oriented in terms of career paths, but far less prepared for studying the environment and skills of the arts. The twenty-first century design student may see design education in a more general context, fitting it with other career goals. To educate students effectively in the skills of conceptual drawing, it is critical to understand what the student brings to the classroom in terms of background, preparation, and goal orientation.

In 1960, just over 2,000 institutions offered degrees and had about half the number of stu-

dents now enrolled and matriculating in colleges and universities. Any business of this magnitude that could double in size while *exceeding* inflation with rises in costs to the consumer has something akin to divine guidance and blessedness. In the past ten years, higher education has seen tuition hikes that are in the range of 50 percent. Even with these measures of success, the fields where education markets their offerings are still growing. The potential for expanding the business of education seems boundless. The NCES reports that among the 30 majors tracked, programs in the visual and performing arts rank sixth among all programs in terms of growth—an astounding level of expansion.

Also according to the NCES, 47 percent of all of the colleges and universities in operation *have only eleven percent* of the 15 to 17 million students (depending on which statistics one uses) matriculating on their campuses. These are the smallest institutions that may have a few hundred upward to 2500 students. These statistics include the renowned college art and design programs. The numbers of people currently matriculating in college is decidedly skewed toward the largest universities with 11 percent of all students going to just 35 institutions—with undergraduate and graduate populations of over 30,000. The statistics demonstrate that students enter universities with expectations of choosing and following whatever educational path to which they may become attracted. These rather universal desires and expectations affect perceptions of university-based design programs as well as the smaller college arts programs that must compete in a diverse educational environment.

Student enrollments are critical to income. Numbers are part of the argument of mission and purpose. Educating more people has been the drive of the largest institutions—with most institutions increasing the total number of students every year. For the last four decades, proportional growth has been in double digits virtually every decade with the exception of a slight flattening of the curve in the early 1990s. Nevertheless, growth has largely been continuous—in spite of fears arising in the mid-1970s regarding the potential decline in college-ready students. A greater percentage high school graduates go on to college than had gone in previous years. Increases have also come in the number of women attending what were once traditionally male-dominated professional fields such as the sciences, engineering, and medicine. Industrial design programs, traditionally all-male with a small influx of women, have seen enrollments of women increase markedly. Some industrial design programs have student enrollments that are 30 to 40 percent women.

Design instruction, the educational environment for design education and the recipients of that education—the contemporary students matriculating in design programs—have all changed profoundly over the last three decades. Both the teaching methodology of design instruction in general and content of drawing classes (the focus of this text) have evolved over time; but there has been no corresponding revolutionary change to respond to a new set of social environmental conditions now existing in design education. The bigger issues of a total curriculum change must be a subject for another text at another time. This text seeks to tackle only part of the need for change— that being the instruction of visualization through drawing. The basic objective of drawing in design professions is communication and is at the core of the approach in all instruction in all design programs. It is fundamental to what instructors hope to achieve through the cooperation and diligence of students of drawing. Therefore, the first chapter begins with rudimentary and preparatory guidance—not just drawing fundamentals—about preparing to draw. Such guidance is essential for students for whom drawing is not a form of second language.

Regarding the higher levels of enrollment in private art colleges, the largest numbers of those traditionally offering specialized visual arts programs are among the majority of institutions, but they enroll a small percentage of the college population that ultimately seeks visual arts and design programs. In fact, students entering large universities, mostly state-assisted institutions, make up the largest aggregate of students entering visual arts programs. They gravitate toward visual arts programs some time *after* admission. No single reason emerges for the changes of mind and heart that compel students to seek visual arts and design. Nevertheless, they enroll in ever-increasing numbers, sometimes without assessing their capabilities and aptitude for the courses of study to which they have been attracted.

In 1973, the Industrial Designers Society of America (IDSA) recognized 16 programs in the United States as having what they deemed acceptable programs for preparing industrial designers. In 1975, Joseph Carriero, then Chairman of a design program at Cornell University, produced a study that included 125 institutions offering at least 1 industrial design course and 44 institutions with programs in industrial design. When he presented his findings at the national conference of the Industrial Designers Society of America (IDSA) in Aspen, Colorado in 1975, Carriero's report was met with disbelief and derision. The organization never offered his report as a publication. Yet today, just over 30 years after Carriero's report, IDSA recognizes 53 programs in industrial design in the United States. Of that total, 16 programs exist in the largest universities in the country. Enrollments in these programs as well as in the traditional college arts institutions are increasing—in general relationship to the trend for all enrollments—*and those students come from the general population of students, without a rigorous selection process in place to assess aptitude for design studies.*

In the visual arts, the fastest rate of enrollments is among degree specializations, doubling since the middle of the last century, and that trend is projected to continue. In addition to these evolutionary changes, students entering college are younger than ever before—dramatically changing maturity and experience levels among matriculating students. Design programs were traditionally discovered after partial matriculation in college and even after the student received a degree. Undergraduate design students in past years were older compared to students in other programs. According to the NCES, there has been a dramatic rise in the youngest high school graduates entering design professional programs and a slight decline in older students enrolling and attending. This is significant because visual arts programs have traditionally benefited from an older population's maturity and experience levels, which were major factors in the establishment of excellence in design programs. To recap: three important dynamic changes are supported by various statistical analyses by the National Center for Educational Statistics:

- There has been a dramatic increase in enrollments in the visual arts and design programs in large universities.
- The student profile of those entering the visual arts has changed to become more like the general profile of all other students, whereas the profile of students in past years were those selected on the basis of aptitude, proclivity for design studies, and experience within visual arts.
- The contemporary student has a worldview and sense of self that should be better understood to serve their needs. While design programs are "field driven," the students may not be so. Their approach to design studies may be far more freewheeling and generalized in terms of application than that of their predecessors.

Problems in Teaching Skills

In most design programs, instructors are heavily taxed to offer skill-based courses—such as drawing—beyond their capacity to place such courses in the curriculum. Computer graphics and other technology-based courses have wedged into their necessary place in the curriculum and have displaced up to 30 percent of traditional skill development courses and other electives. Thus, at the very time when skill development in the curriculum is most lacking among students and fundamental for the ultimate success of visual arts graduates, students are getting far less in the way of hand-skills training and development than they need from almost every curriculum in the country.

There are notable exceptions in this regard. The Art Center College of Art and Design in Pasadena, California has successfully adhered to a rigorous admissions program. It is based on minimal acceptance of the youngest high school applicants and focuses on admitting qualified older students from two- and four-year college programs. Graduates from their carefully managed majors in design are highly sought after by industry. They represent their respective fields with the highest level of skill development available anywhere in the country—and possibly in the world. Art Center does not slack on the intellectual development of its students; most criticism leveled at the school by other programs is largely borne of envy. This book about the development of drawing skills as one component of the change to design education is not directed at the Art Center student or for the faculty of that institution. The students' capacity for visualization at that institution was present at admission and requires development and refinement—not initial skill development.

The issue that faces virtually all of the other college and university programs is how to address the skills deficits of their matriculating students. One thing is certain; developing skills must have two components for which the student is entirely responsible: *practice* and *discipline*. Conceptual drawing is an essential skill of the designer. Any person who attempts to draw, and rigorously continues to draw, will improve and develop some level of skill over time. How much time it would take to become professionally competent without instruction or assistance by scrubbing graphite into endless sheets of a sketchpad is unknown. For this reason and others, this text is addressed to both the teacher and the student involved in design programs. Teachers of design must understand the students they are attempting to teach. Conversely, students should understand the goals of teaching as well as look for those characteristics among instructors that should be applauded as well as changed. The largest amount of material in this book is text and visual images about content. It is not likely that students could take this book and learn to develop conceptual drawing skills without instruction. The intent is to amplify instruction and to make students' individual practices of development more effective.

It is likely that there can never be enough time or enough resources devoted to drawing in design programs at this juncture in the continuing development of design education. Clearly, far too many graduating seniors from design programs have not been able to take sufficient course work or practice enough to achieve even entry-level skill capacity—judging by the endless criticism heard from the professionals in the fields of design. Something different must be done or at least attempted to address this problem. It is fruitless for professionals within the fields of design to anguish over the state-of-the-art of design education. Higher education has become a competitive business focused on the bottom line just as much as any other business. The bar will not be set higher for entering students and it will not be raised for graduation. The challenge is in identifying new ways to raise the capacity of students once they are enrolled and intent upon graduation from a design major.

Colleges and universities, regardless of their programs, are no longer operating on an attrition-based model. They do not discharge or flunk-out students who do not meet expectations in order to achieve excellence among graduates. Today, regardless of the size of the institution, colleges and universities are operating on a *retention-based* model of admissions, matriculation, and graduation. Every avenue is explored to retain every student admitted even though there is and will continue to be a percentage that leave or fail their coursework.

More than ever, young people view college education as a birthright. For the contemporary young student, going to college is an inevitable step in a linear educational path that leads to eventual success in life. They believe that this path assures them of their expectations of personal success. One aspect of design education has gone unchanged; virtually all programs are field driven, meaning that programs are expected to graduate individuals—largely from their undergraduate programs—who are sufficiently qualified to find employment in design professions. Visual arts programs graduate more students than ever, but the proportion who are sufficiently capable for entry level in their chosen fields has become a smaller percentage than ever before.

Conversely, it is far less than clear today whether the matriculating students in design programs share the same expectations as do their predecessors or their professors. Many see design as a form of general education, not professional education. Regardless of a program mission articulated by its faculty, this generalization of purpose in undergraduate design education may be another area of change that is happening not by design but by evolution and default. The design of programs—and their measure of success—depends on the perceptions of that program by the fields they profess to support and supply with graduates. Industrial, interior, and visual communication design programs seek the endorsement of professional corporate and consulting designers. They trumpet the successful applicant employed by prestigious firms and companies. They seek out special projects and programs in collaboration with industry. They regularly invite professional designers to participate in juries, panel reviews of student work, and portfolio critiques. These exchanges between town and gown should be viewed as much for their effective communication about the goals of education overall to professional design practitioners as an educational experience for the students.

There is and has always been an assumption that student aspirations match those of the program and the faculty. It is likely that, when asked, students will be qualified to provide their mentors feedback that is just what those mentors want to hear. However, there is a lesson to be learned from the experience of architecture programs that saw the overwhelming majority of their students graduate into a nonexistent job market for traditional architects. The programs adapted to that market and architecture became a form of general education. Therefore, the other design professions are likely to see graduates move into career paths or bend design content to their own sense of who they are and where they want to go in life. This creates a new interpretation of the value of skills such as conceptual drawing and design visualization. It may be a far more influential path expedited by the skills of design, one that requires a shift from the emphasis on artistic values to a greater emphasis on social values and communication.

Features of the Book

Outstanding designers have generously contributed the overwhelming percentage of drawings utilized in this text. There are also drawings in the text of a less accomplished level of capability. These drawings are important to illustrate development of skill just as the drawings generated by talented individuals illustrate the ultimate level of current practice. They make the point that developing conceptual drawings as part of design process must provide adequate communication with others involved in that process. Designers with adequate, but not exemplary, drawing skills have developed award-winning designs. However, regardless of the level of innate talent, the value of communicating the visual image and its importance in the process has been recognized. In addition, all designers represented recognize the depth to which conceptual drawing must penetrate to cover the visual information necessary for sound decision making.

Demonstration drawings that were generated for this text were deliberately kept at a simplified level. For example, the drawings that explain the relationship of perspective to freehand drawing are much more simplified than the elaborate, thoughtfully presented, and excellent technical demonstrations found in F. D. K. Ching's *Design Drawing* (1998) or John Montague's *Basic Perspective Drawing: A Visual Guide* (2005). The design student's personal library is incomplete without these books. In that sense, *Conceptual Drawing* can be thought of as a companion to these works. It is intended to express one important dimension of visual thinking and to cover that subject with the required depth and breadth.

The reader should examine the various drawings selected for this text from the standpoint of adequacy of communications. Students should "look for themselves" among the various levels of capability and the ability to communicate visually. Most do not have the ability of a Preston Bruning—including most designers who work professionally and make substantial contributions to the fields of design and society in general. Drawing is just one aspect, one very important aspect, of a total design process.

In the arts, there is a saying: "Find your own voice." This statement applies to the broadest range of artists, not just singers. This statement can be applied to the fields of design—every designer has some unique quality that can be developed and will be a personal expression. Students should emulate, even duplicate, the drawings provided as examples in this test—because it is impossible to be exactly like another designer. Emulation, besides being a sincere form of flattery, is an important way of learning. Individualism cannot be suppressed. It emerges in design inevitably with time and continuous practice.

Organization of the Text

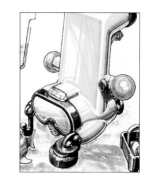

The book has eight chapters and a supplemental section on practicing and developing conceptual drawing skills. The chapters are organized in a linear flow from the most rudimentary and fundamental aspects of learning visual communication skills to advanced levels of presentation, communication, and development of *hybridized*, computer-enhanced conceptual drawings. The book is applicable as a text in the most basic of drawing courses—and is specifically focused on developing conceptual drawing skills. In addition, the book is a reference source on the variety of conceptual drawing styles and techniques. The organization of visual images and their captions relate to the text, but are also meant to stand alone. A student should be able to go directly to specific examples of conceptual drawing and learn from step-by-step demonstrations as well as absorb the methods and techniques of drawing from the array of designers who have contributed their work to the book.

Attached to the rear inner cover of the book is a DVD with seven segments covering: fundamentals; perspective; form development; drawing the human figure; interior conceptual drawing; presentation and communication; storyboarding; and hybridized conceptual drawing.

The DVD provides real-time demonstrations on those subjects covered chapter by chapter in the book. This resource is meant for the student as a guide to practice and develop on an independent basis.

Acknowledgements

R. Preston Bruning is rightfully the first person who deserves mention with respect to his contribution to this book. R. Preston Bruning was a senior designer with General Motors for most of his career. He was—and continues to be—one of the most talented and prolific designers and proponents of conceptual drawing in the design professions. Over the years, Bruning visited, guest lectured, and taught design students in numerous design programs—among them Koncelik's classes at Cornell University and at Ohio State. Pres, as he is known to all, left behind not only the legacy of his talented teaching, but also many examples of his work. Many of his drawings used in this book are examples taken from his own "working" book that he used while teaching students in classes he visited. In addition, Preston left behind for the authors those drawings and sketches he had done over time. This valued archive of his work has been a significant contribution to this book.

In addition to his obvious talent for conceptual drawing, Pres Bruning is an example of the epitome of "empathic drawing" that is the root form of the method that grew out of student work at Pratt Institute in the mid-1950s through the mid-1960s. Pres could draw instinctively—almost without looking at the paper. He drew, arms flying and the paper whirling around to different positions to accept his deft line work, almost with an abandon. No one in the field of industrial design, or in the automotive design works at General Motors for that matter, has ever matched his outpouring of creative energy. It is sometimes the case that designers do one thing very well and do somewhat less well in

other areas of the range of designing. This has never been the case with Pres Bruning. As skilled as he is with the two-dimensional aspect of designing, he also excels at developing form in three dimensions.

It is gratifying to both authors that we have the benefit of Pres Bruning's drawings for this book. Students always achieve more by being in the presence of others who are more accomplished than they might be. Pres, as talented as he is, is never threatening to students nor is he discouraging to them as they watch his instruction. Now, through this book, many more students will have the benefit of his tremendous abilities.

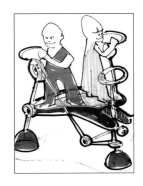

The Ohio State University Class of 1995 in the Product Design major within the Department of Industrial Design was an exceptional body of students who developed a high level of skill in drawing to complement their equally high abilities as designers overall. During the formative years for this text, this class contributed comments and critiques that were essential in developing the materials. As educators, the authors are proud of the accomplishments of all our students and the Product Design Class of 1995 represents the best in all our students and the level of accomplishment educators love to witness among graduates.

The work presented from these students was part of the conceptual process of developing a new computer product sponsored by a leading personal computer manufacturer. Ordinarily, exceptional work comes from one, two, or a few—a small handful of students in one group. This group of students managed to be competitive among themselves in a most positive way and, at the same time, close and helpful to one another. The overall effect was that *everyone* in the group maximized and optimized their development. No one instructor can take credit for student excellence, although it is a tempting. Those students understood the challenges in front of them by recognizing that classes, instructors, and projects in their academic program would not be enough to make them complete designers. Therefore, they took additional classes and worked on their own to increase their skill levels and their understanding of design process. Several were able to secure internships with industry or receive sponsorship of their final senior "thesis" project. These individuals are the kind of students every instructor wants to teach, looks forward to teaching, and enjoys—virtually revels in—their work. They were Koncelik's last class of students taught at The Ohio State University and they also were the major reason it was possible to leave Ohio State with a positive attitude toward teaching and a deep sense of pride about a rewarding association with these outstanding students and the institution.

To break design students away from ingrained habits and help them achieve control of line, **Alexander Kostellow** taught students to draw images from the imagination and how to do them rapidly and in great profusion. Many changes in drawing media continued to evolve throughout the 1940s and 1950s with the addition of magic markers and other tools. Regardless of the tools or media used, rapid visualization became the important conceptual method for designers, and Kostellow's technique helped design students break loose from the labored and time-consuming studio drawing of the past to create images for products, interiors, and graphics in the new industrial age. Without rapid visualization, Kostellow's brainchild, designing would be a ponderous task. With rapid visualization, it is possible for any designer to draw as fast as he or she can think.

Another significant contribution to this book was provided by **Kimberly Elam**. Kim is the Director of the Department of Graphic and Interactive Communication at the Ringling School of Art. She is also one of the more prolific authors on the subject of graphic design methodology. Her book, *Geometry of Design*, had a significant impact upon the development of this book—especially the subject matter in Chapter 4, Developing Three-Dimensional Form. Aside from her scholarly contributions, Kim Elam provided insightful comments about this book, the direction of the writing, and its appropriateness for teachers and students, as well as contributing to the page layout and design of the of the text to enhance legibility and usability. The rare designer is able to combine the capability of visualization with the verbal capacity to explain it to others. Compared with other fields of endeavor, design professions are not blessed with a prodigious literature. This is unfortunate. However, Kim Elam is a notable exception to the rule. Kim is not only an accomplished designer; she is an exceptional author on the subject of designing. It is hoped that her example will be emulated in this new century.

Paul Reeder, younger brother of the collaborating author of this book, is a successful designer in his own right. Paul has pushed the boundaries of his profession by moving from the limitations of form giving into invention and product development. Paul Reeder's company, Zoma, is engaged in the development, production, marketing, and sales of innovative recreational products for aquatic applications. Paul has designed innovative practice equipment for swimmers, swim fins, hand webbing, and designs for water boarding. Again, as with other contributors to this book, Paul Reeder understands uses and communicates through various forms of conceptual drawing. His work is a major portion of Chapter 7, Communication and Presentation. Some of his product development materials—many outside the realm of aquatic application—can be found in other sections of the book.

Dr. Lorraine Justice is the Swire Chair Professor of Design and Director of the School of Design at Hong Kong Polytechnic University. Dr. Justice's contribution to this book is philosophical as well as practical. First and foremost, Lorraine reviewed early text prepared by the authors and provided helpful commentary. She also reviewed the text while it was headed for production. More important, Lorraine Justice opened up the discussion of application of this material beyond the borders of the national environment for higher education in the United States. She illuminated the potential for this material's international distribution and utilization. Asia has looked to the United States as well as Europe for decades for the preparation of designers—and many excellent Asian designers have received their training in the programs of universities and private art colleges in the United States. The tide is turning in the twenty-first century and Lorraine Justice is one American with her fingers on the pulse of educational development in China and throughout Asia. The developmental process is not exclusionary, thankfully. Western designers and educators have a major opportunity to be involved in this developmental process. Books, such as this one, that provide a clear methodology and philosophy for instruction will be a part of this major development.

The authors wish to thank **Ms. Barbara Christopher**, Administrative Assistant, College of Engineering, at the Georgia Institute of Technology. Barbara Christopher has been a friend of this project since its inception. She volunteered to read early text and made numerous helpful comments—not just in terms of writing problems, but regarding appropriate ways to address the intended audience of students she has come to know so well. In addition, the authors wish to thank **Mardia Bishop Reeder** and **Anastasia Hyrkiel Koncelik**, who contributed much in reviewing materials and in suggestions ranging from writing style to use of images. **Amanda Marie Koncelik** acted as the model for the "rudimentary" and "fundamentals" demonstrations seen in Chapter 2 as well as in the CD-ROM demonstrations. Amanda Koncelik's modeling training was helpful, especially because she instinctively knew the proper demeanor for each photographic image required in the demonstrations. **Mrs. Kathleen Litkovitz** contributed

samples of her cursive writing that set the stage for conceptual drawing development.

The authors are extremely grateful to the design professionals who contributed their work willingly to this book—and largely provided the visual content as well as adding to the visual diversity of conceptual drawing. **Aaron Bethlenfalvy, Suzanne Boyden, David Tompkins, Christine Fish,** and **Anne Letherby** contributed work from their professional design activities in product design, web development, and graphic design. **Rob Englert** and **Brian Lawrence** both contributed to the hybrid conceptual drawing content of Chapter 8. A special expression of gratitude goes to **Rob Englert** for his contribution to the DVD content on computer enhancement of drawing. **Noel Mayo**, an internationally recognized designer and educator, greatly expanded the content on interior conceptual drawing—linking it to designs in place that he developed. **Ruth Fowler, Nicole France, Tim Gasperak,** and **Megan Roe** provided work that is from their student days—always a difficult proposition for professional designers who have gone far beyond their accomplishments as students. Nevertheless, representation of student work is an essential component of this text, illustrating the process and the progress in developing conceptual drawing skills. The authors are grateful for the courage and confidence of the students who allowed us to use this material.

The authors and publishers of the book were fortunate to have two excellent professionals assist in the development of the DVD. **Mike Butcher** and **Doug Curran** provided the expertise and creative juice to render this important supplement to the text. Mike Butcher acted as videographer and assisted in editing the video footage. He also selected the still shots from video that greatly enhanced the conclusion sections of each chapter. Doug Curran provided the essential editing of the video footage and molded the segments into a thoroughly engaging set of instructional presentations.

Finally, the authors wish to express their gratitude to the reviewers of this book while it was in

the process of development. Kimberly Elam and
Lorraine Justice have already been mentioned.
The authors also wish to express their gratitude
to **Professor Edward Dorsa** and **Professor William**
Bullock for their many helpful comments and
their support to the development of this text.

Delmar Cengage Learning and the authors
would also like to thank the following reviewers
for their valuable suggestions and expertise:

Richard Buchanan
William C. Bullock
Ed Dorsa
Kim Elam
Lorraine Justice
Ed Ticson

About the Authors

Joseph A. Koncelik

Joseph A. Koncelik is now a retired Professor of Industrial Design from the Georgia Institute of Technology and Professor Emeritus in the Department of Industrial, Interior, and Visual Communication Design at The Ohio State University. Koncelik has been involved in design education for 36 years, beginning with his faculty appointment at Cornell University in 1966 through his retirement from Georgia Tech in 2002. He has held faculty appointments at Cornell University, Ohio State, and Georgia Tech. His teaching covered a wide variety of studio and lecture courses over time, including teaching drawing to beginning-, intermediate-, and advanced-level students. Koncelik began his career in design at General Motors after studies at Pratt Institute and Stanford University. After General Motors, he was awarded a Fulbright-Hays Scholarship to the Royal College of Art and studied with L. Bruce Archer, the renowned design methodologist. Upon returning to the United States, he worked in consulting design offices in New York City before accepting his first academic appointment at Cornell University. Koncelik has been active in design consulting throughout his academic career and has worked with such notable industry clients as: Fairchild Hiller, Herman Miller, Burlington Industries, RCA/Thompson, Rubbermaid Corporation, Lumex Corporation, and others. Koncelik has published two books that were drawn from his long-term research in aging and product development and is responsible for generating 75 publications during his academic career.

Kevin Reeder

Kevin Reeder is an Associate Professor of Industrial Design at the University of Illinois. During the development of this text, Kevin was Associate Professor of Industrial Design in the College of Architecture at the Georgia Institute of Technology. He has more than 25 years experience in teaching and continues to develop materials and methods for the contemporary student in design studies. Reeder has lectured nationally on the subject of conceptual drawing and design visualization, presenting and demonstrating drawing to students and practitioners. Upon graduating from The Ohio State University as the IDSA Outstanding Student in Industrial Design from that program, Reeder went on to Stanford University for his Master's degree. He remained in teaching and consulting in California, working with the children's play and educational product industry until his return as an Assistant Professor at The Ohio State University. Reeder divided his time between the academic world and consulting until he moved to full-time teaching at the Columbus College of Art and Design. After ten years on the faculty in the Industrial Design program, Reeder accepted a position with the Georgia Institute of Technology where he is now Associate Professor of Industrial Design. Reeder is expert in conceptual drawing, teaches that subject at intermediate and advanced levels, and focuses his research on the integration of anthropometry data as well as the use of storyboarding techniques with conceptual drawing and design visualization.

Joseph A. Koncelik

Kevin Reeder

Supplemental Materials

The supplemental section following the eight chapters links the DVD to the text in the book by providing ideas about specific methods of practice. While the DVD is a real-time set of demonstrations, the supplemental section is more prescriptive regarding applying the demonstrations to individual practice that will advance skill development at a faster pace than if attempted without guidance. This supplemental section utilizes still images extracted from the DVD. The DVD and supplement reinforce the major points of development in the difficult process of learning to draw from the imagination. To iterate one of the tenets of the DVD, every individual student engaged in design studies must practice on a regular basis. Individual commitment to practice is the only way any student will advance his or her conceptual drawing skills.

Content of the DVD Segments:

Segment 1: Fundamentals:

Content: Holding the pencil, standing to draw, full-body movement, left/right handedness, power stroke, quality of line

Segment 2: Perspective:

Content: Perspective/point of view, vanishing point locations, emphasizing important information, reducing drawing time

Segment 3: Form in Transition

Content: Geometry, ribs and stringers, setting up the drawing on the long line using ribs, using stringers

Segment 4: Human Figure in Context:

Content: Characteristics of the human figure (generic), figure in perspective, figure proportions, location with product

Segment 5: Interior Space:

Content: Interior single-point perspective, the back wall, proportional measurements, sense of scale as objects recede

Segment 6: Presentation and Communication:

Content: The scope of conceptual presentations, the use of storyboards, desk-side critiques

Segment 7: Digital Integration:

Content: The necessity of speed, transferring images, use of photographic imaging, character of the hybrid drawing

1

The Fundamentals of Conceptual Drawing

Defining Conceptual Drawing

Conceptual drawing is the act of visualizing objects and environments on paper *drawn from the imagination*. Conceptual drawing is a specific type of visualization used in design practice to explore the greatest number of possible solutions to a design problem. This form of drawing is critical to the initial act of exploration that is used to develop the broadest spectrum of possible solutions. This activity employs hand and mind and is a transfer of images from the imagination to paper by the hand's action using a medium such as a pencil, pen, Conté crayons, or markers. The conceptual drawing process also involves computing as the sole method of gener-

ating visual ideas. It is also used to enhance and develop scanned drawings. This process is called "hybrid" conceptual drawing.

Conceptual drawing as a process is difficult. As art educators such as Nancy Beal and Gloria Bley Miller discuss in their book, *The Art of Teaching Art to Children*, and as Cathy Malchiodi states clearly in her book, *Understanding Children's Drawings*, drawing from the imagination is the most difficult of all visualization processes. Drawing from the imagination—as opposed to drawing while viewing subject matter—is beyond the grasp of most individuals and is the test of creative design capability. Child psychologists such as Lowenfeld in his mid-twentieth century

Figure 1-1a
Figure 1-1b
(Kevin Reeder)
These images show two examples of mixed media conceptual drawing that illustrate development of manual drawing skills. The objective, one that will be repeated throughout the text, is to attain sufficient drawing skill to communicate ideas about products, interiors, and graphic designs.

 See the DVD demonstration on intermediate and advanced levels of conceptual drawing in Segments 3 and 4.

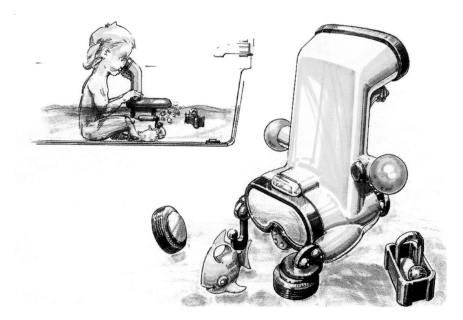

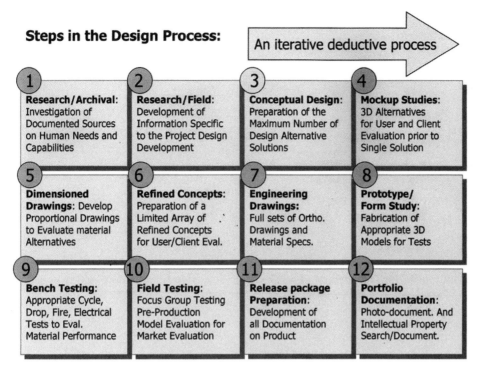

Steps in the Design Process:

An iterative deductive process

1 Research/Archival: Investigation of Documented Sources on Human Needs and Capabilities

2 Research/Field: Development of Information Specific to the Project Design Development

3 Conceptual Design: Preparation of the Maximum Number of Design Alternative Solutions

4 Mockup Studies: 3D Alternatives for User and Client Evaluation prior to Single Solution

5 Dimensioned Drawings: Develop Proportional Drawings to Evaluate material Alternatives

6 Refined Concepts: Preparation of a Limited Array of Refined Concepts for User/Client Eval.

7 Engineering Drawings: Full sets of Ortho. Drawings and Material Specs.

8 Prototype/Form Study: Fabrication of Appropriate 3D Models for Tests

9 Bench Testing: Appropriate Cycle, Drop, Fire, Electrical Tests to Eval. Material Performance

10 Field Testing: Focus Group Testing Pre-Production Model Evaluation for Market Evaluation

11 Release package Preparation: Development of all Documentation on Product

12 Portfolio Documentation: Photo-document. And Intellectual Property Search/Document.

Figure 1-2
(Joseph Koncelik)
This diagram outlines the twelve steps in an iterative, sequential, and deductive design process that includes conceptual drawing as one of the steps. Designers must take a systematic approach to the development of objects, graphics, and spaces. Note that information gathering occurs prior to the conceptual process.

work, *Creative and Mental Growth*, noted a series of stages in the creative development of children based on observations of children interacting with the visual world. Lowenfeld noted that most children stopped using drawing and other forms of image making around the ages of eleven to thirteen. However, as psychologists and art educators have also documented, an instructor who provides examples of how to develop ideas from the imagination, leading the student half the way, frequently unchains the imagination and allows such visualizations to freely develop. Students in university design programs understand the initial difficulty in coping with drawing assignments in the lower-division courses. They struggle to overcome the long interruption in their use of visualization to express and communicate ideas. Nevertheless, most students can make sufficient progress to include design visualization as part of their skills upon graduation.

A variety of other descriptive terms exist for conceptual drawing, including ideation and rapid visualization, among others. Robert McKim's book entitled, *Experiences in Visual Thinking*, used the term "visual thinking" to describe the act of simultaneously imagining and drawing. All terms imply that this act of initial design exploration happens simultaneously *during* the act of drawing.

Conceptual drawing is just as the term implies: an act of drawing enabling design at the very beginning of the creative process. Designs are not preconceived and then "drawn up." Designs occur as drawing progresses. In other words, creativity is an interactive process involving the mind, eye, and hand, not in progression, but in a simultaneous interaction through which ideas are developed and revealed.

Design visualization is a broader term that refers to all levels of image making by any means. Visualization includes conceptual drawing and full presentations, rendering, computer-enhanced drawings (or "hybrid" drawings), and computer-generated images and the components of the design release package for clients and others. Release packages include materials presented to a client and may include renderings, control or engineering drawings, specifications, and other critical materials defining a design solution.

Computers and graphic software have radically changed the academic and professional design environment. With the press of time that is natural to the design process, designers turn very quickly to the computer to generate the form and function of products, graphic images, and environments. Regardless, the manual skill of designing using paper and pencil or pen prior to moving to the

Figure 1-3
(Joseph Koncelik)
The time available for conceptual thinking depends on the time available for all other steps in the process. Speed in the development of concepts is emphasized because the time available is limited. The process can also be envisioned as circular, which is the reason for the link members at the end of each linear string of discreet steps.

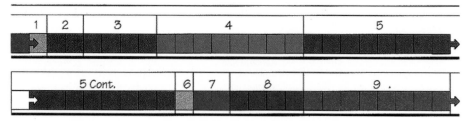

Planning the Research/Design/Research Process over Time

Each Activity Involved in the Complete Design Continuum as a Linear Process over Time

1. Initial Research - 15 Hours 2 Days
2. Conceptual Study - 30 Hours 5 Days
3. Mockup(s) & Initial User Evaluations - 60 Hours 10 Days
4. Design Documentation - 120 Hours 20 Days
5. Appearance Models / Prototypes - 240 Hours 40 Days
6. Product Evaluation - 15 Hours 2 Days
7. Analysis of Evaluation Data - 30 Hours 5 Days
8. Interpretation of Evaluaton Results - 60 Hours 10 Days
9. Report Preparation - 120 Hours 20 Days

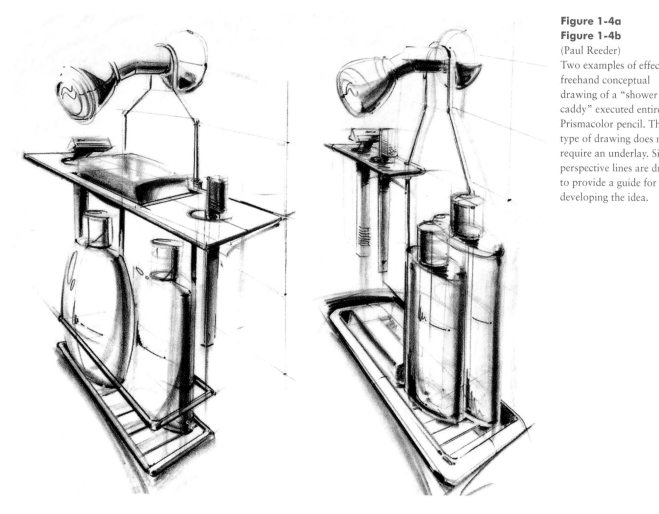

Figure 1-4a
Figure 1-4b
(Paul Reeder)
Two examples of effective freehand conceptual drawing of a "shower caddy" executed entirely in Prismacolor pencil. This type of drawing does not require an underlay. Simple perspective lines are drawn to provide a guide for developing the idea.

computer is not only essential, but this initial conceptual process is actually *faster*. For students in design, developing conceptual drawing skills informs the process of using computers to generate objects and spaces. Without developing drawing skills, computer-generated images are frequently fewer in number, bogged down in the rules of form, cliché ridden, and incorrect in terms of geometry and perspective. When students and professionals acquire conceptual drawing skills, they are more able to recognize errors in the visual image, develop form with a more developed aesthetic, avoid using hackneyed form clichés, and press computer imaging to its limits through a more developed individual creativity.

Returning to the focus of this text, conceptual drawing differs from "quick sketching" and drawing for its own sake in that the value of these forms of drawing is in the aesthetic merits of the drawings themselves. Conceptual drawings have *no intended intrinsic value* except to inform the designer and others about possible solutions to a given problem. Aesthetics involved in conceptual drawing are critical because form giving is an essential part of designing in the industrial, interior, and visual communication design professions. The more beautiful the image, the more acceptable it will be as a form-giving solution to a problem. Conversely, the less able the designer is to generate aesthetically pleasing drawings, the less acceptable will be that designer's ideas and solutions to design problems. For students contemplating their future in design professions, conceptual drawing skills are frequently the defining aspect of a portfolio of work that will enable access to entry-level employment. Employers want to know how the potential employee thinks, how that person's ideas are expressed, and how creative that person is as measured by the number of proposed conceptual solutions presented at the beginning of a design assignment. All academic design programs are "field driven." This means that the standards of the field inform the standards of the program. The manual skill of

conceptual drawing is, in today's academic environment, variable in terms of offerings and instruction; the student is still responsible for developing adequate skills regardless of the amount of instruction and the rigor with which skill development is pursued and required.

There is an implicit assumption regarding the instructional purpose of this text that a proficient designer must have adequate-to-excellent conceptual drawing skills. Further, design process, beyond problem definition and initial research, begins with conceptual drawing. This form of drawing is cost effective, efficient, and fast. As most professional designers are aware, no form of computer-generated imaging competes with hand skills in terms of speed and efficiency at the onset of design.

Conceptual drawing is essential in the process of generating as many potential directions as possible for solutions to a problem. Conceptual drawing is cost effective, expeditious, and critical in developing understanding of the spectrum of possible design solutions. Conceptual drawing is a way to include all parties involved in the design process in the examination of potential solutions—especially clients or users of design services. Competent designers do not propose single design solutions during the beginning phase of problem solving. As a deductive process, designing proceeds logically from the general to the specific—from a wide variety of possibilities to a single solution to a given problem. (See Chapter 7.) Conceptual drawing is a means to broaden the view of potential solutions to a problem that have the potential for success and meet the requirements of everyone associated with the process of design.

Figure 1-5
(R. Preston Bruning)
A freehand mixed media drawing of a highway cruiser designed to operate on an automated highway. This is the reason for the swiveling seats—a driver and passengers can engage in activities while the vehicle operates under automatic control.

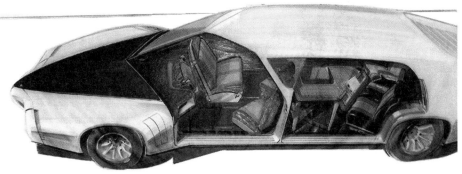

Figure 1-6
(R. Preston Bruning)
Preston Bruning's teapot and breadbox drawing illustrates the level of freehand drawing that is the ultimate goal in developing excellence in conceptual drawing. Note the control of the line used to depict a surface on which both objects rest; the line also indicates the perspective. Also note the freely drawn circle to depict the spherical part of the teapot and the ellipses that describe the ends of the breadbox.

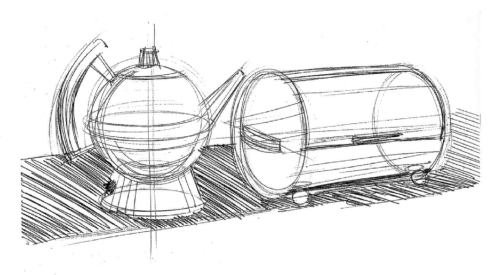

There is little in the literature on drawing that either describes or instructs on the subject of conceptual drawing. It is likely that the obvious focus on rendering and technologically supported design visualization in the literature is more easily conveyed because these forms of drawing are heavily routine, sometimes have mindless conformity, and are systematic. Conceptual drawing has rarely been seen as a teachable subject. As a means of visualization, it has been viewed as "black box," a purely intuitive act that cannot (possibly should not) be explained.

In drawing on the intuitive side of creativity, actually teaching conceptual drawing has been viewed as either inborn in those who do it or unteachable. Obviously, this text is an attempt to challenge such notions. Conceptual drawing is the hardest form of two-dimensional image making any person can attempt. As stated previously, it is difficult to pull purely imaginative form from the mind and visualize it on paper. These skills have

Figure 1-7
(Joseph Koncelik)
Initial assumptions that thumbnail sketches are rough and absent of quality are disproved by this collection of seven small sketches representing various conceptual ideas as well as explorations of form for the development of a toaster oven consumer product. Note that the perspectives are not exaggerated, giving the objects the appropriate sense of mass. Also note the indications of materials such as glass and bright metal.

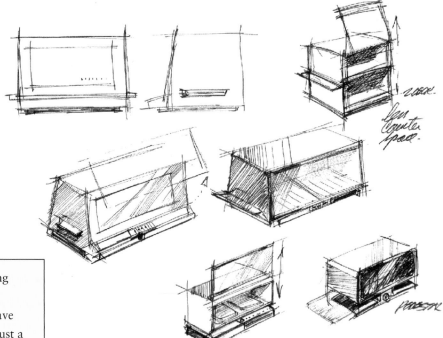

TIP - Always make sure that the drawing instruments are in good shape. Pencils should be sharpened and you should have several of a specific type on hand, not just a single pencil or pen. ▪

been believed to be beyond most individuals and that belief is supported in the literature on art education and child development. When one has skill in conceptual drawing, that skill is the dividing line between truly creative individuals engaged in design process and those who provide just adequate design service. The designer with limited competency cannot develop multiple solutions to design problems. Conceptual drawing is how a designer musters the creative energy to develop multiple images for solutions to design problems— a skill that is vital at the beginning stages of design.

Design visualization covers the range of image making in the two dimensions required to provide sufficient information for the design process to move from development to production. For the sake of argument in this text, design visualization does not include three-dimensional form development or prototype construction that are also critical to depict and describe a graphic piece, product, or environment. Conceptual drawing should be regarded as the most basic level of design visualization.

There are many other forms of visualization and ways to develop visual images that are related to hand skills or supported through technological imaging such as rendering at all levels of finish, mechanical perspectives, exploded view drawings executed using mechanical projection methods, and computer-generated image making. As stated

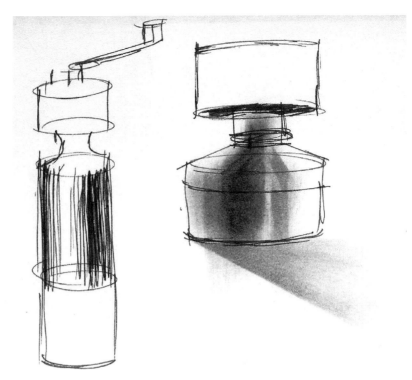

TIP - Thumbnails are drawings too! Focus on creating good drawings no matter the scale or how fast they are done. ▪

TIP - Drawing objects in a transparency and using the thumbnail to measure the proportions of an object are both important tools to achieve designs that communicate well. ▪

Figure 1-8a
Figure 1-8b
(Joseph Koncelik)
These two drawings illustrate that even thumbnails can use mixed media. The first drawing has two objects in ink line, one of which uses gray pastel to indicate the cylindrical surface and shadow. The drawing of a kitchen range uses two sides of vellum that accepts marker with ink and pencil lines. Both drawings were done in a matter of minutes—without sacrifice of quality.

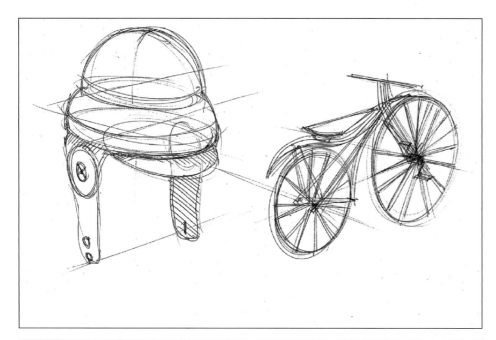

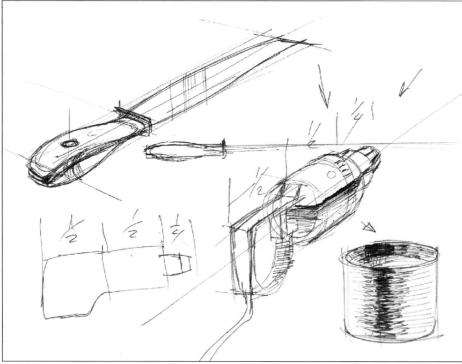

Figure 1-9a
Figure 1-9b
(R. Preston Bruning)
Early-stage thumbnail drawings can demonstrate dimensionality, as in the Bruning drawings, left. The drawings, below left, are explorations of proportion so that more refined conceptuals can be generated with a clear understanding of the relative size of product components.

quite successfully in Ronald Kemnitzer's book, *Rendering with Markers: Definitive Techniques for Designers*, is far easier to explain and demonstrate. Rendering depends on accurate and time-consuming mechanical perspective, the use of tools and templates, the possible use of photographic images for overlay tracings, and many other forms of mechanical devices and means to create accurate, potentially photographic images of an environment or object. All of these are important means to an end—producing a singular final design.

The purpose of conceptual drawing is to explore alternative design ideas. The purpose of more elaborate and mechanical forms of visualization is accurate depiction of a finalized design. Frequently, students of design mistakenly gravitate to mechanical forms of rendering at the onset of design "ideation" to avoid exposing possibly inadequate freehand drawing skills even when quick descriptive drawings are more appropriate. In the compressed schedule of most design assignments and tasks, it is too costly to begin with labor-heavy methods required for rendering and computer image making at the onset of design concept generation.

The computer has permitted visualization at a high level of rendered development. Owing to virtually automatic rendering capabilities, design students increasingly rely on this valuable asset as the primary tool for conceptual development.

TIP - Designers never discard aesthetics—the look of a drawing—regardless of the speed with which the drawing is done. Thumbnail drawings may be done quickly, but they still represent the designer. ■

previously, design visualization that is mechanical, especially rendering, has been covered extensively in the literature. Rendering, as explored

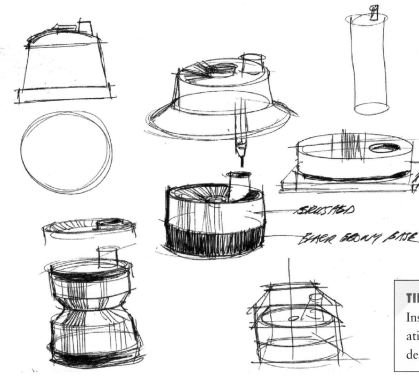

Figure 1-10
(Joseph Koncelik)
Additional thumbnail explorations show attention to the representation of form as well as explorations of proportion. Although the products depicted have passed from general use (manual drafting pencil sharpeners) the drawings help explain the "parts and pieces" necessary to develop the design more fully.

TIP - Never be a "one-idea designer." Instructors as well as clients expect your creativity to be continuous no matter what the design problem. ▪

The problem with using computer graphics at the beginning of design problem solving is that achieving even one "quick sketch" takes huge amounts of time for preparation and execution. In fact, quick sketching is something computers just do not afford designers. Pen and pencil line drawings are far superior and faster as methods for conceptual design development.

Recently, Noel Mayo, the noted industrial designer and Eminent Scholar in Industrial Design at The Ohio State University, was asked by industrial design students how much time he gave to conceptual drawing in the design process. Noel replied, "We do those drawings in the car coming back from the first client meeting." In other words, Noel said that design process does not permit a great deal of time to explore a range of solutions. Designers must quickly develop a range of potential solutions to problems—both for the purposes of communication to clients and because of the cost of design services.

For the purposes of this text, conceptual drawing—within the context of design visualization—emphasizes "freehand drawing" and limits the use of mechanical perspective to conceptualization when and where the subject of design is complex, or the subject is interior design where perspective methods speed up the process of idea generation. The fundamentals of mechanical perspective are covered in Chapter 2 to instill a basic knowledge of perspective that must become an innate part of drawing concepts in three dimensions. Many of the line drawings shown in this text will have the perspective guidelines shown even though the drawings are done freehand.

As the user of this text will quickly learn, conceptual drawing is not limited to simple pen or pencil sketching, although line drawing is the basis of this form of visualization. Conceptual drawing extends to mixed media drawing with freehand perspectives, uses of backgrounds, colors, figure representations, integration of information about measurements of the human body, sections, and exploded views—virtually all of the tools and forms of expression found in more elaborately constructed renderings. For the gifted designer, freehand conceptual drawing is the preferred form of drawing, all the way to finished forms of final design representation. In other words, the lines blur between rendering, representational drawings, and the initial purpose of conceptual drawing. This text will begin with rudiments and fundamentals. As the subject matter develops and the chapters progress, finished drawings are presented that expand the characteristics of conceptual drawing.

TIP - Thumbnails are a good tool to explore uses of media without making a commitment to a major drawing that might be discarded. ▪

Figure 1-11
(Joseph Koncelik)
The world of science fiction and extreme imagination can produce ideas about products, environments, and graphic images that advance the state of the art. This image depicts a cooperative play object—games and toys that do not work without the participation of two children.

Figure 1-12
(Joseph Koncelik)
In the initial stages of conceptual drawing and idea formation—sometimes called ideation—the working mechanics of a device are less developed than the overall idea. These quick drawings allow ideas to be easily accepted or rejected.

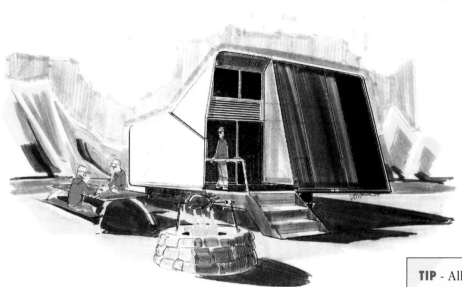

Figure 1-13
(Joseph Koncelik)
Again, the vision of living on other planets gives rise to ideas about our own. This image depicts a collapsible vacation home that folds in on itself when not in use. Of significance in this drawing and those on the previous page, there are no erasures and no over-drawing or tracing from a rough. This helps expedite the process of generating ideas with none so precious they cannot be discarded.

> **TIP** - All ideas are valid in the conceptual drawing process. Never discard ideas before they are visualized. ▪

Design Drawing Literature

Design drawing moves some distance from personal expression because of the need to communicate ideas to others. This "fork in the road" separates the path for the artist and the designer. Drawing for the sake of the art is a visual challenge the artist poses to the self. The process of making art begins with developing images on a surface that are replications of the real world—drawings of the ever-present still life of fruit in a bowl represent that beginning point. Designers, on the other hand, must convey ideas to others—clearly—that are images of physical forms and spaces that do not exist. This is the essence of conceptual drawing. Conceptual drawing of design ideas, on the other hand, must be understood by others and be convincing and not arbitrary. Often when designers present conceptual ideas, everyone who sees those ideas is critical and negative. The more obscure an idea, the less able the designer will be to convince others that the idea is reasonable, much less acceptable. Conversely, the better the conceptual drawing and the clear representation of ideas generated, the greater the interaction of others and the more positive the response.

Drawing as communication then, must be clear and representational. At some point in the process of learning how to design, it becomes essential to learn how to express ideas clearly to others. The designer thinks visually. Robert McKim understood this very well and presented his influential work on the subject in the previously mentioned, *Experiences in Visual Thinking*. McKim's book was an effort to convince engineering students at Stanford University of the necessity of visualizing ideas—and the value of doing so as a means of generating ideas.

McKim's work—through his texts—became a standard in design literature for every design instructor and for many students. McKim was influential in Stanford University's combined program between the visual arts and the Department of Mechanical Engineering—where his teaching resided—between the cracks. Through McKim and other mechanical engineering professors such as Dr. John Arnold and Dr. James Adams, the author of *Conceptual Blockbusting*, the study of engineering was seen to include creative pursuit where students became acquainted with the idea that visualization complemented their technical and scientific experiences.

In addition, the Department of Mechanical Engineering at Stanford experimented with studio experiences for beginning engineers, similar to the classes design students would take in visual arts

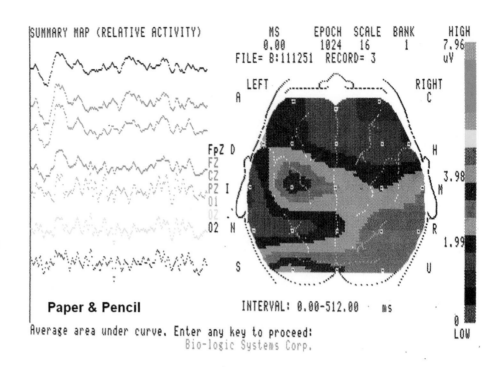

Figure 1-14
(Joseph Koncelik)
While a graduate student at The Ohio State University, David Kerwin conducted studies of brain activity while subjects used different drawing instruments. The objective was to assess which instrument was easiest to use. Kerwin used a "brain atlas" computer that provided images of brain activity during the act of drawing. He had students use pencil and paper, a digitizing pad, a mouse for input, and the directional cursor keys on the keyboard. These images are the results obtained when his professor and thesis advisor, Joseph Koncelik, participated in the study.

programs. Using this teaching style helped ensure an almost total retention of students in the engineering department. McKim's work helped create this environment that reinforced the concept that visual arts can be an important complementary form of intellectual development for science and engineering students.

Two other books explored conceptual thinking and visualization and the link between thinking processes and the need for drawing or visualizing ideas. *Design Yourself* and *Rapid Viz* are two of a series of publications by Kurt and Corrine Hanks intended to both broaden the scope of and help individuals master graphic arts techniques. Another similar work is that of Beitler and Lockhart's, *Design for You*, which discusses and shows the impact of design as a way of thinking. *Rapid Viz* focuses on developing skills using the simplest technique—pens and pencils on paper. The books have a broad base of appeal beyond

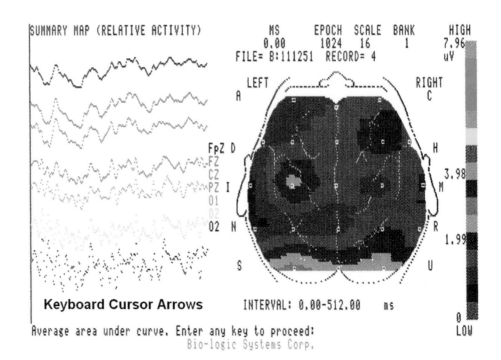

Figure 1-15
(Joseph Koncelik)
For the majority of novice students—those in the beginning classes of their design program—brain activity was very high and areas of the brain in both the left and right hemispheres showed high levels of activity, well into the yellow and red indicator colors of brain activity. For the professor, however, very low levels of brain activity registered. This was due to the length of time (thirty-five years) the subject had been drawing. Skills, it seems, become "second nature" with practice. Just as the athlete can be "in the zone," so the experienced designer does not consciously think about how to draw a concept.

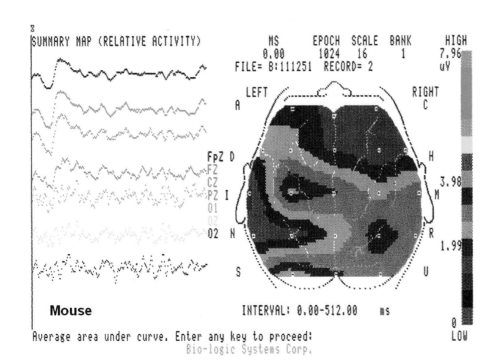

Figure 1-16
(Joseph Koncelik)
While all of the brain scans from this experienced subject show low levels of brain activity, there are noticeable, distinctive patterns of similarity. The lower-right side of the brain seems more active in virtually every case, but the left side is also active. The telltale difference between these scans and student scans is the lack of activity in the frontal areas of the brain—a place for activity that suggests learning is taking place. It seems that learning becomes a process of absorbing new information, which is then gathered and used. Drilling or practice is necessary when something is completely new and unknown.

the field of graphic design and have enjoyed success in the broader marketplace over the years. Drawing on thinking similar to Robert McKim's, *Rapid Viz* demonstrates the capacity to open up visual thinking.

The field of architecture has made the greatest contribution in the literature to understanding drawing as a tool in the design process. This literature covers drawing applications from the purely mechanical to the expressive. Some, not all, of this literature spans the gap of differences between design professions and provides important insights about drawing for all designers. Perhaps the most useful of these texts is Francis D. K. Ching's. In his earlier work, *Architectural Graphics*, his book, *Interior Design Illustrated*, and his later book and accompanying CD, *Design Drawing*, Ching explores the development and use of drawing—including "drawing from the imagination," a rarity among the books available

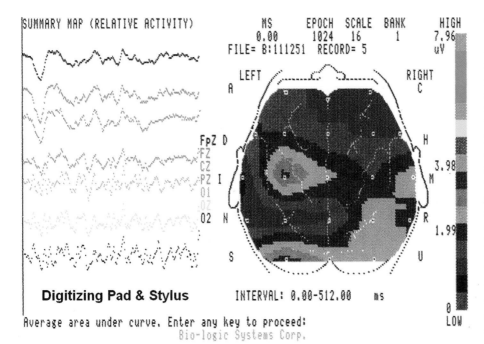

Figure 1-17
(Joseph Koncelik)
Questions arise from studies like these. Clinical studies of brain activity are divorced from specific mental functions such as drawing. Is all learning similar? Do all those who continue to draw acquire skills that become part of the brain's "firmware?" Beyond the questions, it is clear that both sides of the brain are actively engaged in some meaningful way—if not clearly understood—in the development of drawing capability. These scan studies show the association between skill and creativity. Clearly, the designer who possesses a higher level of drawing skill will be more fluid in the transfer of ideas to paper. Drawing becomes an inherent part of the process, not the objective of design development. Highly skilled designers do not separate the function of drawing from the creative act of designing.

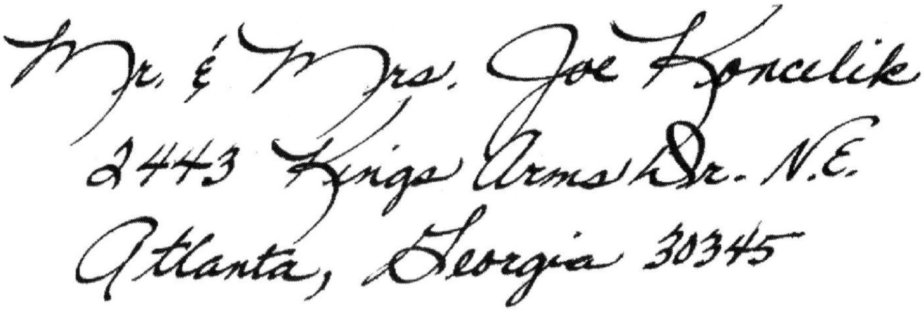

Figure 1-18a
Figure 1-18b
Figure 1-18c
(Kathleen Litkovitz, Joseph Koncelik, R. Preston Bruning)
So-called "empathic" drawing is the basis for the generation of conceptual drawing. The action and eagerness of line placement is derived from the free-flowing form of cursive writing. With continuous practice, curvilinear free-flowing form can be generated in the same way as the uninhibited personal styles of cursive writing. Penmanship is a discipline that enhances writing and informs the process of conceptual drawing.

casting, and other drawing techniques and methods. The latest edition of the book parallels the development of "hybrid" drawing—drawing utilizing scanned line drawings enhanced by computer graphics software to develop color and lighting of surfaces. Lockard followed up the publication of *Design Drawing* with a companion publication, *Design Drawing Experiences 2000*. This book contains sixty exercises that cover conceptual and representational drawing for architects. The exercises help supplement the teaching of architectural drawing procedures and skills.

Another area of design activity where useful publications on the subject of conceptual drawing have been produced is landscape architecture. *Drawing and Designing with Confidence: A Step-By-Step Guide*, written by Mike W. Lin, is directed primarily toward landscape architects. Lin provides information about the requisite graphic, drawing, and rendering skills of his profession. Design is eclectic by nature and the lessons for landscape architects are not lost on other design fields. In this sense, Lin's book parallels this text in that he emphasizes speed in the drawing process to develop confidence. He also professes a relaxed approach in developing the skills of conceptual drawing.

to designers. The accompanying CD-ROM with video clips demonstrating drawing approaches and techniques is an important contribution to the advancement of understanding and skill development.

Design Drawing by Allen Kirby Lockard is a useful reference book for students and professionals in architecture and contains lessons for students in other areas of design studies. Kirby provides step-by-step depictions of architectural concepts through perspective methods, shadow

There are numerous books on drawing and a myriad of rendering technique books. They are all helpful contributions to the learning process, especially if personal capabilities are well developed. Most of these works provide ample illustrations of good drawing, but little in the way of a specific or clear methodology for the translation of an idea into a visual form. These publications are a visual resource and include several illustrative books on science fiction themes and what have been termed "artist's conceptions."

These books were generated out of the materials that give background and environment for the motion picture industry, especially the science fiction world of Syd Meade and the talented designers who contributed their creativity to the *Star Wars* trilogy and its continuing saga in prequel films.

These books are enjoyable to look at and benefit the developing design student by providing more enthusiasm for the subject. Syd Meade is the most noted of movie set illustrators and has generated these fanciful visualizations for several years. Meade has published a number of books on his work and there is an anthology on his work titled *Steel Couture – Syd Mead – Futurist Sentinel*, which is a collaboration between Mead and Strother McMinn. This literature includes the following books: *Blade Runner Sketchbook*, by Scroggy Huebner, Kaplan, Knode, Mead, and Scott; Johntson's *The Star Wars Sketchbook*, and a follow-on publication much sought after by aspiring design students, *Star Wars Return of the Jedi*

Sketchbook, by Johnston and Rodis-Jamero. Another book in this genre is Bresman's *The Art of Star Wars, Episode 1 the Phantom Menace*. There are numerous examples of these visual resources that are valuable references, including the book, *Usagi Yogimbo Book One*, by Sakai and Shay and Duncan's *The Making of Jurassic Park*. This literature also includes Zimbert and Mead's *The Official Art of 2010*. All of these books are marvelous adjuncts to drawing instruction—especially for students who are beyond the beginning stages of conceptual drawing and can integrate the techniques of professionals as they develop their own approaches to drawing and personal style.

The techniques developed in the books on figure drawing and cartooning, such as the books by Loomis titled *Figure Drawing for All It's Worth*, that demonstrate how to draw the image of a person are useful in their sequential demonstrations and building-block methodology. Other books that take a systematic approach to the learning experience in the arts include a series of books by

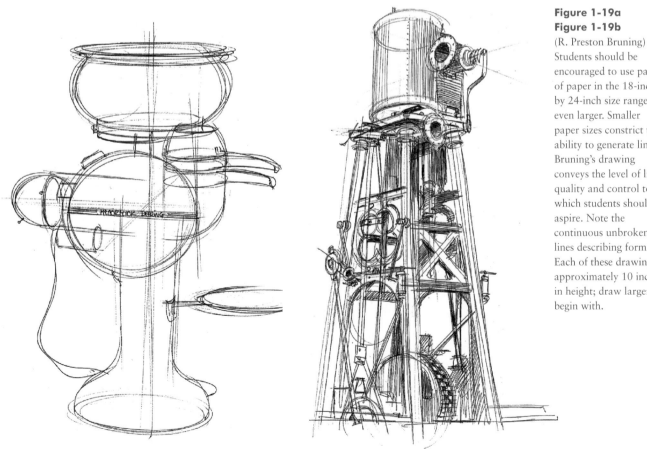

Figure 1-19a
Figure 1-19b
(R. Preston Bruning) Students should be encouraged to use pads of paper in the 18-inch by 24-inch size range or even larger. Smaller paper sizes constrict the ability to generate lines. Bruning's drawing conveys the level of line quality and control to which students should aspire. Note the continuous unbroken lines describing form. Each of these drawings is approximately 10 inches in height; draw larger to begin with.

Barrington Barber, including *The Fundamentals of Drawing: A Complete Professional Course for Artists*. The impression one gathers from the literature pertinent to drawing is that it is eclectic and diverse. Yet, very little has been written that is specific to conceptual drawing as it is practiced in the design professions, other than architecture.

Design books are frequently filled with fully rendered images, but little in the way of divulging process. Unfortunately, picture books fail to convey instructional value because looking at a finished rendering or an excellent drawing from a talented designer does nothing to inform the beginning student of design about how the designer initiated the drawing and then proceeded to develop the finished piece. The *Star Wars* collection works better as a reference for advanced students than it does for the beginner. Other books used by design students to develop drawing capacity—especially the drawing of the human figure—include the many books on cartooning. The exaggerated dynamics of cartoon figures do not sufficiently represent the poses and gestures of the human body in relationship to task environments or products in use. (See Chapter 5). Nevertheless, many renderings and

finished drawing utilize rather exaggerated figure forms drawn from these publications to provide a sense of scale—if not an overstimulated sense of the dramatic. Don't discourage students from using cartooning techniques because any point of departure that helps students develop their visualization skills is a place to begin. Using "cartooning" as a method of learning figure dynamics and poses can be useful and the subject is explored in Lee Buscema's *How to Draw Comics the Marvel Way* quite well.

Some writings on visualization for communication purposes are quite good from a utilitarian point of view. Among the truly useful books in this category are those such as *Rendering with Markers* written by Ronald Kemnitzer,. Kemnitzer takes a very methodical approach to developing one aspect of design drawing skill. He explores various uses of marker technique and various applications. He includes demonstrations and progressions of marker application and includes the work of several talented designers. Of the many how-to-draw books available, Kemnitzer's stands out as essential for design students.

Drawing from the Right Side of the Brain, written by Dr. Betty Edwards, and her latest version,

Figure 1-20

(R. Preston Bruning)
While drawings should be larger rather than smaller, objects should not be drawn larger than they really are. This can convey erroneous information about size to others involved in the design development process. In these sketches, Bruning developed form deftly using line and achieving space to convey geometry. The objects were small to begin with and were drawn at approximately 60% of full scale.

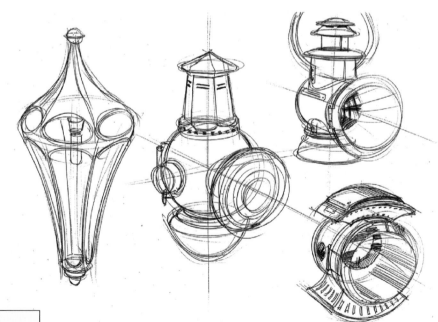

TIP - Drawing objects in a transparency and using the thumbnail to measure the proportions of an object are both important tools to achieving designs that communicate well. ■

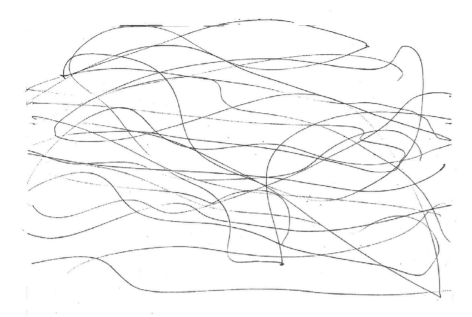

Figure 1-21a
Figure 1-21b
Figure 1-21c
(R. Preston Bruning)
All line work informs the designer about the development of his or her ideas. In these drawings, Preston Bruning used "scribbling" to find a form solution to a vehicular design problem. The form of the vehicle "Bod-Pod" was extracted from free-flowing line work and then refined in a later drawing (below). This vehicle was produced in a prototype form and exhibited at the Epcot Center in Florida.

The New Drawing on the Right Side of the Brain, are revolutionary approaches to the subject of the human capacity to visualize. Edwards draws on information from the rapidly expanding field of brain research to generate her ideas about teaching visualization and improving drawing—especially among individuals who put aside their interest in drawing until adulthood. Edwards uses documentation and information about the understanding of brain function to postulate methods for developing visualization based on distinct differences in the capacities of the left and right side of the brain. Left-brain function is seen as controlling/producing the capacity to think abstractly and develop logic. Right-brain function is seen as the creative side of the mind; producing the human capability of visualization as well as other creative and artistic proclivities. Edwards develops exercises that can produce remarkable results in improvement in skill by tapping into right-brain capability.

The approach Dr. Edwards takes in her writings is certainly novel among all of the approaches found in the

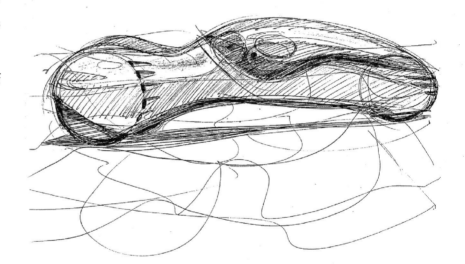

literature. Two essential ideas are explored and advanced by Edwards. The first is recognition of human development expressed in the literature regarding child development psychology and art education. There is a pattern in human development that incorporates the use of visualization in early childhood, and which is typically abandoned by the age of thirteen. Most adults gravitate naturally to other means of expression through verbal development, writing, and mathematics. Edwards realized that many adults reach out to recapture their experiences in visualization; this has made her books immensely popular and important.

The second idea is that there is a connection between visualization and the sciences advancing brain studies. Understanding visualizing as a human capacity, not just as something a few talented individuals can do, makes developing drawing skills less mysterious and remarkable and gives that development the potential to become universal. This idea has immense importance for educators in design professions who are confronted with ever-increasing numbers of students pursuing design studies without the requisite "talent" seen among limited numbers of their predecessors three generations earlier. In this sense, Edward's writings are original, influential, and inform design education about new

approaches that should be explored in the classroom.

As it must certainly be clear to any instructor of drawing, all visualization exercises will improve capability. As brain research has continually advanced, it has become clear that the act of creating a visual image requires the active use of both sides of the brain. Brain functioning in the cerebral cortex toward the front of the brain on both sides, left and right, shows measurable brain activity as someone attempts visualization. This was proved in the studies conducted by David Kerwin at The Ohio State University during his thesis research using a "brain atlas" computer to investigate the differences between using various drawing media and computer technologies. Kerwin's studies demonstrated that the novice design student has high levels of brain activity on both the right and left side during the initial learning process when developing drawing skills. The graphic images from Kerwin's studies shown in this text are images of the brain taken while a man with thirty-five years of drawing experience participated in the study. In this instance, brain activity was again on both sides but very low. It seems that brain activity changes with experience and skill acquisition. Skills become a lower level of functioning in the brain and release easier access to creative thought.

Figure 1-22
(R. Preston Bruning)
Bruning's drawing of a Word War II dive-bomber exemplifies the height to which line quality and control can be brought with perseverance. In this freehand drawing, line work is used to describe the form of the aircraft as well as create an effective background of sky and clouds.

TIP - Always keep the light source in mind while developing the concept. This will help shape dimensionality and give the drawing punch! ▪

TIP - Drawing smaller helps designers master the ellipse because it is more easily drawn and can be seen in context more fully. ▪

Figure 1-23
(R. Preston Bruning)
All form is derived from geometric shapes and volumes—even the most complex of forms. (See Chapter 3.) Preston Bruning's drawings, left, illustrate how form is developed using geometry—even in the quick sketch mode of conceptual drawing.

Edwards was certainly at the leading edge of this new way of approaching the development of visualizing skills. Her books are a testimonial to how much the study of brain functioning has advanced. Educators cannot ignore this information. They need to know about child development and human development to teach visualizing in general and conceptual drawing in specific.

No discussion of the literature surrounding drawing and design can be totally comprehensive because the literature expands every day. Rather than pursue such a goal, this overview of literature is to highlight the contributions that provide insights into the nature of creativity and conceptual drawing. Every literature search becomes an inductive process—looking for specific references that result in an expanding compilation of sources. Students of drawing and design are advised to read about visualization to gain a better understanding of their own developmental processes. Students should build a reference library that includes sources they will often use. These few references should help begin such an endeavor.

The Rudiments of Freehand Drawing

An increasing number of students from general populations in university settings are attracted to design studies. Most design programs are populated with students who have limited exposure to design prior to enrollment and relatively no previous drawing experience. Without selection procedures in place, design studios are overflowing with students demanding to be taught how to draw, because they require that skill to progress in design studies. The common belief among beginning-level instructors is that providing a time-intensive experience with arts-based curricula focused on observation-based drawing experiences and use of expressive media such as charcoal or Conté will bring up the level of drawing skills that are lacking. This experience does to a certain extent. Unfortunately, this approach does not instruct or provide knowledge of conceptual drawing as a form of communication about drawing from the imagination.

Wherever design programs are found, it is common to see dozens of students slumped on the floor in hallways, in foyers beneath skylights, under spreading oak trees on the quad, and in other locations attempting to reproduce a building facade or a tree. These students struggle with applying a charcoal stick or Conte' crayon onto newsprint or other surfaces. The hope is that this process will eventually have students produce images that are recognizable or representative of the objects and environments that are subjects of their observations. The practice and training of the eye to see and reproduce is a valuable lesson that is an important contribution to visual

Figure 1-24a
Figure 1-24b
(Joseph Koncelik)
Penmanship is no
longer a discipline in
school, so students
have been permitted to
hold writing—in this
case drawing—
instruments as they
wish. Students arrive in
beginning design-
drawing classes using a
wide variety of hand
postures to grip pencils
and pens. If allowed to
continue this way,
students cannot
acquire conceptual
drawing as a skill.
Changing these habits
is essential to students'
progress and success.

 See the demonstrations provided in Segment 1, Fundamentals, on setting up to draw, use of the media, standing, sitting, and posture and useful practice. (See the Supplement on Practice in the text.)

TIP - The absence of penmanship has resulted in students holding drawing instruments incorrectly. Rather than the fist grip or the spaghetti-fingers grasp, students must hold the drawing instrument in a way that will help to improve their drawing. ■

thinking. The flaw in this approach is that this form of drawing is disconnected from conceptual thinking and drawing in the first place and students perpetuate bad habits—or learn new ones—in the quest to improve their design capabilities. To effectively develop conceptual drawing skills related to the imagined object and the imagined environment, a different approach to instruction must be used.

Even before fundamentals are discussed, certain rudiments must be observed before exploring other issues of line control and geometric form development. The set-up of the drawing task must be discussed before discussing fundamentals. Issues related to body position, including posture, hand and arm motion, and even the way in which the drawing instruments are held are so basic, they must be called *rudimentary*. These rudiments must be accepted as necessary or the instructional information that follows cannot be taught or learned with any degree of success. Rudimentary knowledge is prerequisite to understanding fundamentals. Hence, this discussion begins with the approach to the drawing task and

the physical aspects of learning to draw for the purposes of designing.

In spite of differing opinions and conventions, there is a right way and a wrong way to build the skill of freehand drawing—especially as it pertains to developing the visual communication so necessary in conceptual drawing. It might seem at first blush that any way a person picks up a pencil and begins sketching objects and spaces is a useful way to learn. The most important aspect of the "uncultivated" approach is that it indicates the strong desire to learn to draw. However, without instruction, guidance, and critique, results will be limited in success and inadequate from the standpoint of developing professionally acceptable visual communication. The student of design visualization—and more specifically, conceptual drawing—must accept that there is a discipline involved in drawing. Unless the student of drawing decides to become deeply involved in that discipline, there will be little progress toward the specific goal of professional competency.

Many years ago, elementary schools taught penmanship and cursive writing. As the culture of

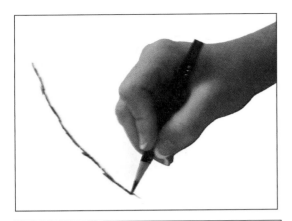

TIP - Continuously rotate pencils as you draw. This keeps the pencil point sharp longer! ▪

Figure 1-25a
Figure 1-25b
(Joseph Koncelik)
Most students at the beginning college level start drawing where they left off as preteens, describing the exterior of form with labored short line strokes. As the photo on the right demonstrates, the first step in regaining a disciplined approach is having students correct the way they hold drawing instruments. The next step will be more difficult: achieving line quality through repetition and practice.

TIP - *Avoid making chicken scratches. Lift the palm of your hand from the paper and move the drawing instrument through arm motion.* ▪

TIP - *Don't hold the pencil or pen in a death grip! Line control requires a light touch.* ▪

discipline in various forms evaporated from primary and secondary education, the specific discipline of penmanship disappeared. Five decades ago, all children were taught to hold a pen or pencil in a particular way and to write letters in a specific direction. If the reader of this text is fortunate enough to have letters from their grandmothers and grandfathers, the evidence of that discipline is clearly visible. The writing style and legibility of the text is beautiful and readable. Teaching a discipline of writing did not disable the psyche and stunt creativity. Instead, such discipline released creativity; students were never prevented from forming a personal style. Some of that teaching is returning to schools in new and different ways—especially as learning is expanded through computing and other technologies.

In other cultures, for example, Japanese, the discipline of calligraphy requires specific posture and hand positions with respect to handling the brush and ink. Japanese calligraphy has an aspect of Zen philosophy in that a discipline can take a

person beyond the material world and even an attempt at mastery is a revelation of the spirit. Much in that approach and in the depth of that thought should apply to the discipline involved in conceptual drawing.

Related to penmanship is the first singularly important aspect of learning how to draw: holding the pencil or pen. Instructors who have been taught the discipline of drawing watch the painful distortions of the hands of hundreds of students in every class they teach. Most students were never taught how to hold writing or drawing instruments. It is critical to get something this basic on the table, so to speak, before undertaking the more difficult aspects of making images that are conceptually interesting, accurate representations of an idea or ideas and making images that are aesthetically pleasing.

The pencil, pen, marker, or other instrument of producing lines is held lightly between the thumb and forefinger, and balanced on the index finger. The hand should be tilted to move the pencil across

Figure 1-26a
Figure 1-26b
(Joseph Koncelik)
Body language in class conveys attitude toward the subject matter. Students slumped at the desk or checking the time likely view the design drawing class as a subject like any other—one taken for grades and credit. Students who commit to studying design must choose to be engaged with the subject matter and see it as essential to their success beyond the classroom—because it is. With the compression of time and subject matter in contemporary design studies, it is important to take advantage of every minute spent learning to draw.

TIP - You are responsible for your own attitude toward class and your own productivity! Be awake, pay attention, and forget about the clock! ■

the page in a single swift motion, from an imaginary point A to an imaginary point B. The hand should not curl over the top of the pencil nor should the pencil be held in a fist or between any other fingers on the hand. Accomplished designers turn the pencil, rotating it as they draw the line to keep its point and even out the deposit of lead, ink, or wax. With markers and pens, this action is not necessary, but the lightness of touch and the motion of the hand and arm are important.

Another rudiment of drawing is posture. Again, the "old school" exercise of sitting properly at a desk is similar to the requirement for proper posture for drawing. Another analogy is sports, as mentioned earlier. Whether hitting a baseball or addressing a golf ball, there is rigorous discipline relating to posture during these acts that must be observed or the balls will not be struck properly. For some unknown reason, these disciplines of posture are acceptable to all who want to learn to play these sports. In the classroom, however, a teacher walking in on the first day will see the overwhelming majority of students slumped at

TIP - Draw in three stages – line work, applied color and value, and then finish line work. Conceptual drawing is essentially line drawing. ■

Figure 1-27
(Joseph Koncelik)
The approach to learning drawing includes posture and positioning of the torso, hands, and arms. There is a relationship between desk height and elbow height. A comfortable relationship between the two enhances the ability to draw and curtails fatigue. There is also an important relationship between the position of the drawing surface and the eye of the designer/student. Getting too close to the work prevents observation of the whole of the drawing in progress.

their desks, resting on their elbows, their hands propping up their chins. When drawing begins, there is usually little change in posture, and while the golfer knows that he or she must address the ball properly to hit it, the would-be designer doesn't know that proper posture is essential to learning this skill.

Another important—and frequently overlooked—aspect of the relationship of the hand and arm to the drawing surface is that of the height of the surface in relationship to the position of the elbow. Elbow height is an anthropometric (body measurement) issue much investigated by home economists in relationship to work in the home. Elbow height should be just slightly higher than the work surface. Obviously, the body flexes and the arm reaches to address the drawing task from top to bottom of the drawing surface. Nevertheless, the beginning position with appropriate elbow height expedites and eases the drawing task. It also establishes an appropriate distance from the eye point to the drawing surface, allowing the designer to see the whole of the drawing as it progresses. Students who are collapsed at their desk with arms resting on the drawing surface cannot achieve the best possible results. Establishing an appropriate and correct posture—either sitting or standing at the drawing desk—allows for the rapid drawing motion that helps develop the skill of superior line quality.

It is suggested that at the beginning of the learning process, students stand to draw—not sit. This unusual request will be met with some resistance, but most students are willing to "address the drawing surface" properly at least at the onset of any skills-development exercise. Breaking habits formed over several years is difficult, but moving the body up and away from the surface to be addressed helps create a new set of behaviors. Again, the sports analogy is useful. Hitting a ball requires as much action from the legs and hips as it does from the arms and hands. Moving the body with the motion of the pencil—anticipating the motion through the body—helps generate control.

Without knowledge of the action of the body in the act of drawing, the slumped student resting

Figure 1-28
(Joseph Koncelik)
In beginning drawing classes, it is recommended that students be asked to stand to draw—especially when conveying the content and discipline of the empathic approach to conceptual drawing. Standing virtually eliminates the potential for boredom and keeps the student engaged with the work. Students will be more attentive and their development of line quality will be quicker in the initial learning stages.

TIP - Standing to draw when you are a beginner helps you see the full page and develop proper movement of the drawing instrument. ■

on elbows has a pencil clutched in a claw-like grasp with the arm lying on the drawing surface. Lines are made in a series of chicken scratches—as if clawing at the paper to reveal the "bug" of an idea. In addition, from the standing position, it is possible to survey the whole drawing as it is rendered. It is possible to position the drawing on the page with visible information about the edges of the paper. It is possible also to survey the perspective of the drawing to see if the convergence of lines is appropriate. (Information about perspective and positioning follows the section on fundamentals in this chapter.)

To initiate a novel experience for students by requesting this change in behavior, the instructor has asked the class to rise, push away their stools, and stand up to begin the drawing process. The instructor has also advised the students how to hold the drawing instrument and everyone is ready to begin drawing. Changing the behavior that accompanies the drawing task has another useful effect: the student's attention is directed to the instruction they are about to receive. Unfortunately, some American students believe that their physical behaviors have little or nothing

Figure 1-29a
Figure 1-29b
(Joseph Koncelik)
Both sitting and standing postures are shown that allow the right-handed design student to move the hand and arm freely across the page. Keeping the eye point back from the drawing surface allows vision of the entire length of line.

TIP - Look ahead of the pencil as you draw. ■

to do with learning. Asian culture takes an opposite approach. Position and posture has everything to do with learning. It seems obvious if not completely logical that the connection between posture and a physical act such as drawing would be connected—and they are.

To ignore the discipline of posture, body position, and proper grasping of the drawing instrument negates the effectiveness of all the other fundamentals. Zen Buddhists say that a person must be one with the act contemplated for that act to be performed—one with the spirit of the bow, one with the brush and ink, or one with paper and pencil. Japanese calligraphers talk about holding

the brush in a specific way and with the hand exerting a particular pressure on that brush. As the Zen artist would say, hold the brush as if holding a delicate bird. By accepting that idea, the person merges with the discipline without fighting it. The discipline becomes part of the person and understanding follows. Such emphasis on discipline of this kind creates initial difficulties because it is different from engrained habits. In the end, however, the discipline permits a freedom of expression unattainable without it. There will come a time when all of the fundamentals become second nature—imbedded—and they require no deliberate thought. Accepting the discipline of proper body position and grip of the drawing instruments will ultimately enable a freedom in the act of drawing, better comprehension of how

Figure 1-30
(R. Preston Bruning)
Leaping forward in terms of drawing development, this mixed media drawing—using a photographic background—illustrates the various components that will be covered in this text, including the use of the human figure to provide scale and context.

TIP - Back away from your drawing as you draw to see how your latest addition of line or tone relates to the rest of the drawing. ■

to draw, and, finally, skill and possible mastery of visual communication. Other rudimentary issues to follow that are important to instructing conceptual drawing include: handedness, sitting and standing to draw, body movement, paper movement, where to look while drawing, object sizing, and use of erasures.

Right and Left Handedness

Everyone who seeks to become proficient in drawing should understand the fundamental flow

TIP - Look ahead of the pencil as you draw! ■

of line direction that is easiest to produce for either left-handedness or right-handedness. Lines drawn in the direction of greatest ease for the left and right-handed drafter are opposite. Hand and arm movement for the right-handed student is bottom-left to upper right, and reversed to bottom-right to upper left for the left-handed student. Following these directions makes lines easier to draw. Secondly, the same motion from top to bottom can be used with relative ease.

To test this, lock the arm at the wrist and draw a line swung from the elbow. Reverse the direction as if changing the drawing instrument to the

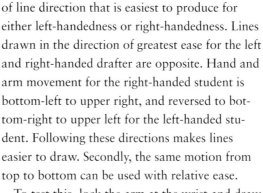

Figure 1-31a
Figure 1-31b
Figure 1-31c
Figure 1-31d
(Joseph Koncelik)
Right-handed and left-handed people have different "power strokes." As shown in these photographs, it is easier for the right-hander to achieve control of line by moving the drawing instrument from bottom-left to top-right. The left-hander's power stroke moves from bottom-right to top-left.

other hand and notice the difficulty in producing lines of any control or consistency. This means that the view of an object, the direction of the perspective, the choice of direction of lighting, and all other aspects of drawing are easier to produce if the person drawing them understands that left-handed and right-handed directions govern points of view. This concept is so simple; it is unsettling that most drawing instruction doesn't inform students about it. The student should practice making lines in each of the two directions to prove the ease this method ensures.

Standing to Draw

Sitting down to draw limits arm and body action and movement. It is also extremely difficult to determine the correct perspective with the novice designer's nose an inch from the paper. Good instructors know when the spirit of their drawing class is fading: the students will be sitting down resting their heads in one hand and trying to draw with the other. Body language tells the perceptive instructor that it is time for some calisthenics, a change of pace, or perhaps time to let the class know you are displeased with their

attitude if students are nodding off as they attempt to draw. A positive approach might help; include jokes about the time and how heavy their pencils have become.

When students stand up, standing initially reinforces wakefulness and attentiveness. Standing means that the line work will have the potential for greater power, accuracy, and control. Perspectives are more easily examined by the student and controlled and corrected from the standing position. Moreover, the student will be engaged in the work, not detached and waiting for the pain of the exercise to end. Line quality depends on understanding how each line in a good drawing is defined. All line work is deliberate, practiced, and carefully produced. Each line is designed with the attributes of consistency. Every line must have the desired weight, a beginning, and an end. Quality line work has character and never seems haphazard.

Moving the Body

The act of drawing can be compared to athletics in that power and control come from total body movement. Draw from the Toes. Watch any good

Figure 1-32a
Figure 1-32b
(Joseph Koncelik)
The "stand-to-draw" requirement at the initial stages allows the student to use full body movement to generate line work, thus achieving the swift continuous stroke necessary to develop quality of line. It also permits the student to stand back from work to examine individual progress.

See DVD Segment 1: Fundamentals.

TIP - Ask a classmate to critique your work from time to time. Peers can be refreshingly blunt about your work and that level of curt honesty is very helpful. ■

Figure 1-33
(Joseph Koncelik)
Children naturally use their entire body in the process of play and in sports. The arms, torso, hips, and legs all contribute to the ability to achieve power and control. This same natural ability should be used to gain control in generating line work.

another; the paper can be rotated to allow lines to be developed with ease and confidence. If the paper is not moved, students will contort their bodies and take uncomfortable positions over the page to draw all lines. The drawing time will then increase and the line work will deteriorate. Drawing is easier if the paper is turned to allow for the ease of motion made with either the right hand or the left. Students will learn to draw with greater ease and quickness if their bias toward left or right is taken into account.

Looking Away from the Pen or Pencil Point

When practicing rapid visualization, it is beneficial to keep the mind's eye focused on the endpoint of the exercise and not the path the pencil is taking point by point. Students should train themselves to look at the point the line will extend to—not at the tip of the pencil or where the pencil is going. When a student begins to worry about the line he or she is in the process of making, the line will surely waver; it will be unsteady rather than confident and uniform.

Skilled practitioners of conceptual drawing "zone out" when they draw. Their mind is on the idea and not on the drawing—because the drawing will happen virtually of its own accord. The beginner who concentrates so hard on achieving a good drawing tends to focus on the specific line being scratched into the surface of the paper. In so doing, the idea fades away and control of line evaporates into a motley collection of scrubbed-in chicken scratches.

Watching the tip of the pencil is equivalent to watching the motion of a bat or a racquet as opposed to watching the ball. One must trust that the bat or racquet will actually get to where it must go to strike the ball properly. Thus, the

instructional video on a sport, such as driving a golf ball, hitting a forehand shot in tennis, or hitting a baseball, and the same principal is always stated: power is generated from good footwork and leg movement. The power necessary to generate good drawings is not in the fingertips but in the whole body. Proper approaches to empathic drawing involve locking the wrist and using arm and torso movement to generate line work. Watching a fine drafter at work, students will notice that the whole body enters into the act of drawing, not just the fingers and hands. Preston Bruning and other accomplished drafters seem to be dancing. George Bellows, famed artist of the "Ash Can School," was a fine athlete who ran back and forth from his paintings as he worked. Drawing is an aerobic exercise when done correctly—and it is great fun.

Moving the Paper

Before a student draws anything, unless it is part of a ream of loose sheets, the paper should be removed from the drawing tablet or pad. It is easier to make lines in one direction than it is in

TIP - Removing the page before beginning a drawing prevents making unwanted tears in the page after the drawing is finished! ■

 See Segment 1: Fundamentals

student must look away from the pencil and see where the line is intended to go.

In children's art, it is interesting to note that the youngest children use a continuous line and those children's drawings frequently have great character. While objects in children's drawings are only caricatures or cartoon simulations of their experiences, the drawings usually have great charm because children are not fearful of placing any line anywhere on the page. However, do not underestimate the difficulty of accomplishing quality line work. Line work is the basis of all good design drawing and requires a very deliberate effort to master.

Drawing Larger Rather than Smaller

Some believe that the so called "thumbnail" sketch is a good way to begin drawing or conception of an object. Thumbnail sketches are useful when a student has a good deal of practice "under the belt" so to speak and the student has progressed to a higher level of communication with drawing. Unfortunately, for the beginner, small versions of an object do not translate into larger drawings with greater detail. In addition, drawing is not learned by avoiding the act of drawing. Empathic drawing practice requires that objects be drawn up to full scale so that lines can be extended fully using the full-body aspproach of drawing from the toes. Use newsprint pads or loose sheets of newsprint (preferred) measuring 18 inches by 24 inches for a single drawing on a single page.

Figure 1-34a, Figure 1-34b, Figure 1-34c
(Joseph Koncelik)
The dilemma of line control is solved if the paper can be moved to take advantage the individual's power stroke. Whenever a drawing is begun, the very first—not the last—act is removing the paper from the pad or tablet.

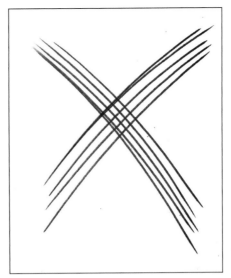

TIP - You will know you are losing the ability to control your line work when your hand is curled into a claw with the pencil upside down. Rotating the page helps prevent loss of line control. ■

Figure 1-35a, Figure 1-35b
Figure 1-35c, Figure 1-35d
(Joseph Koncelik)
Creating line work in opposite directions is a problem solved by removing the paper from the pad. Turning the page allows for lines (above right) to be generated in opposite directions. Otherwise, as shown in the top-left photo, arms and hands are twisted awkwardly and poor line quality results. Turning the page allows continuous ease of line generation.

Figure 1-36a
Figure 1-36b
(Joseph Koncelik)
Consistent line work is achieved by coordinating the hand and eye. The designer looks to that point where the line should extend and draws—with confidence—to that point. In time, the eye will always be just slightly ahead of the pencil point on the paper.

Never Draw an Object Larger than Full Scale

There are exceptions of course, but virtually all objects should be conceived in the scale they are in reality. Larger-than-life objects misinform the viewer, which leads to significant communications problems later when designers are working with clients. The underlying basis of all good design drawing is quality of line and mastery of line. Obviously, there are other methods of drawing such as tone drawings or surface rendering. None of these methods allow designers the rapidity, control, and communications potential of the empathic approach to rapid visualization.

In the early 1960s, a student in Industrial Design at Pratt Institute brought a drawing to the product design class that was a rather well-drawn electric razor—except the razor was 300 percent larger than it was in reality. The instructor, Gerald Gulotta, saw the drawing and remarked, "Fantastic… you mount this razor to the wall and run your face up and down against it!" The lesson was not lost on the students; the drawing communicated something different from what the designer had intended. A balance must be struck in the size, proportion, and point of view depicting an object on a page in order to convey specific information about the object to those who will be literal when interpreting the visualization.

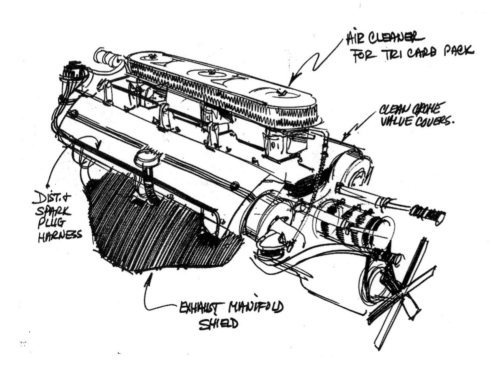

Figure 1-37a
Figure 1-37b
(R. Preston Bruning)
It is worth repeating that line quality is essential to good conceptual drawing and that consistent line work is the hallmark of excellent drawing—as in these two examples drawn freehand.

Figure 1-38
(R. Preston Bruning)
Bruning's "Hose Carriage" is drawn from a high
eye point, perhaps an elevation of twenty feet or
more. The drawing illustrates several points made
in this chapter about control of line. There is
geometric development of form with free-flowing
line and no erasures.

> **TIP** - Conceptual drawing is drawing from
> the imagination. However, storing images
> derived from observation builds a mental
> library of form. ■

Do Not Make Erasures

In rapid sketching, *all* lines are
meaningful. The number of lines
used to create an object informs the
instructor. This is an aspect of drawing that relates to learned behaviors.
Erasure is seen as correction of
error. It is time-consuming to correct every line that seems unacceptable. It is also a process that
corrupts the surface of the paper—
making additional line work inconsistent and rough. Erasure is, in
actuality, a process of highlighting
used to enhance or lighten one area
over another. In effect, it is drawing
without line. Most important,
sketching is enhanced by the extra-
neous lines and provides clues to the
thinking process behind the drawing and the
design represented.

Figure 1-39
(R. Preston Bruning)
Preston Bruning's drawings illustrate every aspect of line control and development of
a consistent perspective, the drafting of consistent freehand ellipses (wheels), and the
development of geometries that inform the process of creating the shapes and masses
of form in this highly complex early fire pumper.

The Fundamentals of Freehand Drawing

Freehand drawing is the ability of the designer or
artist to depict objects in space without the aid of

Figure 1-40a
Figure 1-40b
(Joseph Koncelik)
In the early stages of drawing development, using the concept of "calisthenics" to stretch and warm up is most helpful. At a later time, it may not be necessary to engage in this limbering up before the act of drawing. However, practicing removing the page and drawing lines in the power stroke, rotating the page with each line drawing, enforces the idea of page rotation. The figures at right are an attempt to achieve straight lines by drawing in one direction and then turning the page 180 degrees to place the other lines.

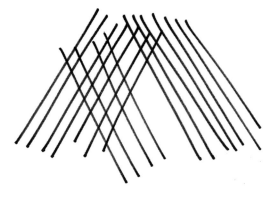
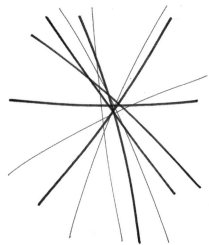

> **TIP** - Turn the page to maintain control of line! ■

mechanical perspective or drafting tools. Freehand perspective drawing is best developed along with mechanical perspective and is learned through repeatedly practicing drawing objects in space. Contrary to misconceptions and "vogue" concepts about how drawing is learned, drawing is neither exclusively a "right brained" exercise, nor are people who draw well necessarily right brained in their orientation. Mathematicians, scientists, and engineers have been known to draw well. Fine art courses were once a central part of the curriculum at West Point Military Academy. Graduates of the academy were widely known for their engineering skills—and their ability to render clear, precise,

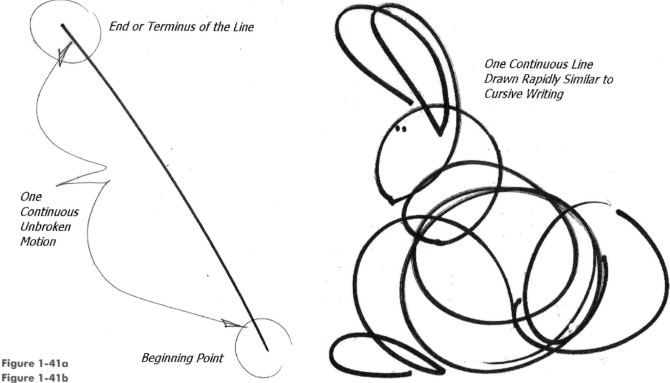

End or Terminus of the Line

One Continuous Unbroken Motion

Beginning Point

One Continuous Line Drawn Rapidly Similar to Cursive Writing

Figure 1-41a
Figure 1-41b
(Joseph Koncelik)
As stated in the text, control is achieved by drawing the line in one smooth rapid motion from beginning point to terminus, or end point, as shown on the left. On the right, a single swirling line is used to describe a fanciful rabbit—similar to the calligraphy of cursive writing—with the exception of added dots for the eyes.

detailed drawings and plans as well as maps. The ability to draw has a connection to the ability to compute, to think generally, to plan, and to visualize that subject matter not yet realized. Conceptual drawing is the ability to imagine objects, shapes, and space and to convey these ideas to paper as a drawing without having to see and translate these objects from the real world. Some individuals possess an inborn talent to see objects in their mind and can translate what they envision to paper almost without effort. Most, however, must acquire the skill of drawing through repeated practice and through training the eye—and the "mind's eye"—to capture an object and translate an image of that object to a piece of paper.

Every form of drawing is helpful in the development of skill, including representational drawing, still life drawing, and drawing the human figure. The mind stores all information about the visual world as though it were a reservoir. In the act of conceptual drawing, all these experiences flow together to enhance the creative development of form. Every designer and artist uses and blends information from his or her visual experience to create new conceptual ideas about form. The more experiences a person receives—visual experiences—the more creative that person can be in developing personal ideas. In addition, artists and designers love to draw; it is not a chore or a job. If drawing practice seems dull or routine, it is a clear signal that the student should look for another field of endeavor. There are three important fundamentals necessary to develop drawing skill and to make drawings that communicate well to others. These fundamentals are detailed in the following sections.

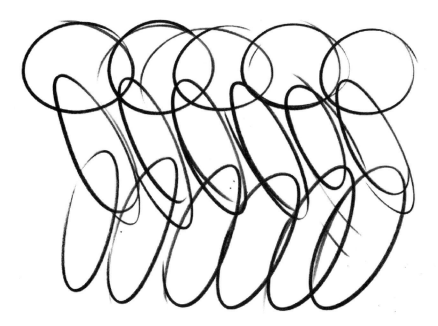

Draw Continuous Elliptical & Circular Shapes

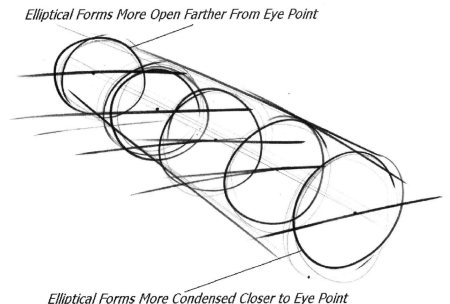

Elliptical Forms More Open Farther From Eye Point

Elliptical Forms More Condensed Closer to Eye Point

Figure 1-42a
Figure 1-42b
(Joseph Koncelik)
The top figure is a series of ellipses drawn in a continuous motion—again turning the page to achieve ellipses drawn in the opposite direction. The bottom figure represents a series of circles in perspective drawn on a single axis line. As each circle is drawn farther up the axis line, they progressively become more "open" and more like a circle than an ellipse. All lines should be one continuous motion with no corrections. The exercises should be repeated to build the skill of line control.

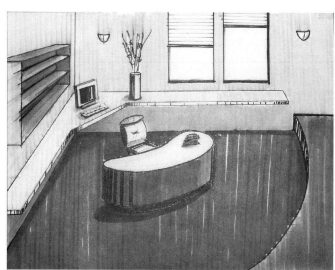

Figure 1-43a, Figure 1-43b, Figure 1-43c, Figure 1-43d
(Joseph Koncelik)
Typically, in the first days of classroom instruction, instructors attempt to gauge students' level of capability by assigning a drawing problem without going deeply into drawing instruction. The four drawings above represent such an attempt—with relatively typical results. In an effort to make the drawings "right," students labored over the line work, spending hours attempting to create the best drawings possible. In each of the drawings shown, the eye point is high off the floor so that space is determined by the distance between objects and not the "overlap" of objects that will come later in the instructional process. When an eye point is high off the floor, the drawing time increases and perspectives are harder to make consistent. The positioning of chairs to table surfaces (left side, lower drawing) has an unrealistic spatial relationship. Material thicknesses have not been fully considered—nor are they as "automatic" as they will become with continuous study and practice.

Control of Line

A good-quality line has a beginning, a middle, and an end. When one examines the line work of accomplished draftsmen, it is evident that every single line has a character because it has a point of origin, a continuous flow over a distance that may vary in weight, and an end point called a terminus. Some drafters emphasize the endpoint of their lines as if they were periods at the end of a sentence. The beginner attempting

to draw an object will usually attempt to scratch out the object with a series of short choppy lines using only the tips of the fingers—believing that this method enables control. Since the line work has not been rendered with confidence, the object depicted also lacks confidence in the way it is drawn.

Every line on the piece of paper must be of consistent line weight, must not be shaky, and must have a firm positive direction. Drawing

> **TIP** - Conceptual drawing is line drawing. Use line to build form. Develop techniques for creating shading and backgrounds using line. ■

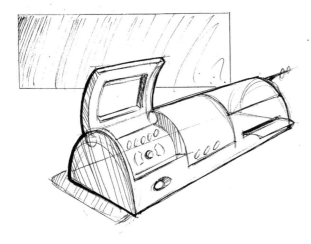

Figure 1-44a
Figure 1-44b
Figure 1-44c
Figure 1-44d
(Nicole France)
In this series of drawings by a single student, there is greater confidence in the line work, in the sense of perspective, geometry, and overall form development in specific materials. There are no magic pills to take that will instantly allow the production of professional quality conceptual drawings. The primary issue is control of line—mastery of line to the extent that the student does not have to divorce the cerebral process of designing from drawing. They are one and the same.

instructors frequently refer to these three aspects of line work in a drawing as *quality of line*. Achieving good line quality to produce quick sketches and realistic visualizations of ideas means relearning how to draw. Control does not evolve from slow, careful line production; it comes from fast, rapid movement of the drawing media on the paper surface. Rapid visualization requires the same control as cursive writing. Rapid movement of the pen or pencil gives the letters their character. Thus, line control in rapid visualization requires that the drafter learn how to place the line on the page with confidence and dispatch!

Each of these drawings cost the student time that they will not have to spend on a single drawing of a single concept as they increase in skill. While these show the typical skill levels of students in beginning design studies, they are very commendable efforts. The drawings show use of markers—a skill in the use of media—somewhat deemphasized as computing provides alternative rendering capabilities. The use of markers is identical to any other form of line work; they must be applied quickly with confidence. At these early stages of drawing development, the marker work is usually too slowly applied, causing excessive "bleeding" of the ink across boundaries of line and shape.

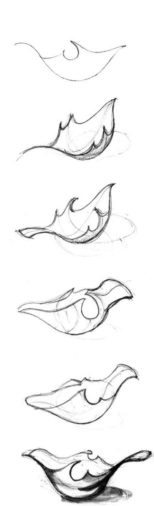

Figure 1-45
(Ruth Fowler)
Natural form is frequently the springboard for the development of objects and products. Ruth Fowler has used a leaf form—showing a sequence of developmental drawings—through which she creates the form for a creamer.

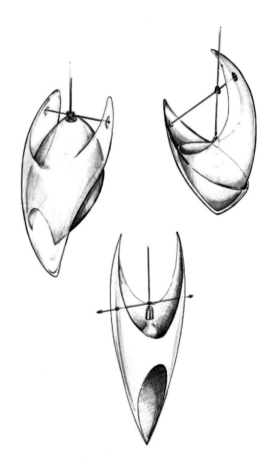

Figure 1-46
(Ruth Fowler)
Natural form has also influenced the conceptual drawings for a hanging light fixture. In addition, these drawing are examples of personal style and how consistently style emerges regardless of the design problem or the subject matter.

TIP - As a general rule of thumb, use heavier line weights on the outer edges of a conceptual product and lighter line weights on the interior. ■

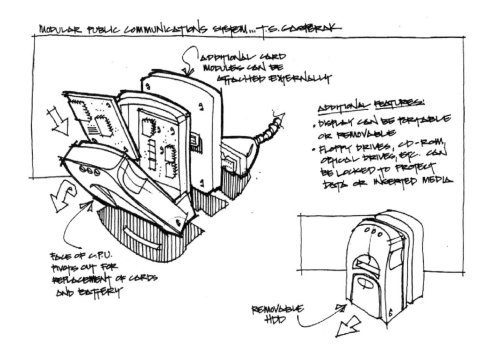

Figure 1-47a
Figure 1-47b
(Tim Gasperak)
This is the work of an advanced student in the senior year of product design. At this point, the student has progressed to achieve a personal style. The use of text in hand-lettered form is consistent with the style of the drawings. Drawings are well composed and the perspectives entirely appropriate to the general mass and size of the objects.

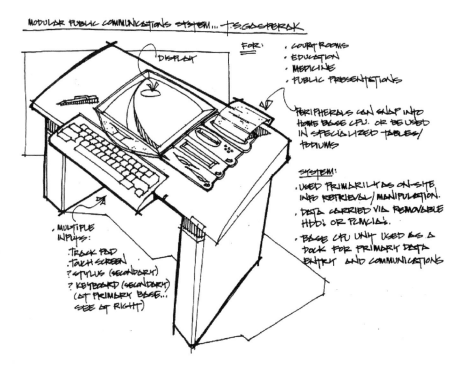

The drawings on this page show progression to an intermediate level of capability. These drawings demonstrate the direction students must take to achieve excellent results. There is a consciousness of materials, production methods, and the thickness of materials that must be part of the conceptual drawing process for a product designer. There is appropriate placement of controls and displays. In addition, there is a conscious effort to organize the page and enhance the representation of objects through composition.

Note that the transition begins with a simple outline drawing but progresses in the second drawing in the sequence to include a centerline and the suggestion of a cross-section that permits the designer to "read" the form from side to side and back to front.

Figure 1-48a

Figure 1-48b

(Tim Gasperak)

One of the most important points about developing conceptual drawing skill is that designers must be able to convey several ideas to potential clients and others engaged in the process. At this stage in this student's development, that capability has been achieved.

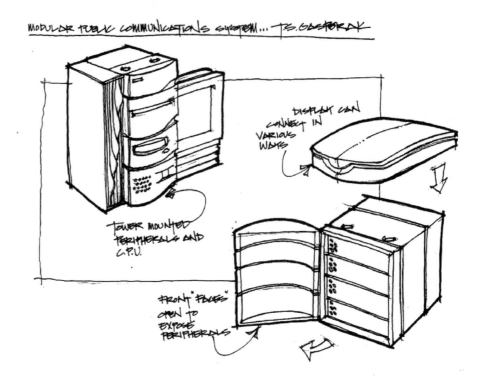

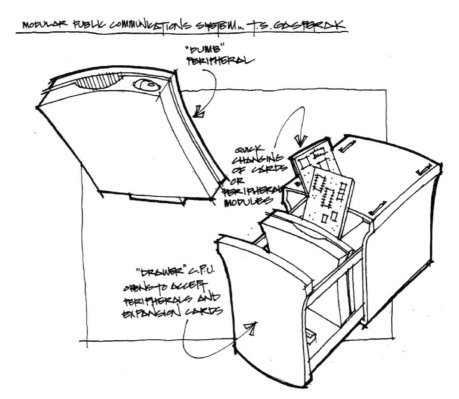

Sense of Geometry

The sense of geometry refers to the ability to see objects as a relationship of simple geometric forms. Every object can be reduced to geometric shapes that are connected, run together, truncated, or fused to create a more complex object.

(See Chapter 3.) To draw an object, it is necessary to analyze it visually, develop a sense of the proportions of the object, and reduce it to simple geometric forms. All complex three-dimensional design drawings begin with an analysis of three-dimensional form in space. Students of design

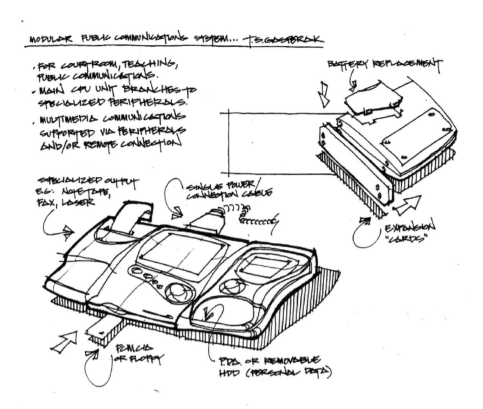

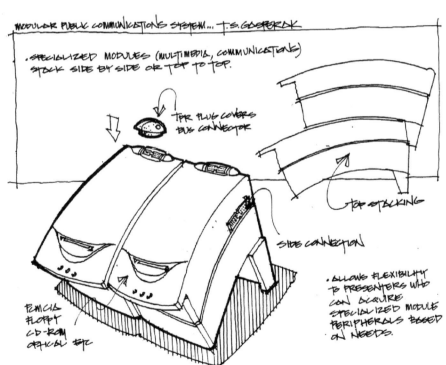

Figure 1-49a
Figure 1-49b
(Tim Gasperak)
At a certain point in the development
of conceptual drawing skill, the
designer must be able to "draw in" the
observer through the quality of the
drawing. These drawings abound in a
kind of intrigue generated through the
interplay of image and text.

drawing must begin to see the inner geometry of objects and not just the outline of form. The human eye sees edges, and this capability results in measurement of focus. It is logical that initial drawings are conceived as outlines of objects.

Nevertheless, development of geometry requires a different form of seeing—seeing the inner geometry of form to produce a three-dimensional appearance upon the drawing surface.

Figure 1-50a
Figure 1-50b
(Tim Gasperak)
The solidity of form is emphasized through the use of heavier line on the exterior of form than the line used on the interior. Also note the "elevation" of objects from the surface through the use of shadow. This device offsets the object from the page—adding interest—and increasing the novelty of the forms used.

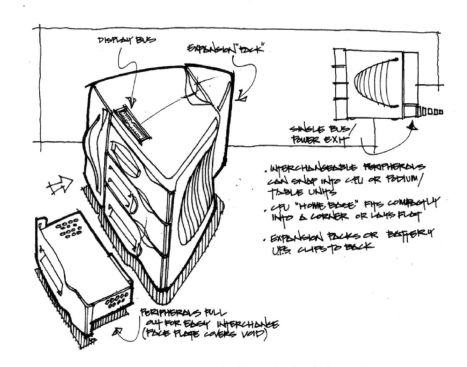

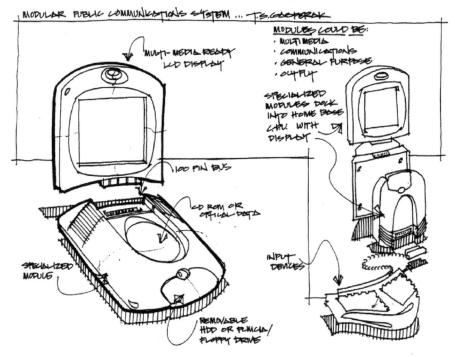

Sense of Perspective

To the accomplished artist or designer, a piece of paper has depth. Many artists and designers actually see the depth they want to convey as they look at the blank drawing surface. Michelangelo talked about seeing figures in the marble that he simply released by carving away the unnecessary stone. The surface of the paper is a front plane with limitless space behind it. As the pencil, pen, or other drawing instrument moves, it moves into

Figure 1-51

(R. Preston Bruning)
Bruning's Fordson tractor demonstrates
his ability to develop the appropriate
ellipse forms for the wheels and then to
provide the traction plates on the surface
of the wheels properly—not a capability
of the novice, but one that should be
emulated. Again, control of line is the
reason such a drawing—without erasures
and done in ballpoint pen—is a solid
depiction of the vehicle.

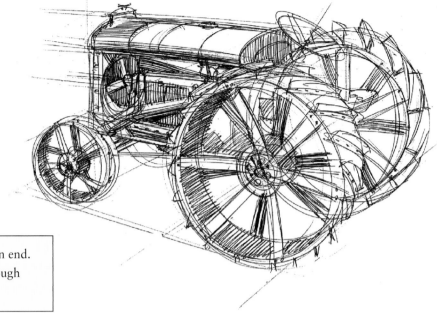

TIP - All lines have a beginning and an end.
Lines also have emphasis created through
changes in line weight. ▪

Figure 1-52

(R. Preston Bruning)
Bruning's American Austin motorcar's
special qualities stem from his vivid
recollection of the vehicle from
memory—not from a still life or from a
photograph. This ability to capture
images of interesting objects and designs
augments the ability to conceptualize.
Designers store a vast repository of
images from which they extract and
apply form solutions to other objects.

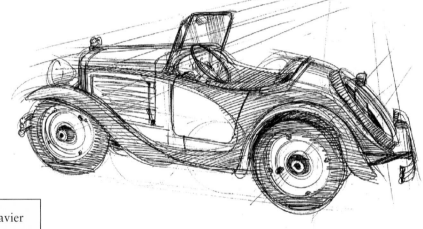

TIP - As a general rule of thumb, use heavier
line weights on the outer edges of a conceptual product and lighter line weights on the
interior. ▪

the paper toward a theoretical vanishing point.
Mechanical perspective methods are useful tools,
but cumbersome and time-consuming in the conceptual drawing process. One purpose of learning
mechanical perspective is to develop an innate or
inborn sense of where lines should go on a surface so that one draws a three-dimensional object
properly without the use of the technique. In
using mechanical perspective, the beginning student of design should begin to see the line work

penetrating the surface of the page and not
remaining on the surface as a form of two-
dimensional grid.

Conclusions About Fundamentals

It is possible to define conceptual drawing as the
communication of ideas about objects and environments that are drawn from the imagination.
Beyond the definition of such visualizations,
there must be intent and purpose. There are five

Figure 1-53a
Figure 1-53b
Figure 1-53c
(Anne Letherby)
Two junior-level student
drawings for presentation and
a full-scale model of a
handheld VHF radio/receiver.

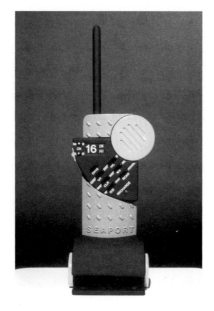

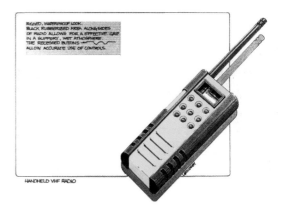

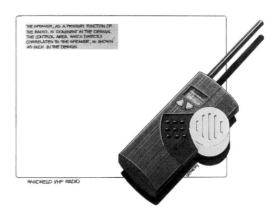

TIP - Practice at least one hour every day, seven days a week! ■

objectives that must be met in developing adequate conceptual drawing skills.

1. Designers require a form of communication that allows representing the largest number of potential solutions to a problem in the shortest amount of time. Conceptual drawing is a derivative of earlier forms of "empathic drawing" that are meant for rapid visualization.

2. Clarity is important in the visual depiction of objects and spaces. The purpose of art may be communication with the self, but the purpose of conceptual drawing and design visualization in general is the communication of ideas to others.

3. The process of designing is one that includes both designer and client. Conceptual drawing should be a means for mutual decision-making—and for eliminating surprises to clients that are typical of "black box" approaches.

4. Regardless of the speed of drawing, conceptualization must convey the aesthetic direction of the design for both products and environments. It

is a mistake to assume that rapid visualization is so-called "rough" drawing. Conceptual drawing should always be of a high quality sufficient for exposure to others.

5. The process of conceptualization is also a means to innovate. Conceptual drawings should progress beyond aesthetic renditions of external form or "surface rendering" to demonstrations of novel technical solutions to problems. Such technical explorations include but are not limited to, for example, ideas about use of materials, mechanical innovation, and relationship to the end-user.

Establishing purpose raises issues about how to achieve adequate visual communications. This text departs from the norms of accepted practice in instruction that avoid a formality in discipline. The "conventions" discussed in this chapter begin with rudimentary physical behaviors and attitudes on the part of instructors and students. Approach to the work is critical—including the physical approach of posture, addressing the work surface, and manipulation of the media tools. Fundamentals issues include practice, evaluation, and criticism, and the method by which one achieves the "elements" of freehand drawing: line quality, sense of perspective, and sense of geometry.

As stated in this section of the text, there are other methods, practices, and teaching styles used for developing conceptual skills. The authors establish a set of "conventions" that have been proven in the classroom—not only regarding instructional methodology but also in terms of specific application of media to the drawing surface. Few texts if any deal with the initiation of learning visual conceptual skills—the most difficult skill (according to sources in the field of art education) to develop. Drawing objects and spaces from imaginary sources is supremely difficult, but is exactly what is required of the designer. As skills develop, so does the imagination. The more accomplished the designer becomes, the more ease the designer brings to the work, and the greater the creative output. Evidence from brain scan research supports these contentions. Facility becomes imbedded. It becomes so much a part of how the designer functions that the quality of drawing is automatic—virtually unavoidable. Students matriculating in design studies who engage with the subject matter in earnest will succeed with the assistance provided through this text and the support of competent instruction.

The organization of this text does not separate instruction from learning; the information,

> **TIP** - Wheels on vehicles are an indicator of size and proportion. ∎

Figure 1-54a
Figure 1-54b
Figure 1-54c
(Kevin Reeder) Senior-level mixed media drawings on white opaque paper and (lower-right) over a blue-line drawing—permitting several variations—depicting the controls and display for a compact earthmover.

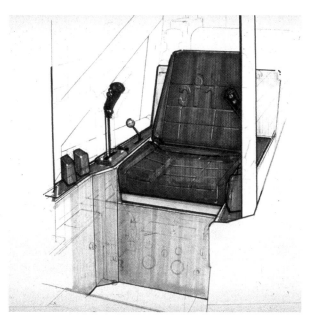

Figure 1-55a
Figure 1-55b
(Aaron Bethlenfalvy)
A senior thesis project was the design of a specialized bicycle for police use. The finished conceptual drawing reflects ideas about suspension members and structure that are carried out in the full-sized prototype—placed on display in front of a full-sized tape drawing.

examples, and process are all meant both for teachers and for students—participants together in the act of developing drawing as a communication tool. The instructor must set aside the mindset that is akin to the drummer in a slave ship beating out the rhythm for the oarsmen. If drawing improves inside and outside the classroom, it does so when instructors understand the idea of participation as opposed to teaching through authority. Authority used in the classroom does

not replace good instruction and being prepared to demonstrtate drawing in class.

Students must set aside the notion that drawing is a "class." Everything intructors pass on will take place in a specific amount of time. There is a defined relationship to instruction that puts the student on the receiving end of knowledge to be dispensed as if it were so many magic pills. This will be repeated, but when the student finds their hands are propping up their heads and they are

Figure 1-56
(R. Preston Bruning)
The rapidity of conceptual drawing
disallows the use of mechanical
perspective, but depends on a complete
understanding of perspective construction.
In Bruning's drawing above, all the
perspective lines are drawn freehand and
demonstrate various points of view—from
a high eye point in the drawings of the car
and tractor, to a very low eye point in the
drawing of the early steam engine.

counting down the minutes until class ends, they
should not be in that drawing class. What happens
inside the classroom is a focused effort to move
development in ways that cannot be achieved without instruction. Sessions outside the classroom that
entail practice are essential as well—just as an athlete prepares by running, weight training, and rigorous calisthenics.

Beyond developing the fundamentals is the full
range of visualization capability required of a
designer. Design visualization uses drawing to
achieve many levels of presentation of ideas, from
the initial development of rudimentary ideas to
the full presentation of finished and detailed
designs for product, interiors, and visual
communications.

Figure 1-57
(R. Preston Bruning)
A very small section of a much larger
drawing in marker illustrates the concept
of a hovercraft transport. The depiction of
water spraying off the sides and stern of
the vehicle is effective as a series of lines in
broad-tip marker.

Figure 1-58

(R. Preston Bruning)
This freehand perspective drawing is a transporter vehicle concept in mixed media on newsprint. Conceptual drawing includes all aspects of a concept—including fantasy. This drawing clearly shows how well the competent designer captures scale, the relationship between the user and the product, and sensitivity to materials. Note how well the drawing of glass is handled.

There is no level of drawing—from the napkin to the finished work on vellum—that is exempt from a standard of excellence in drawing. There is no place in initial conceptual development for chicken scratches and a great deal of arm waving to take the place of a clear representation of an idea. When students say, "Don't look at the drawing, look at the design," those students have missed the point of conceptual drawing and visualization. Ideas are never divorced from the presentation. There is no poor presentation of a brilliant idea. Instructors cannot be expected to see through poor drawing skill to fathom the genius that lies behind the lines; the genius is always *in* the lines—especially where developing visual design is a crucial component of design responsibility.

The content that expands beyond the basics requires development and a depth of explanation placing each segment of content in chapters. Chapters 2 through 5 discuss the following content in depth: perspective applications in the freehand mode of drawing; developing three-dimensional form; lighting and surface finish conventions; and objects in the context of human use and environment. Chapter 6 specifically deals with conceptual interior drawing and the techniques and tools relevant to that area of visual conceptualization. Chapter 7 has the greatest number of visual images dealing with presentation and communication,

providing advanced forms of freehand conceptual drawing. It also is a collection of "case studies," collections of drawings in sets that respond to areas of problem focus and the development of solutions. The work of students as well as professionals is presented to expand the student's frame of reference concerning approach, style, and shaping of visual content in the form of presentation. Chapter 8 is the final chapter with "hybrid" conceptual drawings, the use of computer enhancements combined with scanned line drawings. Chapter 8 acknowledges the power of computing and the generation of images using computer graphics software. Hybridized drawings are the intermediate step between manually generated conceptual drawings and the development of three-dimensional images using computer technology exclusively. The benefit of this method of image generation is that it takes advantage of the speed of line drawing and the variations that are possible using computer software.

This text does not deal with product or interior rendering. Rendering is a specific form of illustration that usually is produced after the conceptual process has taken place. Renderings are useful visualizations and have their place in the design process. However, the focus of this text is developing communication skills to convey ideas to others so that the process of design can be initiated with an understood requirement

Figure 1-59
(Kevin Reeder)
A conceptual drawing for a heavy equipment control and display console. This drawing conveys the essential relationship of components that would be part of a mockup to evaluate user-control relationships.

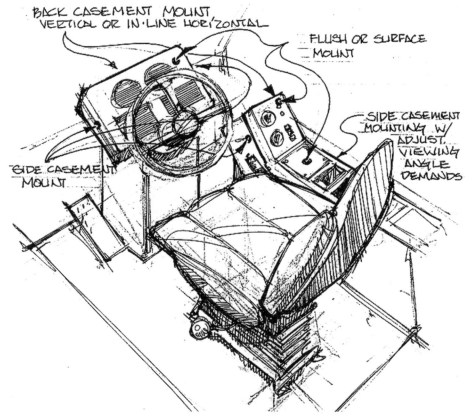

to exchange ideas with others. Rendering takes place when ideas are solidified and a single solution is in hand. There are exceptions to this rule of thumb, especially in the film industry and in stage set design where the look and feel of an environment or a situation must be conveyed. In product development and in the interior design process, conceptual visualizations require multiple explorations that are reduced in number through a deductive design process.

Through the time spent in teaching, instructors discover that everyone has a learning clock and no one learns anything at the same rate of speed. That is the inherent flaw in all educational programs—especially if one employs a retention model. Theoretically, in a retention model, all students should be able to learn all or most of the material. Regardless of the time frame of curriculum design that is either a semester or quarter system, there will never be enough time in either to achieve the theoretically desired result.

All too frequently, grading systems do not measure comprehension and performance; they measure output over time. Learning to draw in the classroom has the same issues regarding rate of comprehension as does learning calculus. The only difference is that output over time is far more easily measured on tests where there are single answers to questions as opposed to an assessment of the performance of students learning to draw. College math uses a curve to grade because the rate of speed required to learn all the material is much faster than the time allowed in

TIP - There is no such thing as cheating in the development of drawing. Copy anybody who has superior drawing skills. It is impossible for any individual to duplicate someone else's style. Every person will develop their own. ■

a single course. The fastest learner in a class may be able to comprehend and either recite or produce test results that cover 60 percent of the material. That performance could benchmark the best grade with others who learned less over time, getting lower grades.

This whole construct of pedagogy means that most students do not learn much at all and, because they are younger and adept at short-term memory, do not retain much of what they learn. That affects all other courses for which the previously noted calculus class is a model for appropriate instruction. The ability to learn something faster than someone else has nothing to do with

Figure 1-60
(Kevin Reeder)
A conceptual drawing for a child safety seat intended for use on airliners. This drawing has been executed on high-quality tracing paper with a tone background achieved through the use of gray pastels.

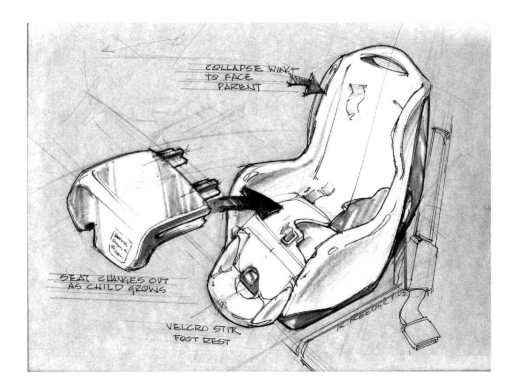

intelligence, nor does it govern competency. Too frequently, the fast learner is seen as the intelligent student. It is far more important that students retain what they learn and can apply what they learn—especially in the realm of design. Thus, the calculus simile is an important example of what not to do for those who teach drawing, a subject that has become foreign territory to the design student.

When students were selected for their capability to visualize, the initial drawing course was a means to determine which students had what level of skill. There were usually different levels of ability and different preferences for visual subject matter. An assessment could be made to determine where students should focus their studies in discrete design fields. It matters little, in this construct, whether the quarter or the semester system determine time available because the ability to draw is already present. When virtually every student enters a program without drawing skill as a given, the problem of instruction becomes more like teaching any other subject. If the pedagogical philosophy of retention is a tenet of the measurement of performance, then every student should learn enough about drawing to progress to the next step of application to a specific area of

intended study. For the purposes of this text, those areas are seen as industrial (product) design, interior design, and visual communication design. However, there is no difference between these intended fields and any other where the subject matter of visualization is important. The engineering disciplines require some ability to visualize—and many engineering programs still maintain links to art and design for that purpose. At the core of this expectation of learning is the question of what can be achieved.

To answer the question of what can be achieved—with any sense of affirming the concept of professional orientation—it is necessary for design educators and students, who share in this responsibility, to address the following seven pedagogical guidelines.

1. The issue of time and rate of learning must be suspended as ways to measure student performance where and when initial skills development is involved. For some, the process may take longer than for others, but achievement occurs nonetheless.

2. Design programs should produce pre-entry forms of study and practice that are aimed at skill development prior to program admissions.

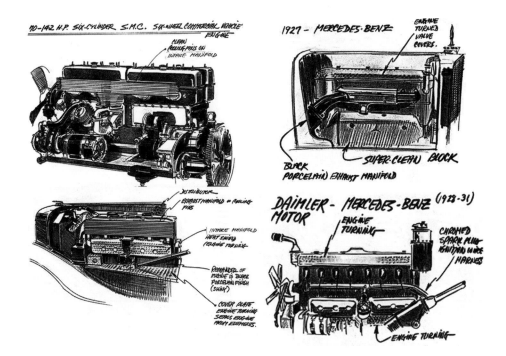

Figure 1-61
(R. Preston Bruning)
Simple black-and-white drawings of
vintage engines with notations regarding
the significant components of these
innovative power plants. The drawings
demonstrate excellent use of line and the
use of markers to indicate shape. The
automotive industry has used designers to
"clean up" the messiness of engine design.
These "under-the-hood" designers have
contributed not only aesthetics—derived
from vintage engine designs—but also to
functionality and ease of maintenance.

3. A series of consultation sessions—not critique sessions—should be employed to review work with students both at the point of entry to a program and on a continuous basis after admission and enrollment.

4. Potential students who seek admission to design programs have a responsibility to utilize the resources provided to develop skills as much as possible *prior to* program enrollment and matriculation.

5. Practice and discipline must be instilled in every student who enters a professional design program. It is their responsibility to follow practice guidelines and understand that not everything that must be learned will be presented as course material during class.

6. Graded course performance objectives are meaningful beyond initial skills development objectives when a level of adequacy has been established. Grading makes sense when the student has developed the capacity for skillful and creative visual solutions to complex design problems.

7. There can be no black box approach to problem solving if design is seen (correctly) as a participatory act in multidisciplinary team situations—resulting in carefully detailed design resolutions in an open, iterative, and deductive design process.

There are many avenues and techniques for advancing this proposition of self-study and continuous self-administered learning. "Learning to learn" has been and remains today a tenet of university education. It has become more important to give the student tools of continuous self-development rather than force-feed visualization content at a rate the student is unprepared to digest.

A good many programs already employ the Internet as an augmentation to the classroom. This important technology can be the vehicle for courses the student should do at their own rate. All that would be necessary is for the student to produce evidence upon application to a program that such a course or series of courses were taken. There is the option of doing the course for credit, but the issue is that continuous practice and the discipline of practice are defeated when they are completed for a reward that has little meaning. It is a situation similar to that old adage, "How does one get to Carnegie Hall?" The answer, of course is, "Practice, practice, practice." However, as mentioned earlier in this section, practice without focus and with only general intent may not produce the results in skills development that are necessary to support program excellence. Therefore, a careful program of instruction must be provided

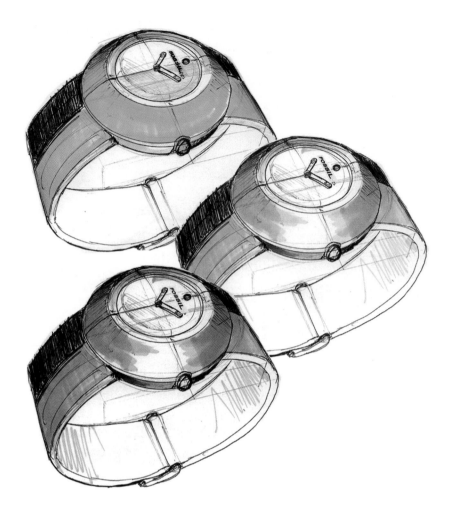

that has clear objectives and both the opportunity
and possibility of achieving them.

Drawing can be learned and drawing can also
be taught. It is not necessary to see the ability to
draw as specifically related to innate talent or
ability. These two realizations make the process
of developing visualization skills faster, more efficient, and applicable as a means of communication of ideas. Somewhere, at some time along the
way, the student of drawing must fall in love with
the act of drawing itself to make the progress necessary for full professional development. It cannot be a chore to practice; drawing should never
be drudgery.

While the process of learning to draw may
seem formidable at first, it cannot remain so. If
the student feels that drawing is an imposition
and something to be tolerated and endured in a
classroom for a grade, that person should question their aptitude for design and move on to a
better application of their intellect and their
labor. While most individuals can learn to draw

adequately in the context of design communication, not everyone really wants to draw at a level
that will permit them access to design professions. On the positive side of this discussion, very
few students find drawing to be tedious. Most,
even those who are not interested in pursuing
design professions, gain from the experience. This
is important for everyone because designers
become better at what they do when clients and
end users of design are more familiar with design
process and design excellence.

Now it is time to pick up that pencil, pen,
marker, or charcoal stick and, without hesitation
or fear, begin something everyone once did as a
child without that hesitation or fear. For those
who have not drawn in many years, the first
scratches on that piece of paper will be disap-
pointing, but be patient and continue working at
it. A great revelation waits down the path of this
learning process. There will be those times when
it seems as if no progress is being made.
Everyone bloodies himself or herself on that

Figure 1-63
(Michael Butcher)
The wrong way to change directions
drawing lines. Without removing the
paper, the designer must either run
around the table or contort the drawing
arm and hand.

See Segment 1:
Fundamentals

brick wall of knowledge—but the wall eventually
yields and afterward, development can occur
rapidly, even beyond expectation. It is also
important to know that no progress will occur
without approaching that personal intellectual

brick wall. It cannot be avoided. When that
occurs, and frustration mounts, it is important if
not essential to keep focused on the goal of
attaining adequate if not excellent conceptual
drawing skills.

Figure 1-64
(Michael Butcher)
The right way to change directions
drawing lines. Removing the paper from
the pad—first—allows the designer to
use the power stroke to make lines.
Rudiments of this sort are discussed in this
chapter and demonstrated in the DVD,
Segment 1: Fundamentals.

See Segment 1:
Fundamentals.

2 Using Perspective in Conceptual Drawing

Perspective Resources Revisited

Every elementary school child knows that things appear to be smaller the farther away they are from the viewer. Every designer automatically understands this concept when employing perspective: when the designer draws objects on a page, certain fundamental principals guide the placement of every line. While some designers rework drawings to alter perspective or to "tighten up" the line relationships in perspective, some errors are contrary to perspective and unacceptable to the practiced eye.

Four excellent reference books on perspective should be part of every design student's library. The classic text is Jay Doblin's book, *Perspective, A New System for Designers* (1977). Used for over three decades, this book is a ready reference for industrial and interior designers, is well illustrated, and supported by a clear instructional text. Most designers appreciate "applications" of principals such as perspective. Doblin's book has remained useful precisely because of its direct relationship to the tasks of designers. If refreshing the perspective knowledge base is required, consult Doblin's text. *Design Drawing*, by Ching and Juroszek (1998) has good references to mechanical perspective construction. *Perspective Charts*, by Phillip J. Lawson (1940) is useful if designers are required to have accurate layouts for products in space or interior views of environments (see Mayo Drawings in Chapter 7). However, these charts are not useful as guides for perspective in the conceptual drawing process. The more recent *Basic Perspective Drawing: A Visual Guide*, by John Montague (2005) captures much of the spirit of Doblin's earlier work and advances the more complex development of mechanical perspective.

To convey ideas about perspective conventions, the examples in this chapter include typical one-, two-, three-, and multiple-point perspective—emphasizing point of view by providing a "simulated" viewer. In the majority of problems posed to designers, one- and two-point perspectives should be enough for use in conceptual drawing.

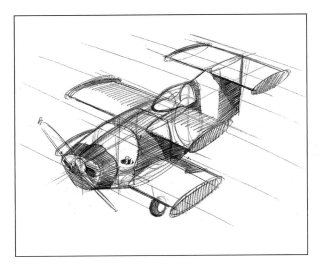

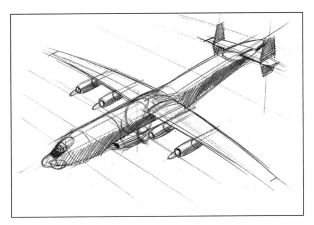

Figure 2-1a
Figure 2-1b
Figure 2-1c
(R. Preston Bruning)
R. Preston Bruning's line drawings clearly show the perspective guidelines used to ensure the consistency of the aircraft drawings. The vanishing points and horizon line are imaginary, existing only in the mind of the designer.

Figure 2-2a, Figure 2-2b
(R. Preston Bruning)
R. Preston Bruning's line drawings of
complex large machines assume an eye
point low to the ground plane, providing a
dramatic, effective view of this large steam
engine. The low eye point perspective is
useful to convey the massive size of the
machine. These drawings use ballpoint pens
and avoid the erasures associated with
pencil line drawings.

Knowing more complicated forms of perspective
informs the product and interior designer and
provides a basis for assessing and comparing
mechanical perspectives. Architects require a
background and knowledge regarding complex
perspective development that is not essential for
other design professions.

Developing Freehand Perspective in Conceptual Drawing

Reading about perspective and using mechanical
means for developing perspective is necessary and
useful, but frequently does not prevent fundamental difficulties that occur in freehand perspective
development. As stated repeatedly in this book,
conceptual drawing is an immediate and fast form
of visualizing. It requires an innate sense of

perspective—and the knowledge of the principles
that will permit accuracy and speed of form development. Studying mechanical perspective is necessary to build a range of perspective conventions
that will allow accurate development of objects
and environments. A primary issue for design students—as well as professionals—is to avoid critical
perspective errors that can go unnoticed by the
novice and avoided by the more practiced designer.
Some of these perspective drawing errors are discussed in the following sections.

Reverse Convergence

In freehand drawing, it is easy to lose track of
how lines that define an object extend back to a
vanishing point. Where lines converge at the front
of the picture plane, object perspective lines seem

Figure 2-3

(R. Preston Bruning)

An R. Preston Bruning conceptual drawing in mixed media. The different media used for this drawing include the following: Verithin Prismacolor pencil line for the basic free-hand layout, design markers, and pastels for the color and form definition as well as the background; line markers and Prismacolor pencils for the definition of details that define the shapes.

If this drawing had been done using a mechanical perspective, the layout would have been complex and the design time tripled. Bruning's ability to envision the form of this aircraft—a "lifting body" aircraft for the transport of large containers and vehicles—and develop it freehand allows him to produce a fully developed color drawing in three to four hours. The generation of alternative designs as well as views of the craft explain the concept visually without the extra costs of time consumption.

The speed in conceptual drawing is an essential part of its efficiency. Competent designers, even those with much less ability than Bruning, can generate numerous variations on a design theme as well as explore details of a single design easier and quicker by hand than when using a computer. Computers find their way into conceptual drawing in composite drawings or "hybrids." See Chapter 8 for examples of hybrid drawings. However, the best image-makers have developed skills in freehand drawing *before* they use computers.

Bruning achieves complex variation in textures in this drawing, including the background of cloud formations and the land below the aircraft. Note the reflective surface of the lifting body and the wing forms.

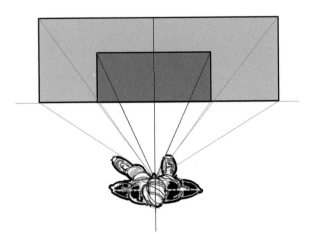

Figure 2-4

(Joseph Koncelik)

The closer the viewer is to the object, the more severe the perspective. The walls of the rectilinear form shown to the left and in figure 2-5 appear to flair outward—especially in the development of single-point perspectives.

One modification to the single-point perspective that can be effective in interior and product (object) drawing is to move the point of view to the left or right off the centerline without developing a second vanishing point. The view of the Bentley automobile (Figure 2-6) maintains such a shift in the point of view, exaggerating the perspective of the forward wheels and the cabin as the viewer's gaze shifts to the right.

Figure 2-5

(Joseph Koncelik)

This drawing is a view of a single-point perspective with the eye point centered on the horizon line. Single-point perspectives can be effective when developing concepts of interior spaces as well as vehicular side views. Single points enable relatively fast drawings without the complexity of determining where two or more vanishing points meet.

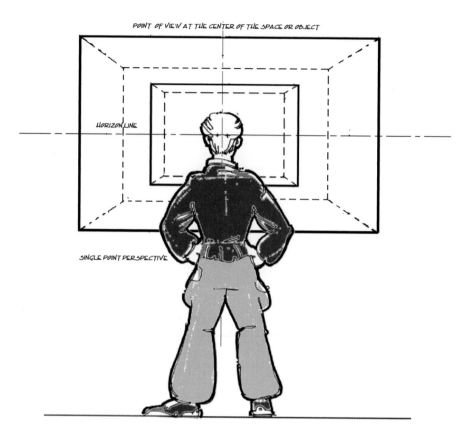

Figure 2-6

(Joseph Koncelik)

The observer's point of view of the observer shown in the rendition of single-point perspective is at the automobile's beltline, lower than the roofline. This view simplifies the drawing and provides interest. The step-by-step drawings of a sport vehicle demonstrate an easy. quick sketching method beginning with wheels on the ground line and progressing through six general steps to a finish level appropriate to this form of concept drawing.

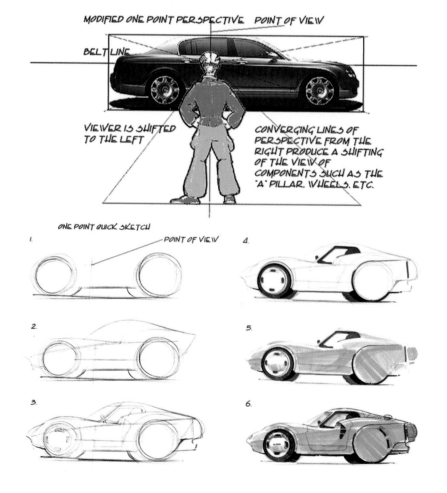

Figure 2-7a
Figure 2-7b
(Joseph Koncelik)
Vehicular design concepts can be generated quickly using single-point perspectives. In this step-by-step example, the first step is drawing a ground line followed by a series of quick sweep lines used as guides to develop the car. Erase no lines. All lines remain visible through to the final rendition in number 5.

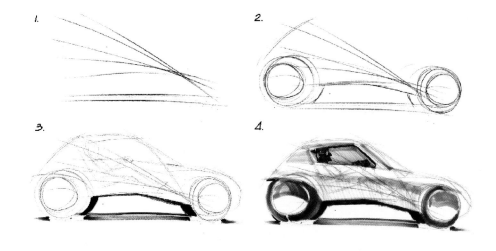

to come together in front of the object and not at the rear at the vanishing points. Lines that should go back on the page to a vanishing point converge to the front of the page, making the object *out of perspective*. For the beginning design student who is working at drawing three-dimensional objects, creating a consistent and correct perspective is one of the most difficult problems faced. The more complex the line relationships, the more difficult it is to identify problems of reverse convergence. One reason for the occurrence of reverse convergence is that the size of most products, appliances, and other fabricated objects prevents most convergence of lines to the rear of the picture plane. Assessing the amount of convergence in freehand drawings, especially in objects "smaller than a breadbox," can be difficult.

Over-Development of Perspective

Severe perspectives may make objects, products, and interiors seem dramatic in the drawing, but communicate incorrect information about the size of the object. Automotive stylists influenced the tradition of product designers through the drawings of William Mitchell, former Vice President of Styling at General Motors. As a young designer, Mitchell became an internal corporate celebrity by producing automotive drawings with extreme perspectives. Prior to Mitchell's approach to automotive rendering, styling was achieved using engineering views—elevation, front, rear, and plan views—of an automobile that were then altered using mechanical drawing and air-brush techniques. Mitchell's drawings, using techniques he developed in advertising design, were an ingenious

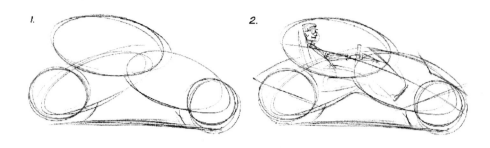

1.

2.

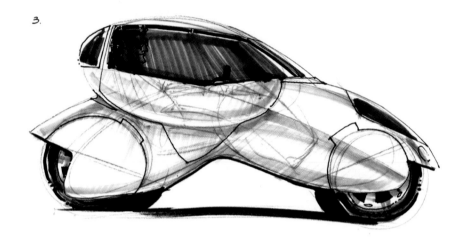

3.

Figure 2-8a, Figure 2-8b
(Joseph Koncelik)
These three step-by-step examples and the
five on the previous page illustrate how an
effective drawing can be generated in only
seconds—a few minutes at the most—
depending on the size of the drawing. These
examples demonstrate the principles of
conceptual drawing. The designs emerge
from the drawing process without
developing a concept first. Each is an
interaction of the designer and the act of
drawing itself; design and visualization are
combined.

With respect to technique involved, the
use of tools is a progression from pencil lines
(Verithin pencil) to cool gray marker of the
tires and undercarriage of the car to beltline
"light cores," explained in Chapter 4, using
a middle value gray marker. The drawing of
the driver appears in shadow before the final
treatment of marker to represent the tinted
window.

While the idea may be fanciful, a
limited amount of time is spent generating
the drawing. Designers can generate ideas—
accept or reject them—without a large time
commitment and associated costs.

Again, to develop these single-point
perspectives, begin with a ground line and
place the wheels on that ground line.
Continue the conceptual interaction by
using lines or shapes such as those depicted
earlier. There should be no erasures in these
quick idea sketches.

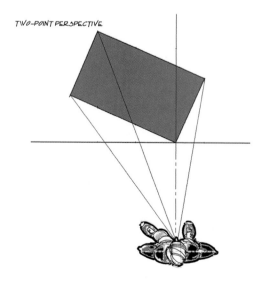

TWO-POINT PERSPECTIVE

Figure 2-9
(Joseph Koncelik)
Two-point perspective is the most prevalent form of perspective development
used to generate product and interior drawings. Place two vanishing points on a
horizon line and shift the point of view to fit the expression of object or space
providing the most visual information. Centering the point of view on an object
is usually not effective—especially if the object is not a sphere or cube.

In this example, a view of two sides of the six-sided volume results from a
shift in the point of view to the right. Note that the eye point determines the
horizon line, which determines when an object appears above the viewer's eye
point. In instances such as this, objects appear to be large—as in R. Preston
Bruning's drawings (Figures 2-2a and 2-2b) of steam-powered machines earlier
in this chapter.

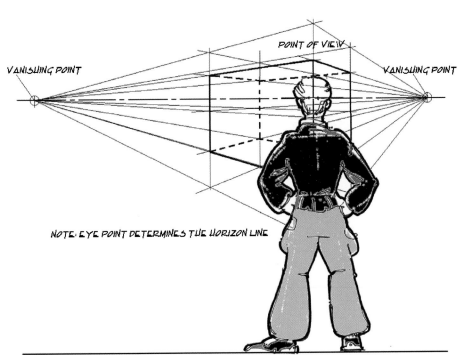

VANISHING POINT

POINT OF VIEW

VANISHING POINT

NOTE: EYE POINT DETERMINES THE HORIZON LINE

Figure 2-10
(Joseph Koncelik)
Two-point perspective is illustrated in these diagrammatic drawings with the point of view on the horizon line and the viewer "in close" to the object. Construction of two-point perspectives on a single page usually renders a perspective that is far too severe to represent most products that are "bread-box" sized or smaller. This is the major reason a "sense of perspective" must be an integral part of the intuitive conceptual process. Objects require guidelines but no mechanical perspectives.

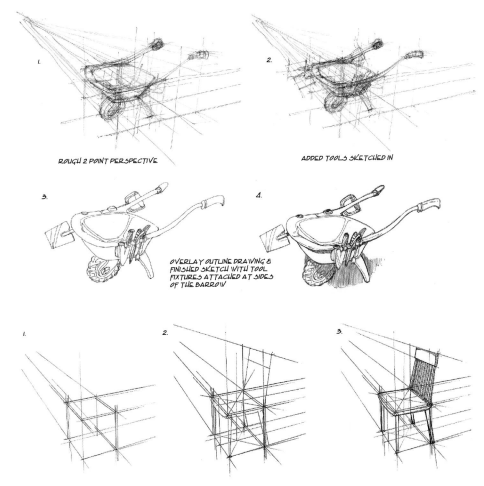

1.

ROUGH 2 POINT PERSPECTIVE

2.

ADDED TOOLS SKETCHED IN

3.

4.

OVERLAY OUTLINE DRAWING & FINISHED SKETCH WITH TOOL FIXTURES ATTACHED AT SIDES OF THE BARROW

1.   2.   3.

Figure 2-11a
Figure 2-11b
(Kevin Reeder)
These sequential perspective drawings depict objects that are *not* ordinarily seen above eye point—a standard side chair and a gardening wheelbarrow with tool attachments. The chair is primarily a demonstration while the wheelbarrow is conceptual. A straight edge helps define the lines meeting at imaginary vanishing points on the chair drawings at the top of the page. The guidelines for the wheelbarrow are drawn freehand with vertical markers used to gauge the proportion of the product(s) from one side to the other to be faithful to the perspective. Rather than attempt shading to indicate the interior curved form of the wheelbarrow, a series of curving lines indicates the depth. The tool attachments are relatively easy to add to the sides of the barrow after drawing the perspective. Note that a series of lines depict a shadow below the barrow, giving the sense of sitting on a ground plane rather than floating in space.

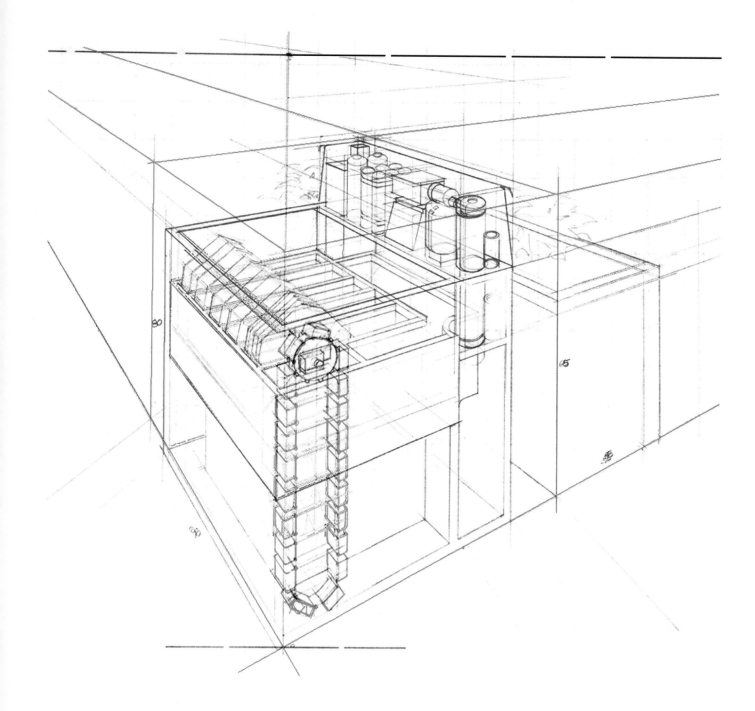

Figure 2-12

(David Tompkins)

When the subject matter contains visual information that is complex, a mechanical perspective is necessary. This two-point perspective underlay drawing by David Tompkins is an underground water purification system with attention paid to the significant relationship between mechanical components and various purification devices and containers. Therefore, the layout must be accurate, and substantial attention must be paid to the dimensional relationships among all parts of the system.

The unusual nature of this system—from a design point of view—is that it is underground. The two-point perspective layout is, thus, below the eye point to provide a sense of the system's location. Even so, the chosen point of view has one vanishing point farther from the point of view than the other, reducing the necessity to draw the two vertical sides equally. This also increases the drawing's dramatic effect.

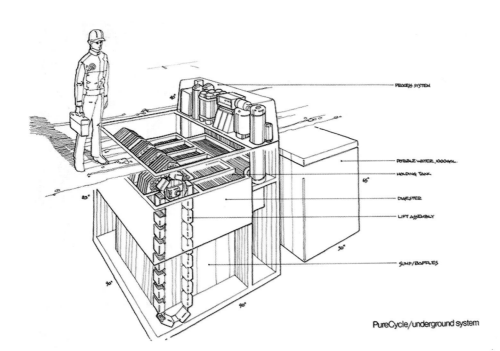

PROCESS SYSTEM

POTABLE WATER, 1000GAL.

HOLDING TANK.

DIGESTER

LIFT ASSEMBLY

SUMP/BAFFLES

65°

30°

83°

90°

90°

PureCycle/underground system

Figure 2-13
(David Tompkins)
The finished drawing created using the underlay (Figure 2-12) done carefully in ink line. To create the sense of scale that would not be apparent otherwise, a figure stands on the ground in the closest relationship that would occur with this underground system. Note that the controls and other devices required for operating the system are above ground to the left of the figure.

An important aspect of this drawing is that it retains a sense of personal style regardless of the mechanical approach. Line work indicates shadow and emphasizes the components that are critical in the device's design.

calculation to elevate his designs to achieve the same recognition he received in his early experience as an illustrator. However, extreme perspectives are not always useful and leads to mis-communication of size and scale to other viewers of the drawing that is inherent in the development of two-point mechanical perspective.

Too Little Distance Between Vanishing Points

Placing vanishing points close to the object may seem to make the object dramatic in appearance, but this simply makes the object appear larger in scale than it is in reality. When objects have steep or acute angles in the foreground, they appear distorted. While some drawings look dramatic this way, the scale is usually incorrect. Only architectural perspectives can utilize such acute angles of line convergence in the foreground. Such techniques are usually inappropriate for representing products, people, and other artifacts that should appear in human scale. The general rule of thumb is that the nearest angle in the foreground should never be less than 90 degrees when drawing a product—or any object that is near human scale. In freehand drawing, the vanishing points of the perspective are quite far apart on the horizon line. The larger the object on the page, the more distance should be between the vanishing points.

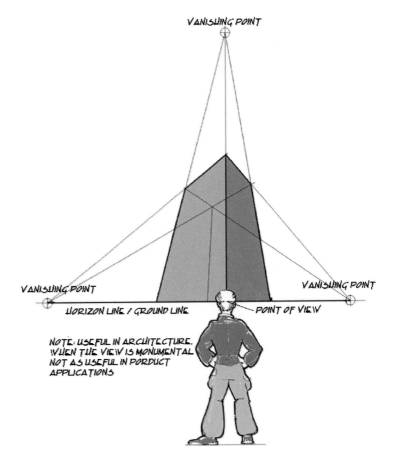

VANISHING POINT

VANISHING POINT

VANISHING POINT

HORIZON LINE / GROUND LINE

POINT OF VIEW

NOTE: USEFUL IN ARCHITECTURE, WHEN THE VIEW IS MONUMENTAL. NOT AS USEFUL IN PORDUCT APPLICATIONS

Figure 2-14
(Joseph Koncelik)
The three-point perspective illustrated in this drawing is appropriate for the development of architectural form. In this example, the horizon line and the ground line are combined, so there is no need to develop the perspective of the floor plane of the object.

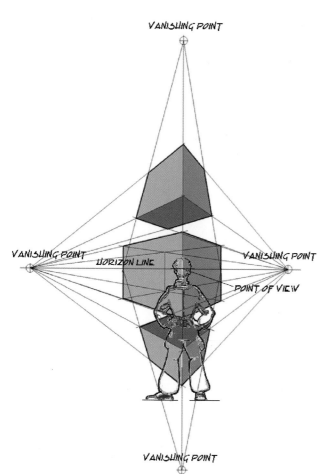

VANISHING POINT

VANISHING POINT   HORIZON LINE   VANISHING POINT

POINT OF VIEW

VANISHING POINT

Figure 2-15
(Joseph Koncelik)
Multiple-point perspectives give the appearance of objects seen in a "fish-eye" lens. These forms of perspective may be appropriate to developing *Star Wars* interiors conveying vast expanses, but they do not lend themselves to product and interior drawing—especially in the conceptual domain.

Many of the drawings provided in this text have perspective guidelines that, if drawn to vanishing points, would require expansive pieces of paper or a full ten- to fifteen-foot wall to construct. In actuality, these sketches are without the benefit of horizon lines, station, or vanishing points because the designers knew where they would be and how the lines would relate. This takes practice, but virtually every student of design can accomplish it.

Placing the "Eye Point" Too High

Another common and problematic judgment made by beginning students of conceptual drawing relates to drawings done when they were in their formative years. High eye points on drawings

Figure 2-16
(Joseph Koncelik)
One of the most common errors among novice design students when creating reverse convergence of object lines occurs when lines of perspective converge in the foreground of the page and NOT at the horizon line. Unless the illustrated form is intentionally a wedge, it is incorrectly drawn.

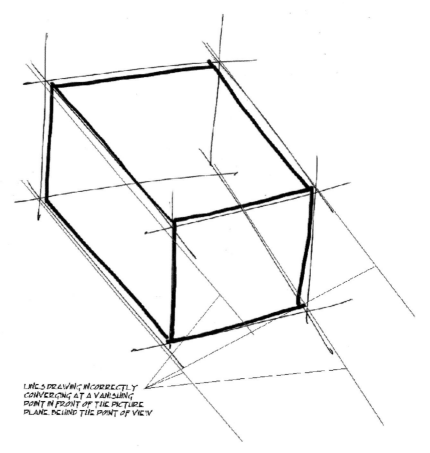

LINES DRAWING INCORRECTLY CONVERGING AT A VANISHING POINT IN FRONT OF THE PICTURE PLANE, BEHIND THE POINT OF VIEW

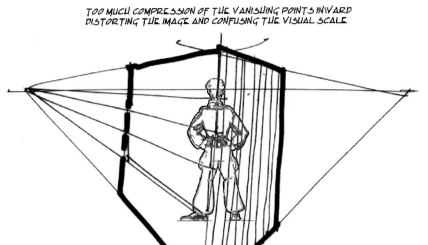

TOO MUCH COMPRESSION OF THE VANISHING POINTS INWARD DISTORTING THE IMAGE AND CONFUSING THE VISUAL SCALE

Figure 2-17
(Joseph Koncelik)
Moving the vanishing points in too close to the object creates an "architectural" perspective. This drawing is too exaggerated in perspective to represent cabinetry, a form that should be in the thirty-inch to three-foot height range. Also note that the object rises above the horizon line, further exacerbating the problem of an exaggerated perspective.

reflect a student's memory of their early childhood drawings their desire to "see every detail" of the object or scene. Getting high off the ground permits the viewer to draw or see all of the surrounding details. Looking down on the world also allows the artist to draw more of the objects and environment to provide as complete an array of visual information as possible.

Two things happen when the eye-point is too high: first, it takes longer to render the object, and second, the view is unrealistic. Few people see a kitchen appliance while suspended thirty feet in the air. Many products show more of the top surface than the front and sides. An important and detracting aspect of this approach is that the designer must render more surface area to

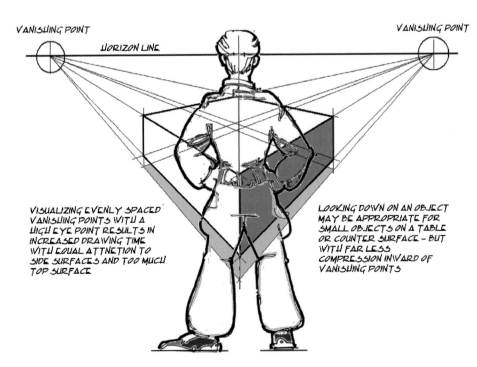

VANISHING POINT
HORIZON LINE
VANISHING POINT

VISUALIZING EVENLY SPACED VANISHING POINTS WITH A HIGH EYE POINT RESULTS IN INCREASED DRAWING TIME WITH EQUAL ATTENTION TO SIDE SURFACES AND TOO MUCH TOP SURFACE

LOOKING DOWN ON AN OBJECT MAY BE APPROPRIATE FOR SMALL OBJECTS ON A TABLE OR COUNTER SURFACE - BUT WITH FAR LESS COMPRESSION INWARD OF VANISHING POINTS

Figure 2-18
(Joseph Koncelik)
Moving the vanishing points in toward the point of view and dropping the ground line, or, conversely, raising the eye point, creates objects that require more drawing time than necessary to carry off an idea conceptually. This diagram demonstrates the increase in total surface area in a drawing that is counterproductive to quick conceptual drawing.

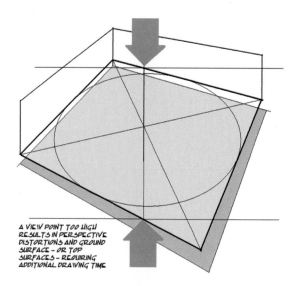

A VIEW POINT TOO HIGH
RESULTS IN PERSPECTIVE
DISTORTIONS AND GROUND
SURFACE - OR TOP
SURFACES - REQUIRING
ADDITIONAL DRAWING TIME

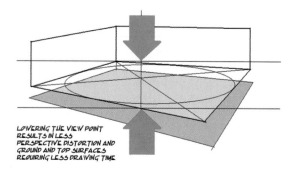

LOWERING THE VIEW POINT
RESULTS IN LESS
PERSPECTIVE DISTORTION AND
GROUND AND TOP SURFACES
REQUIRING LESS DRAWING TIME

See Segment 2, Perspective, on the DVD for a demonstration of the uses of perspective in product and interior development.

Figure 2-19a
Figure 2-19b
(Joseph Koncelik)
These quick sketches illustrate the difference in the amount of surface area that must be developed in a drawing when the eye point or point of view is raised too high. This error happens often among novice design students and is a carryover from childhood drawings. In childhood, drawings are an exploration of a world and require complete information. Conceptual drawing conveys sufficient information to represent the idea—and no more.

complete a drawing when a high eye point is used. This increases the time spent on the drawing and defeats the fundamental purpose of conceptual drawing—communicating ideas to others.

The high eye-point is a common error when drawing interior perspectives. In interior drawing, the conceptual drawing is to give some sense of the theme or aesthetic of a space. The interior is best visualized from a standing eye point, seeing the objects, artifacts, and furnishings of a space in overlap (discussed in Chapter 6, Interior Conceptual Drawing). As noted previously, the problem with such drawings is that no one sees spaces or objects while hovering thirty feet in the air. Most objects are rather close to eye point—some three feet away from the eye point. Most interiors are seen from an eye point six feet above the ground. It is common for beginning interior design students to submit drawings with eye points thirty to fifty feet from the ground. In such drawings, more time spent will be spent rendering the surface area of the floor than on any other aspect of the interior design.

In a properly drawn room setting, most of the furnishings are seen in overlap—one object will be positioned in front of another. An accomplished designer with competent conceptual drawing skills uses overlap to enhance the spatial effect of a drawing. A technique known as "vignette" is also used to provide detail in the central part of the drawing with decreasing detail and rendering as the drawing progresses away from the focal point. Interior designers take longer to produce conceptual drawings than product designers owing to the amount of information necessary to convey impressions and thematic ideas. The set up of an interior drawing from the proper eye point reduces the amount of time required and increases the drawing's impact of the drawing.

Drawing the Circle in Perspective
Drawing the circle in perspective—the generation of an appropriate ellipse—is the true test of the designer's ability to visualize objects in perspective. A circle in perspective is an ellipse that fits within a perspective square. It is possible to construct an ellipse with mechanical perspective. The resulting object is technically correct, but may

Figure 2-20
(Joseph Koncelik)
In this freehand drawing, the eye point is just below the horizon line. The interior space is created by overlap of objects placed on the floor plane. The table and chairs in the foreground overlap—are in front of—the sofa and side chair arrangement close to the wall. Note the consistent use of marker for walls and floor; this avoids the difficulties of laying out marker lines in perspective.

seem distorted and may not even appear to be a circle. Note in the accompanying drawings in this section that a constructed ellipse can be drawn to fill the perspective square as carefully as possible. Another approach is to draw an ellipse locking the wrist and making a complete circular motion in one stroke with the hand and drawing instrument—drawing from the practice "calisthenics" mentioned in Chapter 1.

Construction lines in freehand are left as guidelines and the heavier line is used to pick out the true shape of the ellipse. As stated in Chapter 1, before the beginning student attempts to draw circles in perspective, students should have practice sessions filling a page with circles, not necessarily in perspective, but generated with one continuous motion.

Empathic drawing is the form of drawing where speed is required to generate line and control of line. Once some skill has been achieved in developing circles in this way, it is possible to move on to drawing the circle in perspective. Empathic drawing assists this process by combining the ability to control lines through continuous practice. Swinging the line of the ellipse through the positions of the points of its related perspective square in one motion is the best way to practice drawing an ellipse. In the drawing showing the quick sketch of a circular table with a circular base, the

difficulties of appearance are vividly illustrated. The improper alignment of the lower ellipse and its excessive tilt makes it impossible to place the table shown on any ground plane—a common mistake.

Objects That Are Not Sitting on a Ground Plane

Does the object float in space? Do the stereo, chair, or the case goods cabinet seem to be floating off the ground in space? Objects drawn in three dimensions in perspective *should be generated from the ground plane up*. Objects such as bottles or other containers should be generated from a centerline with a series of ellipses drawn to guide the outer construction of the object. Chairs and tables should be drawn in relationship to a defined ground plane and drawn from the legs, sitting on a floor plane, upward. Products such as stereo tuners or other six-sided box forms are defined by their footprint, the amount of area they take up on a horizontal surface. Students should draw the footprint first. Prior to drawing the table forms, a single square box should be drawn to guide the development of the table base. The table is then "built" from the ground up, and then shaded to emphasize the overlap of the top on the base and to indicate a simple and single light source.

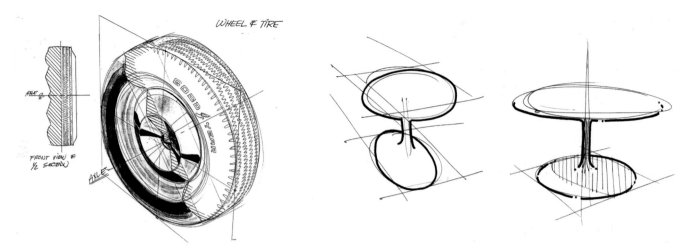

Figure 2-21a, Figure 2-21b, Figure 2-21c
(R. Preston Bruning, Joseph Koncelik)
Ellipses are the true test of the conceptual drawing ability of the designer. Note the "circle in the square"—the drawing of the tire that has an accurate set of ellipses defining the tire's shape. Of the two quick sketches of a pedestal table, one is incorrectly drawn; the other is more accurately drawn because a centerline was used and a better "ground" square defined the base.

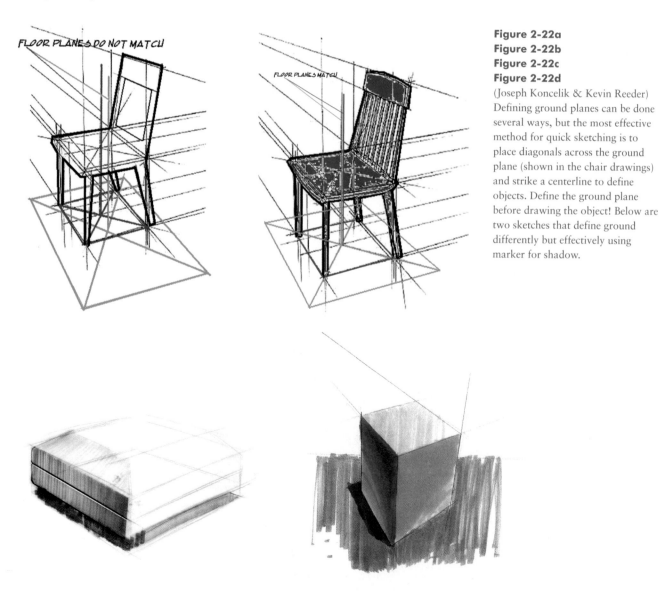

Figure 2-22a
Figure 2-22b
Figure 2-22c
Figure 2-22d
(Joseph Koncelik & Kevin Reeder)
Defining ground planes can be done several ways, but the most effective method for quick sketching is to place diagonals across the ground plane (shown in the chair drawings) and strike a centerline to define objects. Define the ground plane before drawing the object! Below are two sketches that define ground differently but effectively using marker for shadow.

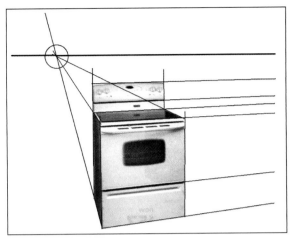

Figure 2-23a
Figure 2-23b
(Joseph Koncelik)
Maximize the exposure of the surface of an object conveying the most important information! Note that the point of view is at normal eye height with one side slightly exposed to view—allowing the definition of the rectilinear form. The front oven door, the range surface, and the backsplash that contains the control and display devices are critical in conveying the household range image.

Choosing the View Maximizing Critical Information

In developing a conceptual drawing, the designer should be as efficient as possible and not commit an undue amount of time to a single drawing. One way to avoid this problem is to select a point of view that is as close to the ground line as possible without distorting the perspective. It is also important to select a view with maximum exposure to the surface conveying the greatest amount of critical information and minimize the exposure of an object or space that does not convey critical information. This chapter shows examples of products where one face of the object receives maximum exposure and other faces (especially in the case of rectilinear forms) receive minimum exposure. The minimally exposed faces provide a sense of the three-dimensionality of the form and the overall shape or massing of the form. By choosing such a point of view and eye point, drawing time is less than it would be when attempting to provide full visual information for all sides given equal or near-equal exposure.

Analyzing the Drawing

Many students continue to make drawing errors because they do not analyze their drawings while they are in progress and after they have completed. Perspective errors are easy to make and, in freehand drawing, cannot be rectified without

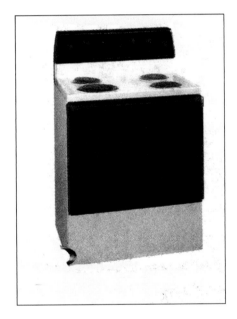

Figure 2-24
(Joseph Koncelik)
Maximize the exposure of object views that are critical to the concept to reduce drawing time during the conceptual process. Pages 68, 69, and 70 depict a similar method to do this: one vanishing point is close to the observer's point of view. The other is imaginary, but the lines of perspective must convey a sense of accuracy. The important information in this appliance image is the range top, oven door, and control and display on the backsplash.

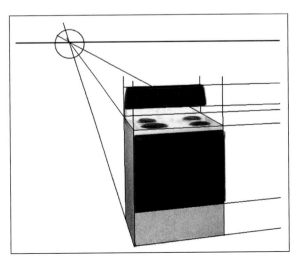

Figure 2-25
(Joseph Koncelik)
A variation on the theme expressed on the previous page with even less visible area of the side facing away from the viewer to the left.

Figure 2-26

(Joseph Koncelik)

The fastest way to defeat the accuracy of a conceptual drawing is to align the door on the washer/dryer combination's surface incorrectly. All surface lines are defined by the perspective lines drawn to the imaginary vanishing point. Students are advised to create clip files from magazines and newspapers that will provide similar views of images. These images can be useful in establishing an appropriate view of products and appliances.

proper scrutiny and diagramming of the drawing. One method to analyze the perspective of a drawing is to *hold it up to a mirror*. It is amazing how errors can be detected when the drawing is reversed for viewing. *Drawings held upside down* also reveal errors in line relationship and perspective.

In conceptual drawing, all line work should remain part of the drawing. Construction line work (frequently related to perspective) is critical to determine the correctness of a drawing. Students are frequently tempted to either erase construction lines or to trace over drawings and leave out construction lines. This is not helpful, especially in the early stages of drawing instruction and practice. Study examples of R. Preston Bruning's quick-study line drawing (Chapter 1) to see the effect of leaving all line work in place.

Conceptual drawings are not expected to be finished drawings in the initial stages.

Always back away from a drawing to gain some distance from the surface of the paper and the object being drawn. It is easier to analyze a drawing from a distance and if the full page is within the scope of viewing.

Conclusions About Freehand Perspective

Perspective in freehand drawing requires the development of an innate sense of perspective that can be applied to a variety of drawing/design projects or problems to accurately convey objects and space. Simultaneous and intuitive drawing of objects in a correct perspective presents significant challenges to the novice and several common errors must be overcome. These include the

Figure 2-27

(Joseph Koncelik)

Doubling the appliances becomes a relatively easy drawing operation following along the lines of perspective to the imaginary vanishing point. It is possible to extend such a drawing to include a micro-environment of products defining an interior space.

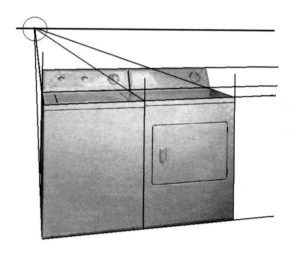

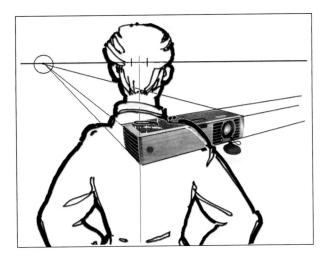

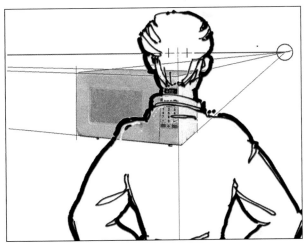

Figure 2-28a, Figure 2-28b, Figure 2-28c, Figure 2-28d
(Joseph Koncelik)
Products "smaller than a bread box" need to have a view established that
is the most common way of seeing the object. For the projector at the top of
the page, the view would most likely be at table top—giving information
about the front surface as well as the top, where most control and display
devices would be located. The microwave oven would be either at countertop
or above the eye point when housed in a cabinet or mounted below
cabinetry.

following major points about integrating perspective within the freehand drawing skill set.

1. Avoid creating a "reverse convergence" of lines of perspective that close in the foreground of a picture plane rather than converging at the vanishing points on the horizon line.

2. Do not attempt mechanical perspectives within the dimension of a single page of paper; this will force the vanishing points in close and distort the object. A stove is not a skyscraper, but exaggerated perspectives can give that impression.

3. Select an eye point in relation to a space or an object that is as low to the ground line as possible; for an interior, that height off the ground line should be standing eye height or somewhere in the domain of five and one half feet off the floor. Products that are appliance sized and sit on the floor should be viewed at no higher than standing eye height and can be just low enough to permit the visibility of top surfaces. Products in the hand-held or breadbox range of sizes can be seen at an eye height where the top surface is next to a horizon line.

4. Make sure objects in space do not appear to be floating in a gravity-free environment. Establish a ground plane to fix the object in space.

5. The test of design drawing is being able to draw the circle in perspective. Drawing an appropriate ellipse in relation to the square in perspective is difficult and requires practice. Drawings

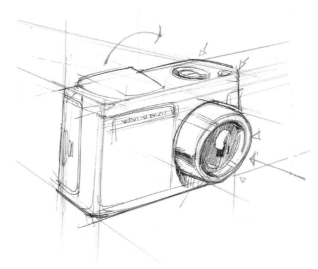

Figure 2-29a, Figure 2-29b, Figure 2-29c, Figure 2-29d
(Joseph Koncelik, Kevin Reeder)
Handheld products require little in the way of perspective—excessive perspective would be inappropriate. Cellular phones might be seen at virtual eye level. Cameras vary in size, but when drawing such products, follow the same guidelines as for image making. The two camera drawings are quick sketches with one an overlay of the other.

are "given away" by ellipse construction that is not accurate with respect to surfaces on which they are to be placed.

6. Emphasize an object's surface, which provides critical information to the viewer; give this surface maximum exposure. Minimize the exposure of other surfaces that convey the three-dimensionality of the object. Equalizing emphasis to all exposed surfaces increases the conceptual drawing time.

7. Analyze drawings as objectively as possible. Receiving critiques from others is important and

See DVD Segment 6, Presentation and Communication, for additional information about presentation of drawings.

Figure 2-30a, Figure 2-30b
(Joseph Koncelik)
Critical analysis of conceptual drawing is always essential. It is crucial to analyze drawings as they are done. These two images depict a rather clever means to identify drawing problems in a sketch: hold the drawing up to a mirror and tack up the drawing upside down.

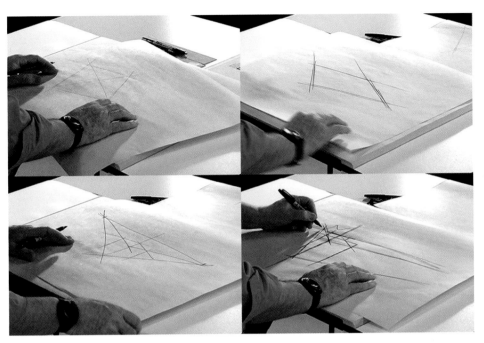

Figure 2-31
(Michael Butcher)
These images represent the sequence of operations and some guidelines for developing perspective in freehand conceptual drawing, beginning with limiting floor place and progressing through positioning of the point of view to capture critical visual information.

See DVD Segment 2, Perspective, for developing freehand perspective appropriately within the context of conceptual drawing.

should not be avoided. The designer can analyze drawings by viewing them in a position other than on the drawing board. Hang the drawing upside down to analyze the perspective or view the drawing as a mirror reflection. Reversing the image will also reveal perspective inaccuracies.

Perspective is an important attribute of conceptual drawing that permits the designer to convey a sense of the object or space realistically. No orthographic projection of a product can convey the image of an object as well as a perspective drawing. Individual practice at drawing freehand perspectives is useful, if not absolutely necessary. Drawing objects one likes helps generate skill, as Preston Bruning demonstrated in the number of "museum piece" transportation drawings in this text.

Figure 2-32
(Michael Butcher)
The perspective development of products reaches the most critical stage in the development of the ellipse form and its integration with other geometries. This sequence shows the development of a quick perspective sketch and the uses of an overlay to correct the drawing and finish the surfaces.

See DVD Segment 2, Perspective, for uses of overlays to capture and correct perspective images.

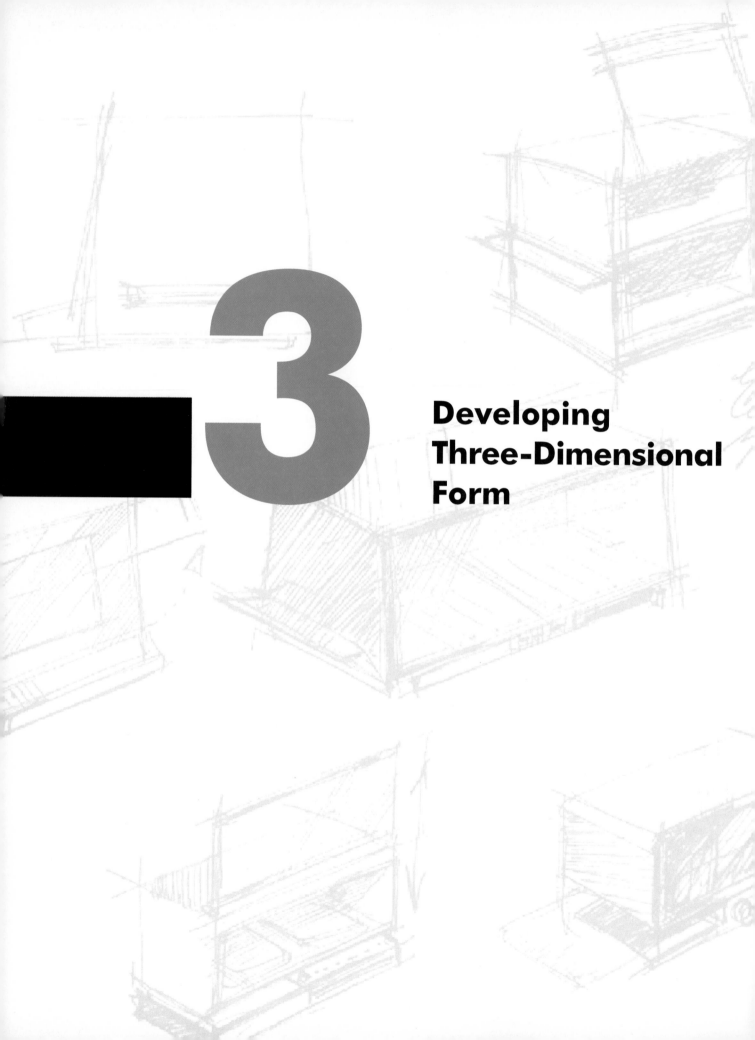

3

Developing
Three-Dimensional
Form

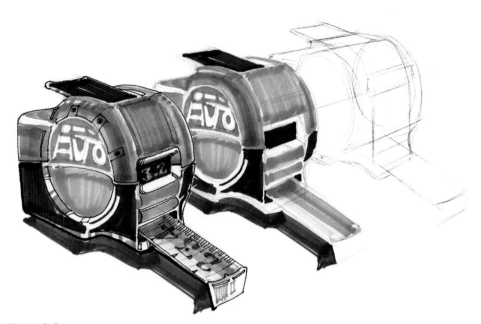

Figure 3-1
(Joseph Koncelik)
Geometry is the key to understanding all manufactured form. Every tool, consumer product, and even complex vehicles—as will be seen in this chapter—are composed of geometric shapes and volumes. In this quick conceptual sketch, the device holds a measuring tape coiled around a cylindrical drum using a coiled spring for tape retraction. From right to left, this sketch uses geometry as a point of departure for the development of the overall form. This quick sketch incorporates changes, such as defining the form with line work in the "finish" stage. The tape's release, retrieval, and stoppage are central issues in conceptual development. In this sketch, releases are on the top of the body rather than side or bottom locations. A digital readout is also placed on the front of the product—a location that changed in further sketching. Sketches at this level of drawing allow designers and their team participants to accept or reject ideas without a great deal of investment in the drawing process.

The Geometry of Form Giving

Cultivating a sense of how form should appear in conceptual drawing so it seems geometrically correct as well as visually balanced and in proportion comes after developing drawing skill. Developing a sense of geometry is not intuitive, nor is it based solely on talent. There are specific methods for creating appropriate geometries that are aesthetically and proportionately correct. The ability to fuse geometry with conceptual drawing skill must be learned simultaneously.

This chapter covers various methods for developing geometric and complex transitional form. There are two- and three-dimensional systems that are of great value to the designer. Kimberly Elam covers some of this material in her text written in 2001. This text, in this chapter, extends the information about creating geometric form and using proportioning systems—such as the proportioning systems used in vehicle development or the use of the "ribs and stringers" method drawn from ship and aircraft construction. It is important to develop continuous practice and use of systems of proportioning, geometry, and transitional conventions so that they become an intrinsic part of the conceptual drawing process.

What the Eye Can See

The human eye is an amazing visualizing organ of the human body. It is specifically "designed" to perform in a particular way—yet it does not perform at all or performs poorly in some aspects of visualization. The eye is "edge sensitive." The human eye sees color far better than some animals but it does not see the ultra-violet or the infrared ends of the spectrum. Other visualizing organs found in animals and insects are far better at seeing pattern, texture, and movement. Some species of nature's varied living organisms have eyes that contain far greater acuity. However, regarding perception of objects and space, the human eye is a "camera" device built to focus on the periphery of form—the edge of form that defines shape.

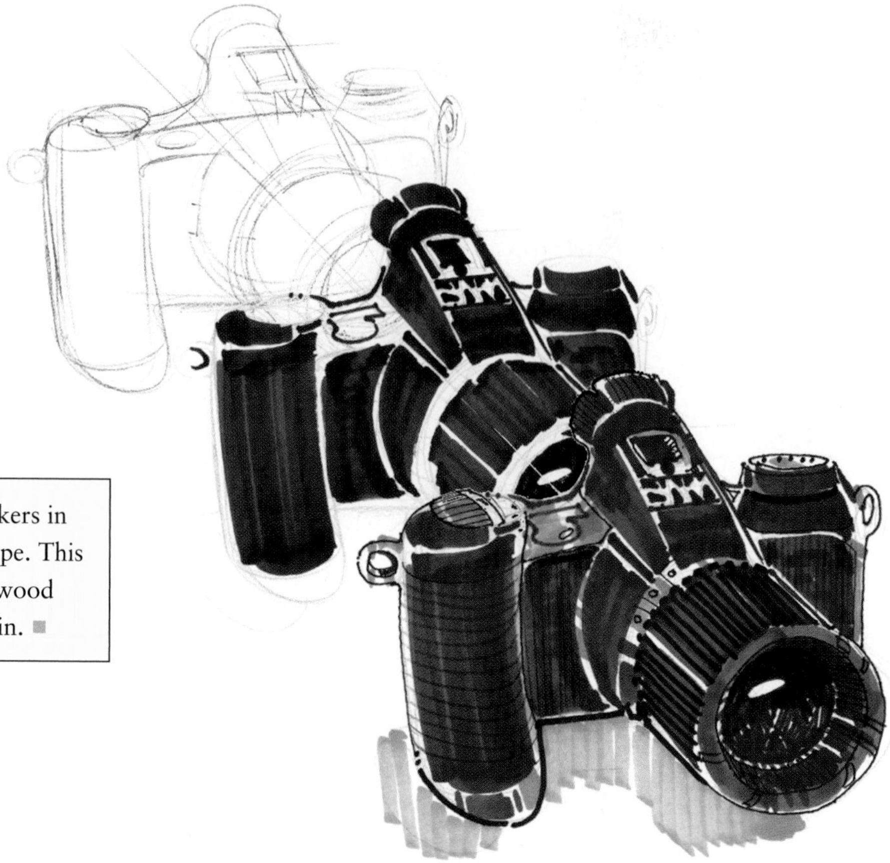

Figure 3-2
(Joseph Koncelik)
Camera lenses define camera shape. Here
again, in a "line, color, finish" series, the
cylindrical shape of the lens determines
the overall geometry of the camera. Note
that this drawing is totally freehand with no
use of guides or tools. Drawings of this type
take only minutes to do and allow the
designer to move on to other ideas that are
variations of the same theme.

TIP - Apply color and tone from markers in
the direction of the surface of the shape. This
is similar to finishing the surfaces of wood
by sanding in the direction of the grain. ■

Figure 3-3
(Joseph Koncelik)
This three-step "line, color, and finish"
drawing of a powered portable jigsaw
begins using a modified rectilinear form as
the base and a cylindrical form that is the
vertical member in the front of the product.
Surface treatment may obscure the
geometry in the end, but it is clearly the
basis for developing the form. Use markers
in the direction of the surface to heighten
the three-dimensionality of the object.

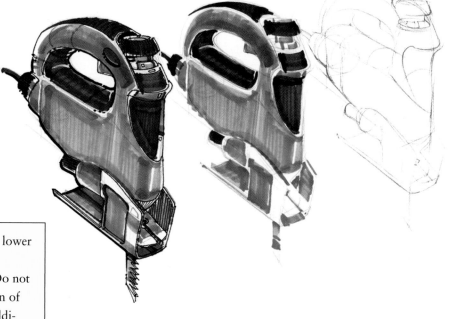

TIP - Use heavy line work to define the lower
outline of the form and lighter lines to
describe the top surfaces of the form. Do not
mix markers. Allow the first application of
marker to dry or set before applying additional marker to enhance the "core" areas of
reflection. (See Chapter 4.) ■

Figure 3-4
(R. Preston Bruning)
A drawing by R. Preston Bruning
exemplifies the use of line to
describe form. The drawing
illustrates the creation of form
using geometric shapes and
volumes. The finished automobile
drawing illustrates the designer's
capacity to capture proportion.

Perception of objects and understanding of space is oriented toward that human capacity to focus on the edge or exterior of an object.

It is natural that when children draw, they create an outline of the edge of any object. That is how the eye sees and how it focuses on objects. For example, the child—as well as the novice at drawing—depicts a person by first drawing a line around the exterior of the visual part of the form. The form's exterior description defines the placement of eyes, mouth, ears, and other details without any definition of the face or body structure. When children draw houses, they delineate the exterior that defines the doors and windows, affixed within the outline as if they were ornaments hanging on a surface. It is completely natural, and a logical relationship to how the eye works, to begin drawing this way. Unfortunately, the novice designer producing drawings that are outlines with ornamentation will depict objects lacking in proportion, structure, and scale. Objects and spaces must have structure, scale, and geometry to seem correct.

Continuing to draw without changing the process of drawing itself results in images that lack believable three-dimensional geometry and structure. *To move away from simply drawing of edges, students must reverse the process and rather than begin a drawing from the outside to the inside, they must begin to draw from the inside (the structure of objects and spaces) outward.* This is, perhaps, one of the most difficult changes expected of design students as they start to develop visualizing skills. It means, literally, seeing form in terms of the underlying structure of objects and developing visualized ideas that are constructions of carefully aligned geometric forms.

Geometric Form Development Using Line

Two important mental steps must take place to produce conceptual drawings that are credible representations of imaginary objects. First, the designer must engage in an analytical process to determine the internal structure of an object as well as the basic geometry of volumes that create the relationship of form masses. Second, part of the creative process will be the synthesis of forms, the bringing together and blending of geometric forms that make up the volume of the whole object. R. Preston Bruning's two drawings of an Indianapolis racing car shown in this chapter exemplify this two-step process. The car, as shown in the sketch, develops from basic three-dimensional geometric volumes. In the more refined drawing, these forms are further detailed and blended through the application of "fillets and rounds" to create the full sense of the machine. The accuracy of the drawing depends on visual examination of the car's geometry from all sides—not just the side facing the viewer.

Digressing for the purpose of clarifying this point, this process differs little from that employed in the overwhelming majority of fine art programs. One purpose of the many classes in human figure drawing is to gain the ability to see the figure in terms of massing of form that has structural relationships. Traditional fine arts programs have classes in anatomy and some even

Figure 3-5
(R. Preston Bruning)
Bruning's further development of
form using line and inside-out
construction of objects illustrates
classic product and vehicle designs.
Bruning demonstrates his facility to
create ellipsoid forms—circles in
perspective. The Ahrens Fox
pumper depends completely on the
geometric development of form.

engage in human dissection to understand the
human body in depth. Again, this is part of learning to draw from the inside out. Drawing from
the inside out had its genesis in the Renaissance,
and is exemplified by the myriad human anatomy
studies of Leonardo Da Vinci. The human figure
is complex and has endless possibilities for creative artistic visualization. It is far less complicated to deal with fabricated objects that have a

Euclidean geometry of basic three-dimensional
shapes. Traditional fine arts incorporate the same
developmental premise; the artist (or designer)
must be able to see beyond the edges of objects
and the delineation of spaces to see underlying
structure and geometry. While the artist works
somewhat intuitively using formal education to
build a subjective repository of form, that artist
still visualizes from the inside outward. To define

Figure 3-6
(Kevin Reeder)
The drawing shows a different but equally
skillful application of line that establishes
the scale of objects through perspective and
intensity of line work at the drawing's focal
point. Use of the human figure establishes
scale. (See Chapter 5.) The visualization is
convincing owing to careful articulation of
the geometry of specific components.

The most significant aspect of this
drawing and the drawing in Figure 3-7 is
the use of vignette. Vignette is a process in
which the designer provides the most
detailed drawing at the focal point and
allows the detail to lessen as it moves away
from the focal point. In this drawing, the
figure in the foreground, the vehicle tractor-
treads, and the surrounding ground plane
texture receive the most detail. The
remaining areas of the drawing lessen in
detail the farther away they are from the
figure.

Figure 3-7
(Kevin Reeder)
A similar style as that in the drawing Figure 3-6 this vignette focuses on the front end of the tractor and the figure changing a tire. The background fades away. It provides environmental context, but it is not as important as the visual information in the foreground.

Interior sketching frequently employs vignette. The necessity to provide visual information to convey an interior idea does not mean the entire environment must be treated with equal attention to all details. Focusing attention on the important information, usually in the foreground, and letting the rest of the interior space fade away saves time. It is more effective—from a time-management point of view—to draw interior sketches in multiples using vignettes than to fully render a complete drawing that may or may not be a satisfactory solution to a client's needs. In addition, several drawings done efficiently with an eye toward time management will convey more information than one time-consuming drawing.

these two steps, analysis and synthesis, more specifically, the following terms may be helpful.

Analysis

All man-made objects utilize geometric shapes and volumes. Conversely, all manufactured objects utilize building blocks of geometric form. Two-dimensional shapes such as circles, squares, rectangles, and triangles are the root of developing volume. It is possible to "extrude" a circle to make a cylinder—to extrude a square to make a cube or rectilinear volume—to rotate a circle on a

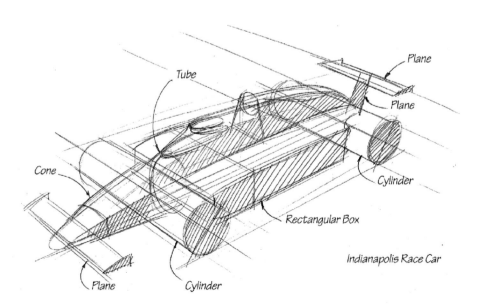

Indianapolis Race Car

Figure 3-8
(R. Preston Bruning)
Preston Bruning's drawing of an Indianapolis racecar demonstrates geometric analysis. Basic geometric forms have a "structural" relationship, including cylinder forms for wheels, rectilinear solids for side fuel tanks, conical sections for the nose, and planes for the airfoils fore and aft.

Figure 3-9
(R. Preston Bruning)
This drawing demonstrates synthesis of
form. The geometric forms of the
previous drawing (Figure 3-8) have been
refined (using an overlay) to create the
transitions between shapes and bring out
the detail that identifies the drawing more
clearly as the specific vehicle represented.

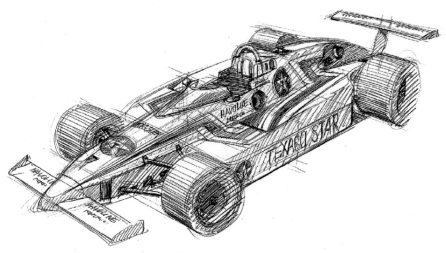

Indianapolis Race Car

single axis and create a sphere. Developing form
in this way combines with perspective to place
objects in a virtual three-dimensional space.

Synthesis

Once geometry in perspective defines the object on
the drawing surface, geometric forms connect with
transitional line work, merging with fillets and
rounds. Such transitional elements exist on every
machine-made object. There are no perfectly
square edges on the exterior of mass-produced
objects. A **round** is the edge that always has a
radius. A **fillet** is the curving surface that connects
one form with another. The blending of the fuselage of an airplane with the wing employs a con-
caved surface known as a fillet. In essence, the
merging of geometries into a specific visualized
design of form is a process of synthesis—bringing
things together to make a cohesive whole.

Understanding Proportion

There is substantial and significant literature on
the subject of proportion. One of the most useful
and carefully documented is Kimberly Elam's,
*Geometry of Design: Studies in Proportion and
Composition* (2001). Elam investigates proportioning systems in use throughout the ages in fine
arts and the design professions and demonstrates
the application of such systems in graphics, products, architecture, and even vehicular design. Her
comprehensive work on this subject details how

the use of proportioning systems can be used
both developmentally and analytically. As
Kimberly Elam states in *Postscript*, in *Geometry
of Design*, about the value of geometric systems
applied to form giving:

"What [geometric organization] offer[s] to the
creative idea is a process of composition, a means
of interrelationship of form, and a method of
achieving visual balance."

Proportioning systems apply to the development of visual communications at the onset of
the design process in the conceptual stages. It is
useful to see such systems applied intuitively in
conceptual drawings of products and interiors
within the time frame that usually occurs after
the onset of the process. However, as Elam points
out in her book on the subject, students must be
acquainted with the use of geometric systems as
they apply to form giving or they are, in essence,
on their own in realizing the value of such content. Without a sense of proportion, designs
become awkward visually—without balance—
and it usually takes more than an intuitive
approach to insure the visual "stability" of form
development.

Preston Bruning's rough analysis of vehicle
design in relationship to the proportion of wheels
is an example of proportioning that is useful at
the onset of conceptual design. Graphic design,
product, and interior design differ in the use of
conceptual drawing as a fundamental step in

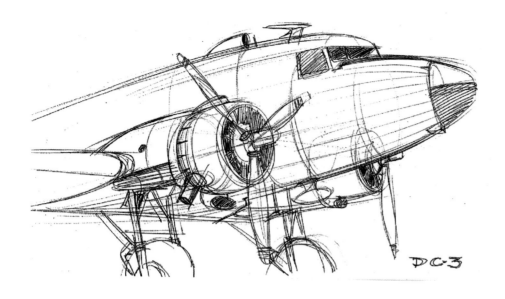

DC-3

Figure 3-10a
Figure 3-10b
(R. Preston Bruning)
These examples show the uses of
geometric form in the development
of quick freehand sketches. Note
that the drawings both show
full description of shapes to better
describe the relationship of one
form to another, as well as provide
a more accurate three-dimensional
appearance.

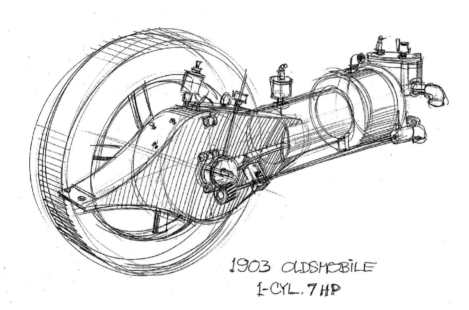

1903 OLDSMOBILE
1-CYL. 7 HP

generating ideas. While it is entirely appropriate for the graphic designer to approach the development of form through a geometric construction, other design disciplines require that a sense of that geometry be developed and imbedded in the process of creative thinking for geometry to be useful. The Bruning proportional analysis of vehicles provides one way to approach a specific order of design related to vehicle development. The geometry of products differs from the geometry of wheels. It relates to the careful construction of objects using geometric form in a carefully constructed relationship. Simply put, developing a sense of the geometric principles for proportioning

is most useful in the process of developing forms with visual balance.

Form in Transition

For the most part, developing the form of electronic technologies, household appliances, furniture, and architectural products is a derivative of geometric form. Knobs on a radio are cylinders. Electronics for stereo systems and VCRs, for example, are easily seen as being derived from rectilinear volumes. Other areas of complex form development require going beyond the use of basic geometric forms. The slippery shapes of the modern automobile and the hulls of watercraft

Figure 3-11a
Figure 3-11b
(R. Preston Bruning)
Bruning's drawings represent
examples of the uses of geometric
form in quick freehand sketches.
Aircraft have complex transitional
forms in the fuselage as well as in
wing surfaces. The line work
Bruning deftly applies describes
form and gives the image
three-dimensionality.

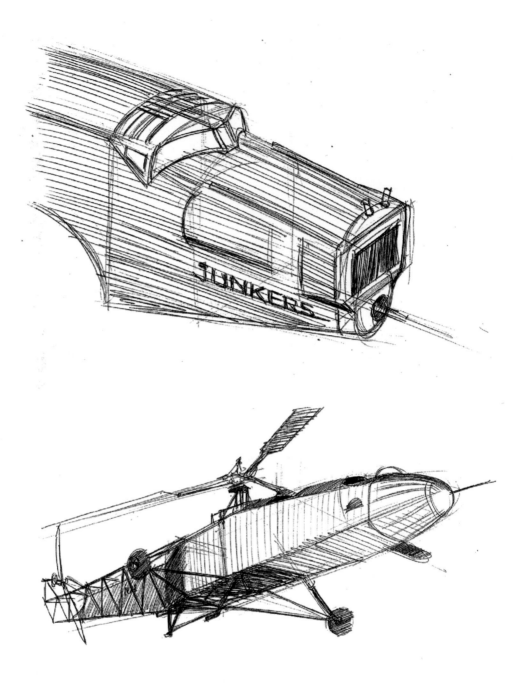

require additional means of visual analysis to complement the use of basic geometry. These three-dimensional forms usually change from one end to the other through a gradual alteration of cross-sections. This is form in transition.

Forms that change from one end to the other require analysis in the same way as the form development of airplanes and ships. The complex shaping of ships and airplanes—the two vehicles that have defined and informed designers regarding form in transition—evolved and developed from the need to create efficient forms that could pass through the fluidity of water and the gaseous atmosphere of air efficiently and without resulting drag that would slow down these vehicles. Naval architecture essentially informed the process of aeronautical engineering and both share a common heritage in form development.

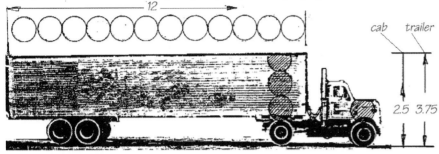

Proportional Analysis of Two Differing Semi-Tractor Trailer Trucks

Using truck wheel size as the guage of general length to height proportions...

A "cab-over" rig with slightly longer trailer section

Figure 3-12
(R. Preston Bruning)
This image demonstrates a relatively simple method of assessing proportion derived from a system created by Homer Lagassey, Jr., a designer for General Motors Corporation. It is the use of wheel dimension to determine the length and height relationships of vehicles. This method is never exact, but it is relative to the overall proportion of a vehicle—establishing its visual balance.

Later, these techniques of form analysis and synthesis emerged within the automotive industry as "streamlining" became part of the functional and aesthetic development of automotive design. Ship builders drew full-scale outlines of their crafts using chalk on the floor of huge open buildings called lofts. The term "lofting," used to create the engineering drawing of ships, airplanes, and automobiles, derives from this process. While much of the process of engineering drawing is now relegated to computers, automobile designers drew full-size side, front, rear, and top or plan views on large drafting tables in the "BC," or Before Computers, days.

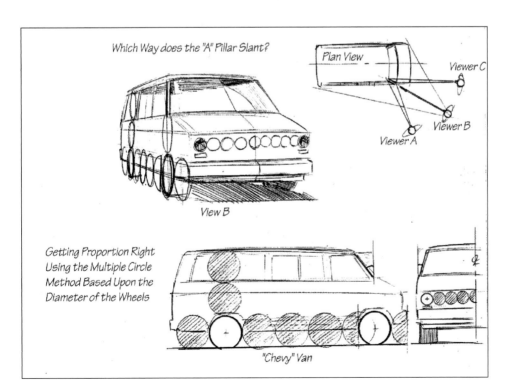

Figure 3-13
(R. Preston Bruning)
Again using the Lagassey method of proportional assessment, Bruning demonstrates an assessment of vehicular proportion using the wheels and headlights as "modules" of measurement. Also note the assessment of the degree of slant of the "A" pillar—the structural support for the windshield—as it is represented in view "B."

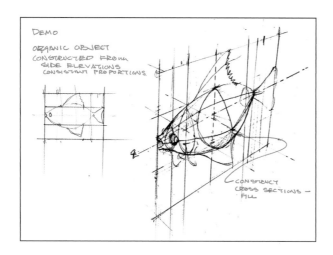

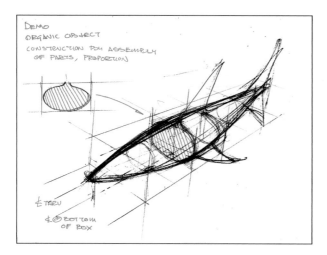

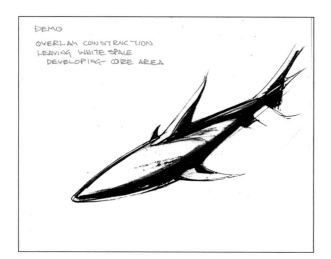

TIP - Natural forms and shapes can be a trigger for the imagination. ■

Figure 3-14a, Figure 3-14b, Figure 3-14c
(Kevin Reeder)
Kevin Reeder's drawings demonstrate another method of analyzing form—even natural form—to establish appropriate proportions in drawing. The key to assessing these aquatic forms properly is understanding the cross-section and its progressive change of shape moving along the centerline of the fish.

Ribs and Stringers

The traditional design and building process for ships and airplanes use a system of structural analysis called "ribs and stringers." Ribs are the two-dimensional shapes drawn at specific intervals that transect a form perpendicular to its long linear axis. Ships and airplanes have an underlying skeleton of ribs that defines the shape in a series of cross-sections placed at specific intervals. Such ribs can be structural linear elements or solid walls that are also called bulkheads. In the traditional construction of ships and airplanes, the ribs or bulkheads serve as supports for a series of "stringers." These linear elements run fore and aft, stem to stern, and define the flowing shape of a hull or fuselage even without a skin. In aircraft construction, sections of thin-walled aluminum sheets are riveted to the stringers to complete the structure. Similarly, in shipbuilding, planking is affixed to the bulkheads—sometimes without the use of stringers—to form the outer hull. The appearance of a hull, either smooth or hard edged, is the **chine** of the hull. Overlapping planking is lap-strake construction. Planking that is joined edge to edge against the bulkheads becomes a smooth outer hull surface. Ships and boats with such a smooth transitional surface are "smooth-chined." Ships and boats with hard edges defining the hull surface and hard-edged lines between the upper and lower sections of a hull are "hard-chined." Many students are familiar with computer terminology that refers to similar methods of rendering using sophisticated software. A "smoothing algorithm" is an automatic form of programming that defines transitions between shapes and geometric objects. Another term used frequently to describe the transitions created in computer-generated objects is "morphing."

These terms and construction methods deserve mention because they are the basis of analyzing and synthesizing form in transition. The more complex a form and varied its geometry, the greater the number of cross-sectional ribs to define the transition. A length of pipe has a continuous cross-section of circles defining its outer cylindrical shape. An airplane fuselage is far more complex. Uniform pressurization of modern aircraft requires the form to be tube-like. However, in many fuselage shapes, the circular section at the nose will transition into an elliptical form and then back again to a tapering conical shape with slightly convex surfaces. This form is a "teardrop" shape.

Without understanding this process, the novice designer may attempt to draw a series of exterior lines defining the shape of a complex object (vehicle) or a shape for a handheld product without understanding how to develop the form as described. As stated, this is a natural assumption of shape delineation based on how the eye sees and focuses on objects. Nevertheless, without understanding—analyzing and synthesizing— the form, the drawing will tend to be flat, without dimension, and lack any sense of three-dimensionality.

It is always helpful to see the construction of the object with all of the lines left in place— including those lines that form the unseen sides of the object. This process ensures that a solidity is imbued into the form that is necessary to understand its construction. Students will also learn quickly that freehand drawing inclusive of such analysis and synthesis makes engineering drawing or control line drawings much easier to do. Drawing from the inside out is critical in the process of understanding, explaining, and exploring ideas in the conceptual stages of development.

Line Technique and Form Development

It bears repeating that drawing the line and basic understanding of control and quality of line are core principles regarding the development of ideas in this text. Prior to learning how to apply media that will further define surfaces for advanced methods of design visualization, it is necessary to

> **TIP** - Try to see all form development from the inside outward. ▪

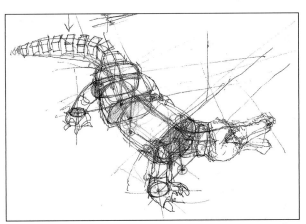

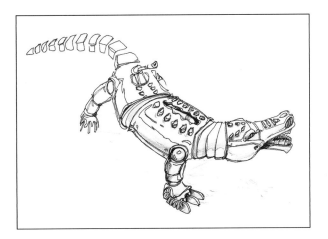

Figure 3-15a, Figure 3-15b, Figure 3-15c
(Kevin Reeder)
In this progression of three drawings, Reeder moves from analysis to synthesis in the generation of a conceptual drawing for a pull-toy. In the previous series of drawings and these above, the form generates from the inside outward to establish a full sense of the three-dimensional attributes of the figure/form.

Figure 3-16
(Joseph Koncelik)
Naval architecture provided the first
method of developing contoured form
using flat members and bending/forming
linear plank members against those
members. "Ribs and Stringer" is the
terminology applied to this method of
aircraft industry construction and also is
applied to the method of creating forms
that are transitional from end to end,
designed to pass through the fluids of
water and air.

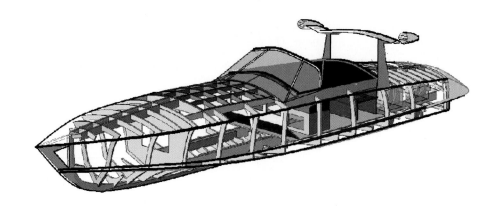

Figure 3-17a
Figure 3-17b
Figure 3-17c
(Joseph Koncelik and R. Preston
Bruning)
The British fighter aircraft of World
War II fame, such as the mosquito
fantasy version, right, were
airplanes with numerous fillets and
rounds replete with transitional
form. Their design clearly illustrates
that "stringers" join along a series
of cross-sectional ribs. R. Preston
Bruning uses that same technique in
two drawings of aircraft models.

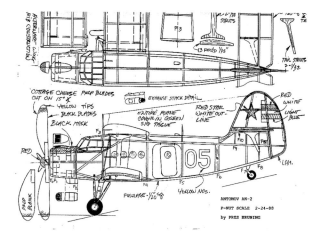

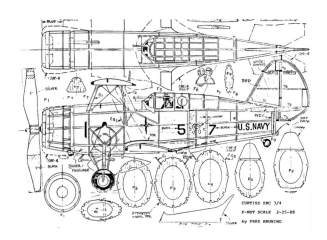

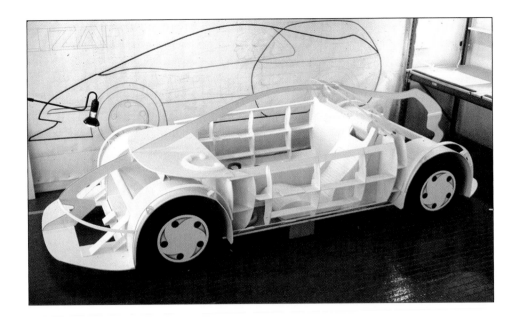

Figure 3-18a
Figure 3-18b
(R. Preston Bruning)
Bruning uses a technique of "ribs
and stringers" to shape a vehicle.
Foam core, a material easy to cut
and shape, creates a centerline
elevation shape of the vehicle and
cross-sectional members join to it to
form a rigid egg-crate structure.
Below, another method for
visualizing the shape of a vehicle
uses bendable wire over an inner
structure.

explore thoughts about the further development
of line technique. Once the structure, volume,
and form characteristics of an object emerge, the
designer's attention turns to describing surfaces.
The basis of all conceptual drawing using mixed
media is that line work is always the descriptor.
This means that pens, pencils, and markers define
line in conceptual drawing. This idiom makes little to no use of tone, blending colors, stippling,
and other techniques that require more time. In
fact, the novice will find that such an attempt
with markers will lead to diffusion of colors,
bleeding beyond the line work, and muddying of

marker colors. Even when backgrounds or areas
of tone and color are applied, they are line work
in close proximity.

Preston Bruning's exceptional pen-line drawings are fine illustrations of the use of line work
to describe surfaces. His "technique" is an extension of drawing lines as a single continuous
motion—except now, the lines are multiples to
describe surfaces and other features of the image.
Several of Preston Bruning's drawings appear in
this section to demonstrate how line describes
form. The use of line to describe form has five
different areas of application:

Figure 3-19a
Figure 3-19b
(R. Preston Bruning)
Examples are shown of the use of
cross-sections placed at intervals
along a centerline to establish the
transition in each of the forms
illustrated. Notice the airfoil section
of the propeller, the semicircular
cross-sections of the pontoon, and
the midsection rib of the steam-
powered "Chiripa."

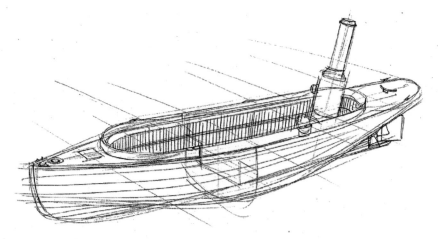

1899 Naphtha Launch "Chiripa"

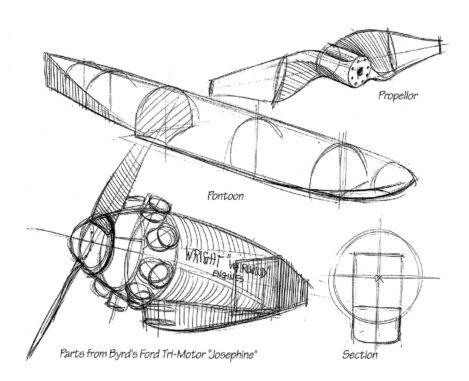

Propellor

Pontoon

Parts from Byrd's Ford Tri-Motor "Josephine"

Section

- *Line describing form surface:* The use of multiple lines, usually running in the same direction,
to illustrate the shape, contour, or geometry of
a surface
- *Line describing light and dark:* The use of line
to define the different sides of a form or geometric volume; frequently differentiated by the
use of denser or heavier line weights to describe
a surface that is oriented away from the viewer
- *Line describing surface texture:* The texture,
given visual definition by line work, defines the

difference between materials, such as the rubber of tires against the polished metal of wheels
- *Line describing shadow:* The use of line in a
fashion similar to that used to describe surfaces
but heavier or doubled-up in specific areas to
show that this surface is not facing a light
source or has a shadow cast upon it
- *Line describing background:* The use of line to
depict an area behind an object showing that
object to be in the foreground and defining it as
the focal point of the visualization.

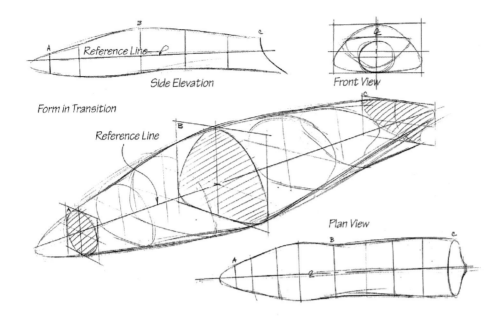

Side Elevation

Form in Transition

Reference Line

Front View

Plan View

Figure 3-20a
Figure 3-20b
(R. Preston Bruning)
Transition in form requires
understanding how the form
changes along its centerline. A
series of cross-sections establishes
the general shape of the form. The
process of developing the cross-
sectional analysis frequently begins
with elevation, plan, and frontal
views of the form.

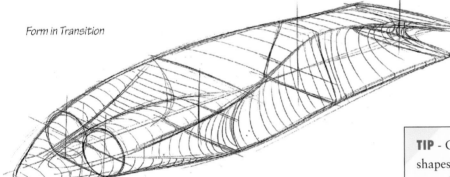

Form in Transition

TIP - Construct the array of cross-sectional
shapes or "ribs" along a predetermined
centerline. ■

Illustrating the five uses of line to describe form was specifically chosen because the five all use a single pen line weight, demonstrating how effectively this technique can be applied to illustrate a conceptual image. All uses of other media derive from this technique—regardless of thinness or broadness of the marker, its color or tone, or the combination of drawing tools chosen to achieve a desired effect. The skill acquired through practice will allow the design student to place lines in close proximity without them becoming a visual jumble—but that takes practice. To illustrate this point, reference examples of mixed media drawing in other chapters of this text and the companion DVD provide demonstrations of line control and technique. These examples demonstrate how the use of drawing tools—such as pens and pencils—is an extension of line drawing in developing surface treatments.

Conclusions: Geometry As a Conceptual Tool

The major point developed in this chapter is that students must shift their approach to drawing from defining the edge of objects first to understanding and drawing the underlying structure of objects—as well as objects that define space. As discussed and illustrated, geometry plays a significant role in the conceptualization of form. Two- and three-dimensional systems of geometric form development and the proportioning of form have been explored to help the student comprehend

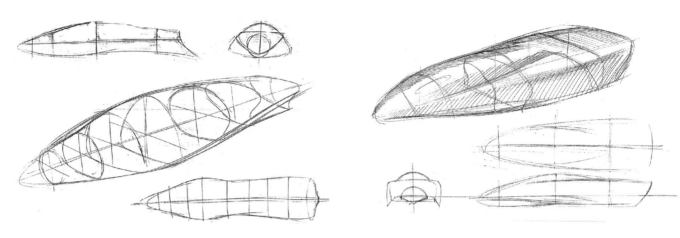

Figure 3-21a, Figure 3-21b

(R. Preston Bruning)

A degree of intuitive sensitivity is required to establish the progression of cross-sections for the development of a form that changes or morphs from stem to stern, front to back. Nevertheless, establishing the elevation and side views provides a major assist in developing the appropriate three-quarter view cross-sectional development of the form.

the inside-out approach to visualizing objects and spaces. With regard to developing three-dimensional form, the use of geometric proportioning systems can begin with developing objects within specific geometries of the rectilinear six-sided box. Viewing objects such as vehicles in terms of their relationship to wheels. as shown in various diagrams presented, is a simple way to develop a sense of appropriate proportion. More complex form development, such as the sweeping lines of vehicles and other transitional form objects, demonstrates applications of cross-sectional

Figure 3-22a
Figure 3-22b

(R. Preston Bruning)

The drawing at right demonstrates a transitional form using perspective guidelines and a single cross-section through the middle of the vehicle. The lower drawing is more finished, and the underlying structure disappears under the surface treatment of the car body. However, the drawing utilizes the same technique to develop the complex transitional form.

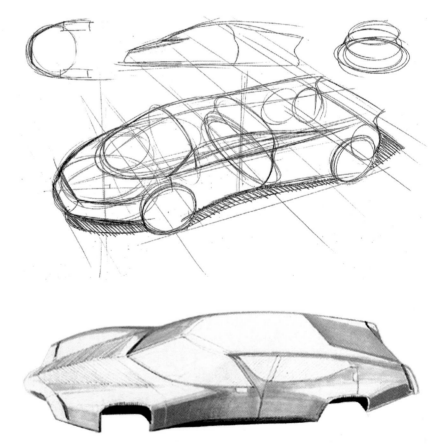

TIP - The more guidelines used, the better will be the development of the three-dimensional form. ■

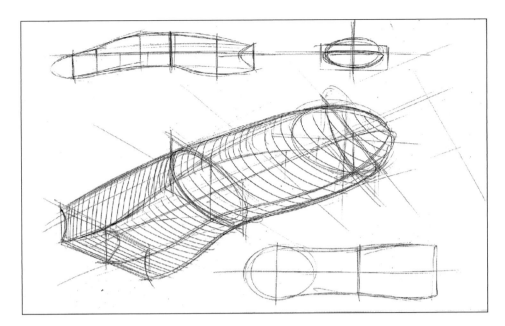

Figure 3-23a
Figure 3-23b
(R. Preston Bruning)
Bruning has a keen awareness of
how form transitions. Simple
cross-sectional ellipses (circles in
perspective) help establish the three-
dimensional character of a small
personal aircraft—an aircraft that is
the smallest jet-propelled airplane
in the world.

analyses and uses of "ribs and stringers" drawn
from ship and aircraft construction.

There is an old saying appropriate to form giving that "if something looks right, it is right." To
make three-dimensional conceptual drawings of
ideas seem right requires attention to geometry,
proportion, and the development of form from
the inside outward. Clearly, as the literature on
the subject of form and geometry indicates (Elam
2001), specific proportions such as those developed for use in the arts are more preferable and

seem to have greater balance and correctness
than do other developments of shape and form
that lack these geometries. From the perspective
of developing the sensitivities and skills that are
essential to conceptual drawing, it is necessary
for the designer to cultivate a sense of geometry
early on in personal development as a designer.
As with other aspects of developing the skill of
visualization, these sensitivities become instinc-
tive in the conceptualization of ideas with practice and over time.

Figure 3-24a
Figure 3-24b
Figure 3-24c
Figure 3-24d
(Kevin Reeder)
Thumbnail sketches are not exempt from the rigor of defining proportion and geometry. Note the studies, right, examining how the "fit" of handles to hands is related to tool design. Also note the attention to material thickness and surface treatments.

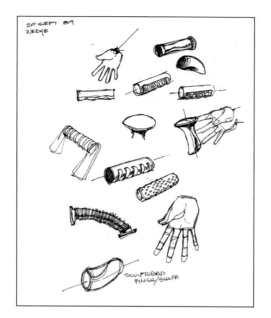

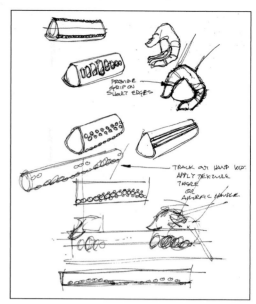

TIP - Thumbnails are part of the communication process with others involved in designing. ■

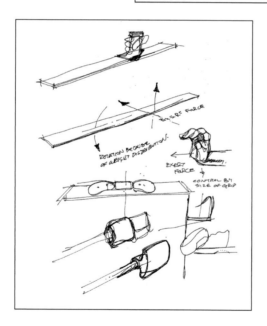

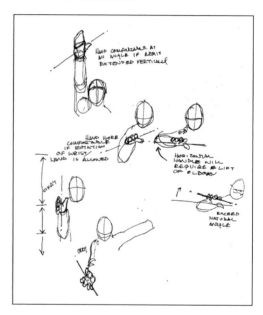

This chapter reinforces one of the most important points of the text: conceptual drawing is a tool to communicate ideas to others. Conceptual drawing is primarily a means to work through ideas on paper. However, the design process is not a soliloquy, a person creating visualizations as a creative exchange with oneself, as much as it is a process in fine art. Communication of ideas in design means passing on clear visualizations to others.

To develop this form of visual communication, there are specific practices, beyond knowing the rudiments and fundamentals, which are essential if student designers want to assimilate and use the skills of conceptual drawing effectively. The following list summarizes the various major points of this chapter:

1. Students of conceptual drawing must change their approach to drawing from the outside to

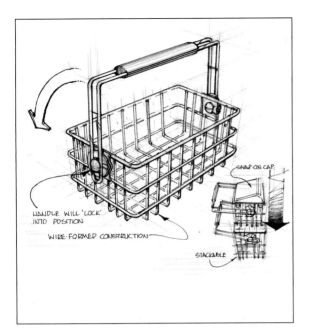

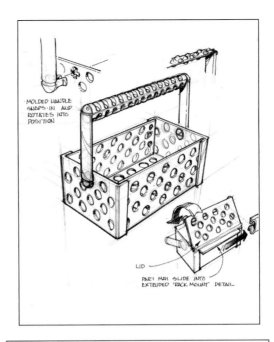

TIP - All practiced designers provide visual information about materials, objects, and spaces through the conceptual process. ■

TIP - Use two thin lines to show a curved corner in a line drawing. ■

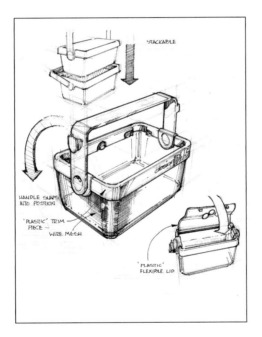

Figure 3-25a
Figure 3-25b
Figure 3-25c
(Kevin Reeder)
Here a relatively simple three-dimensional form appears in terms of its material conformations, fastenings, and mechanical devices—all in line drawing rapid visualizations. Note the detail in drawings that illustrate ideas about openings and closures—all aspects of understanding the geometry of the form.

the inside to an approach that is structural—drawing from the inside to the outside.

2. All objects can be analyzed and depicted in terms of underlying geometry—even the most complex visual objects.

3. Developing a three-dimensional object in space requires understanding that object from all sides, from inside to outside, to provide a sense of the form's three dimensions.

4. Complex shapes make "transitions," or, in the contemporary vernacular, they "morph" from one end to the other. Examples of this morphing of form are present in ships, aircraft, and automobile design—as well as other "streamlined" shapes.

Figure 3-26
(Aaron Bethlenfalvy)
This demonstrates clean, clear line drawing geometry and form development with attention paid to material thickness, proportion, and scale. The geometry of the devices determines operationality. Text (discussed in the final chapter) and surface treatments (such as indications of images on LCD screens) enhance the legibility of form for the observer.

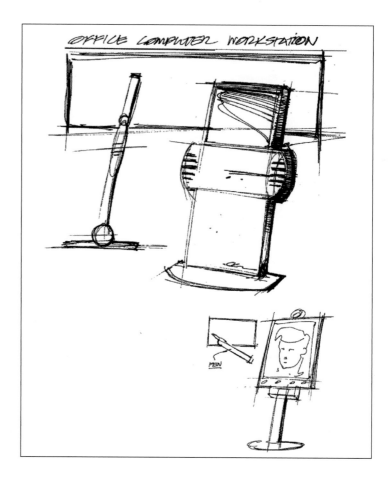

TIP - Copy the drawings of others—including the drawings in this book. There is no such thing as cheating in design studies. No matter how faithfully someone emulates another person's drawing, his or her own style will show through. ▪

Figure 3-27
(Aaron Bethlenfalvy)
From the perspective of drawing style, consistency is apparent from the outline structure of the product idea through the development of images on the screen of the miniaturized components.

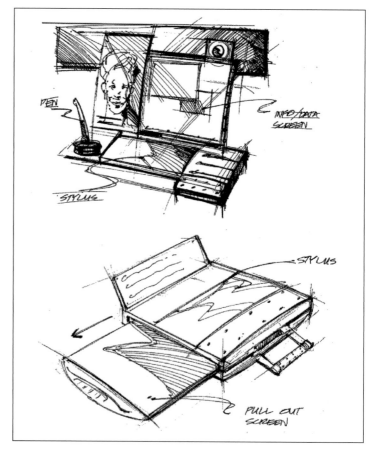

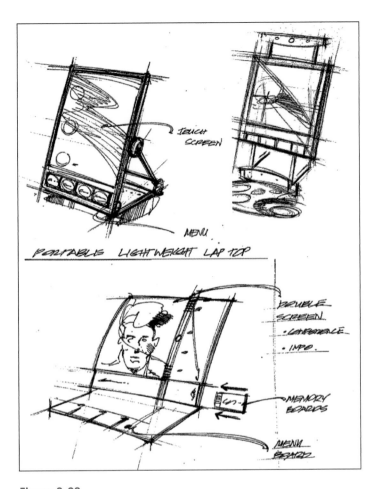

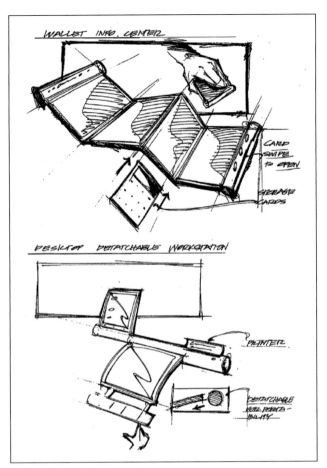

Figure 3-28

(Aaron Bethlenfalvy)

Bethlenfalvy demonstrates the value of fundamentals. Note the crisp lines drawn in a single stroke without pause, hesitation, or lack of confidence. All line work remains in place without erasures. Text complements the drawing style as well as being informative.

Figure 3-29

(Aaron Bethlenfalvy)

In the top drawing, the perspective is slightly more severe than in Figure 3-28 or the lower drawing. Geometry is essential to this miniaturization of computer products as components become independent rather than housed in a large box.

Figure 3-30a
Figure 3-30b

(R. Preston Bruning)

Line drawing can be an effective means of communicating form without the complication of mixed media. These two examples show geometric form development of complex objects. The tugboat engine is more intensively developed and shadowed. The milling machine provides visual information about the visual assembly of such complex combinations of form.

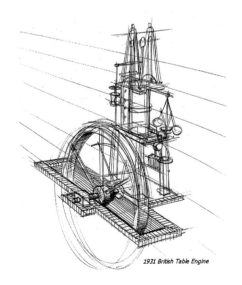

1931 British Table Engine

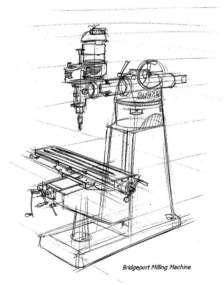

Bridgeport Milling Machine

Figure 3-31

(R. Preston Bruning)

Early aircraft use combinations of metals, wood, and even fabric. Bruning's illustration captures these early material combinations. Note the metal of the cowling around the engine, the glazing of the cockpit, metal struts for landing gear, and what would be fabric-covered wooden ribs and stringers for fuselage and wings. Note also the simple illustration of sky.

5. Form in transition can be accomplished in conceptual drawing by using a system of "ribs and stringers" with the ribs as cross-sectional descriptors of form and the stringers delineating the surface change.

6. There are numerous proportioning devices, such as using the wheel to understand the proportion of vehicles, as well as other complex geometrical devices such as dynamic symmetry, a system applied in the fine arts.

7. Regardless of the complexity of form, line work is the essential elemental means for describing that form. Use of multiple lines in proximity provides effective delineation of surfaces.

Figure 3-32

(Michael Butcher)

An approach to complex form development or form in transition is to think in terms of cross-sectional development and the application of lines or "stringers" to the exterior sides of the cross-sections. This method helps the form achieve visual accuracy.

Figure 3-33
(Michael Butcher)
Once the ribs have been placed on the long diagonal of the perspective and the stringers applied, the exterior shape of the object can be more fully realized.

 See DVD Segment 3, Form in Transition, for information about quality of line.

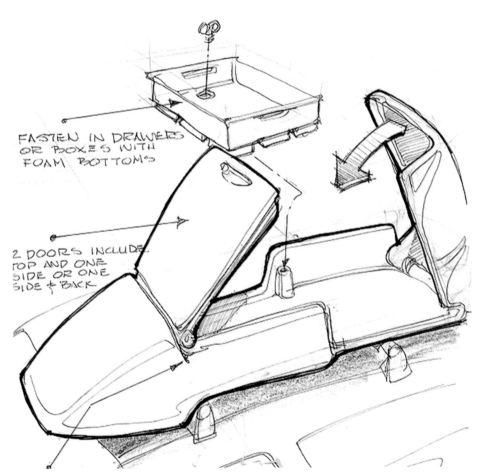

FASTEN IN DRAWERS OR BOXES WITH FOAM BOTTOMS

2 DOORS INCLUDE TOP AND ONE SIDE OR ONE SIDE + BACK

Figure 3-34
(Kevin Reeder)
Attention to the geometry of a form permits the designer to assemble or disassemble components or pieces of that form to further explain design ideas.

> **TIP** - Conceptual drawing is essentially line drawing. Applying any media to the surface of the paper produces results when the designer thinks in terms of drawing line, control of line, and design of line. ■

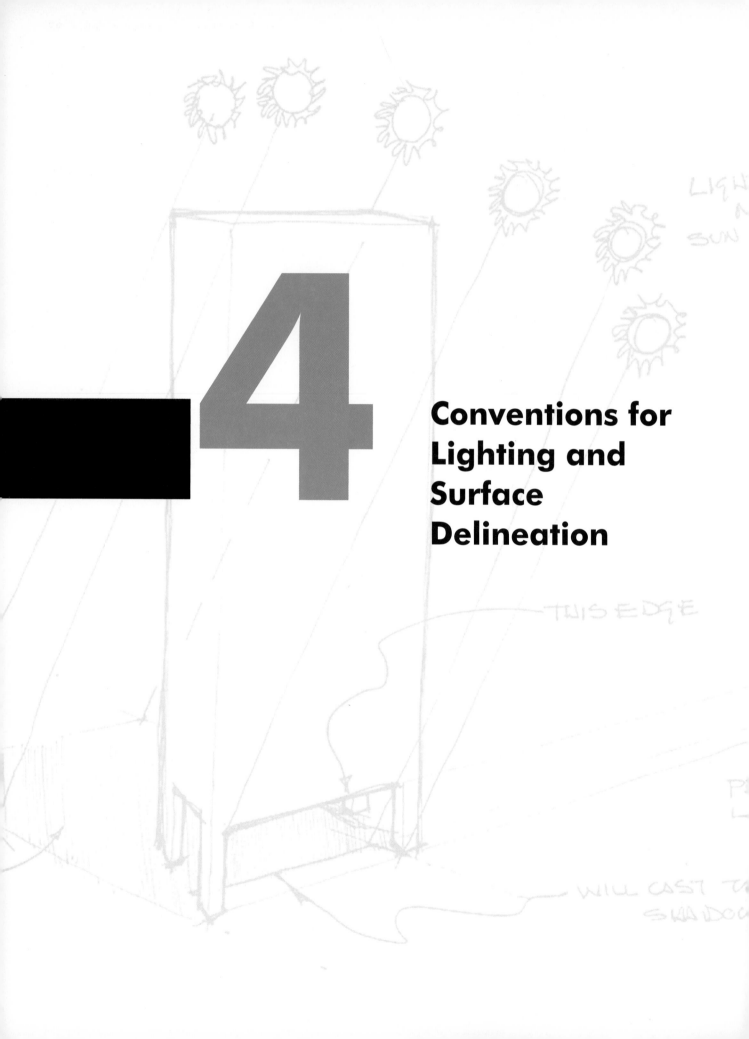

4

Conventions for Lighting and Surface Delineation

This text emphasizes throughout, sometimes in differing ways, that control of line is the essence of mastering conceptual drawing. Several masterful line drawings by R. Preston Bruning demonstrate control of line and its components of confidence, quality, and consistency. In this chapter, that theme continues and the use of line will be demonstrated in various media. The text and visual examples provide techniques for surfaces representing materials and textures in light and in shadow. Line control, the surfaces of objects and spaces, and how objects appear in light are linked components of conceptual visualization that cannot be separated. All surfaces appear in light and receive definition in light. Reflections in surfaces are just another aspect of light or illumination of a surface. Thus, it is appropriate to begin a discussion of surfaces starting with light, shadow, and the effect of light on surfaces.

1. There are numerous ways to utilize every form of drawing media, including the blending of colors in pencil, chalk, markers, and even pigments. For the purposes of simplicity and to develop useable conventions in conceptual drawing, the student is asked to follow these media conventions as would be the case in rendering: Each line drawn on the surface of the page is an independent "stroke" of the pencil guidelines.

2. The line work used to create the specific appearance of surfaces does not utilize blending, pen, or marker.

3. The visual effect of combining varying lines (in width and darkness) is blending without the complexity of color mixing.

4. Tone and surface variation is developed through a build-up of appropriate media on a surface.

5. Drawing tools should be appropriate to the desired effect in the generation of mixed-media drawing. For example, the drafter/designer produces surface texture by placing one marker color next to another and using other tools, such as pastel, to produce blended effects and gradients of color and transformation of one color to another.

These points are essential to instruction and learning. Reducing the number of techniques

Figure 4-1
(Kevin Reeder)
This rather stark photograph of an older computer mouse illustrates how shade and shadow define form and assist in visualizing three dimensions. Top surfaces capture the most illumination, and the vertical sides away from the light source capture the least. The subtle shadow from the mouse on the side of the box is more shadow than would be necessary in a conceptual drawing.

required to communicate ideas on paper will result in faster development of the design student toward adequacy, competency, and eventual proficiency in conceptual drawing. There will always be time for any student to pursue advanced methods for surface treatments associated with rendering. As stated a number of times, the focus of this text is communication of ideas to others.

In this chapter, the representational drawing work used as demonstration includes "mixed media." This means that pencils, pens, markers, and some pastels have been used to develop a drawing more fully. Each media tool delineates surfaces in a way that is easy to accomplish by using that specific tool rather than any other. Designers are always mindful of *control of line and line quality* regardless of whether the line work is describing the shape of an object or used to produce a background to emphasize that object. There are no lines that simply become in-fill. Every line, regardless of its placement in the representation of an object or space, has a definite character or quality. A way to imbed this idea in the consciousness of students is having them remember: "*Design every line.*"

Figure 4-2
(Kevin Reeder)
The gradient of shadow on the vertical surface of this tube form defines its cylindrical shape—as does the flat dark shadow on the surface of the table. Note the shadow on the interior defining the hollow of the tube in the reverse direction of the exterior shadow.

Techniques for Depicting Surfaces

Quality of line work is the most essential ingredient in the total array of fundamental skills designers employ to create form. Without understanding how to develop line and use it in constructing shape and developing perspective, nothing can follow. Mastering basic drawing skills comes before someone is concerned about technique. However, when quality of line and an inherent understanding of perspective and geometry are part of the working vocabulary for drawing, it is possible to extend the skill to include more elaborate techniques involving line use that describes surfaces.

This chapter discusses fundamentals of creating *shade and shadow* as well as surface *representation*. The beginner typically has a tendency to overdo both of these aspects of drawing and use of techniques to depict form at the onset of learning drawing skills. In the visual language of designing,

abstraction or simplification of shading and shadowing a form quickens the process of having the object stand out from the page. Shade on the surface of an object may also be simplified and may be sufficiently represented using only one medium tone marker rather than attempting to render the intricacies of modulation of light on the surface of a form through color mixing. Designers, typically product or industrial designers, use this method to enhance the image on a page. This chapter demonstrates this method in a number of the images.

Line quality is as important in the development of surface treatment as it was in the development of the structure of form in the first place. Students should avoid "coloring in" an object with surface tone or shading because it will be ineffective—and marker drawing makes this type of surface treatment ineffective. More important, a casual approach to using markers to represent surfaces will result in poor drawings; the surface representation will conflict with the geometry of the drawn object or space. Some otherwise reasonable novice drawings frequently suffer from poor use of media to represent surfaces. It bears repeating: *In conceptual drawing, design all lines!* It is important for the student of drawing to review the techniques presented in this chapter repeatedly. Iteration and repetition are essential in the learning experience—especially when learning how to draw.

Rendering is the word in the vocabulary of designers that describes surface representation. Since rendering is a complex subject, the authors defer to other references and texts on the subject for the benefit of students and professional designers. Again, the best reference for students who wish to know more about mixed media rendering is Ronald Kemnitzer's book on this subject, *Rendering with Markers: Definitive Techniques for Designers, Illustrators and Architects* (1983). It sets out step-by-step procedures for use of pencils, pens, and markers to illustrate the surface of form.

There is a vague area with a fuzzy boundary between the emphasis on line drawing, the subject of this text, and that of surface rendering. Rendering is an additional set of practices and conventions that provide a misleading reality through adept use of various media. This text ventures close to that fuzzy boundary but will not consciously venture into the territory of rendering because that subject is adequately covered in Kemnitzer's book and by the large numbers of books that show advanced illustrative techniques from advanced designers and illustrators.

Rendering also does not serve the purposes of conceptual drawing. Renderings are usually a separate request by clients or by management meant for specific purposes—such as display or advertising. It is a time-consuming venture that is usually called for separately from the charge to develop ideas. Rendering *is not conceptual in its nature; it is essentially descriptive and illustrative.* It is an important part of the general spectrum of design visualization. Rendering requires preparation, the use of tools beyond freehand drawing and time.

In the overwhelming number of challenges clients provide designers, there rarely is time to spend on a single highly polished mixed media drawing of a single idea—unless the client or instructor requires it. Rendering is usually requested as an inherent part of the problem-solving process. On the other hand, many ideas that should and must be represented require surface representation—color, texture, and treatment of the illumination striking the object—to provide clarity about the idea being communicated. That conception about surface treatments is stressed in Figures 4-18 a and b through 4-19 a and b where light and dark, color and surface texture are critical aspects of communicating information about objects.

In the contemporary design world, rendering has been shifted to computing. It is faster and far more descriptive to utilize the myriad forms of software available to provide carefully delineated images at the same level as those produced using illustrative techniques in the past. The value of line drawing is that it is faster and cheaper than computing. The value of the computer is that it replaces the time and cost of producing illustrations and full release of package information such as mechanical drawings, dimensioned drawings, and three-dimensional objects that are ready for translation for production by automated machinery. There is a gray

Figure 4-3
(Kevin Reeder)
A simple cylindrical shape viewed in overhead illumination described by the shadow on the interior of the hollow form, the shadow on the side, and the simple shadow on the ground plane.

area; the authors have chosen to call one form of drawing **hybrid** drawings because they combine the speed of quick sketching with the extensive capabilities for rendering using computers. Hybrids are conceptual drawings because they utilize the speed and efficiency of manual and computerized visualization techniques. Refer to Chapter 8 for further discussion and examples of hybrid computer drawing. Also, refer to the portfolio section of the CD-ROM that accompanies this text for full-color renditions of hybrid drawings.

It is possible to bring the use of line work up to a level of finish that provides sufficient detail to be convincing imagery. R. Preston Bruning has provided numerous examples of this level of drawing that have already been placed in this text. More examples of his work and that of other designers (including the authors) are part of the text as well. In these examples, freehand drawing line work provides a sense of surface—utilizing the same techniques of drawing discussed in previous

Figure 4-4a, Figure 4-4b
(Kevin Reeder)
Exterior solar illumination provides stark shadowing where (theoretically) all of the rays of the sun run in parallel. Two rather commonplace objects are seen here in direct exterior illumination.

chapters. This chapter is the "jumping-off point," so to speak, in that line has been used to give geometry and surfaces of form greater impact, transition, and dimensionality. Trading the pen for a marker and using the technique of drawing lines in close proximity with the same speed and accuracy can approximate the rendering of surfaces in more time-consuming techniques. For some of the drawings shown, pastel pencils and chalks have been added to provide both backgrounds and transition in the delineation of surface shape—but line technique is still the underpinning of the drawing.

Two areas of discussion, example and systematic demonstration, follow in this chapter and must be integrated with the repertoire of a designer's skills. As stated, understanding surface delineation requires knowledge of lighting, shade, and shadow. Conventions for lighting surfaces and delineation of the resulting effects on form are shown and discussed. Second, all objects

and spaces are designed with specific materials. Whether it is the fabrics, wall coverings, and floor surfaces that are used to provide a sense of interior space or the metallic and plastic surfaces used in product development, representation of materials is essential in understanding any conceptual design. Ideas in conceptual drawing extend beyond shape and dimension. Ideas about use of materials and the way they are produced as well as fit together or are fastened are always part of the initial exploratory conceptual process.

Shade and Shadow Development
In fine arts, shade and shadow have value in their own right, conveying a sense of drama or heightening the impact of an artistic philosophy or statement. The purpose of shading and shadow in conceptual drawing is always to emphasize the three-dimensionality of the form so that a design is properly communicated to the observer. In drawing generally, all aspects of

the picture are part of a composition. While design drawing does not ignore the principles of composition, the visual image of an object or space is of central if not singular importance. Product drawing is successful when the object appears to separate from the page and take on the presence of reality. This is the opposite intention of how objects are visualized or captured in art. Objects, spaces, and other figures are envisioned as part of the whole and should not be separate from the overall composition on the two-dimensional surface. In communicating objects, composition is fundamentally an issue of placement on the page in relationship to other information such as text, exploded or sectional views, and specifications.

To explain further, the essential aspect of applying all techniques in conceptual drawing is to communicate the object so well so that everyone has the same understanding of what is represented. Again, this differs from artistic intention wherein a drawing may convey many messages. The intention of a conceptual drawing is specific to a single message that all viewers should understand. With regard to light and shadow, the following six fundamental principles should be observed.

Light source—Shade and shadow are the result of knowing the direction of the light source. In design drawing, it is easy to establish the direction of light sources—and in virtually all cases, only one light source pointed in one direction is used. To avoid confusion, especially for novice designers, it is best to depict the light source as coming from the direction of the viewer or in close proximity to the viewer—over the left or right shoulder, for example. Almost every object will cast a shadow on the ground plane; that shadow will not appear adjacent to any surface facing a light source. (See Figures 4-3, 4a and 4b that demonstrate how light defines shadow.)

While this general rule can be broken to enhance communicating the shape of an object, shadow on the ground plane should follow the convention of direction that is a given from the position of the light source. It is not as advantageous to have a light source directly overhead or, in other words, directly over the object represented in the drawing. Top surfaces rarely have the visual information that communicates the representation of the object. With light sources directed at elevation level—at either one side or the other—the resulting shadow effect will have one side lighter than the other, increasing the sense of three-dimensionality. For those interested

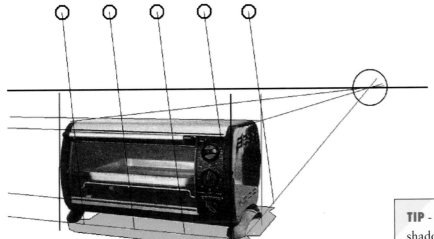

Figure 4-5
(Joseph Koncelik)
Exploring the premise that solar illumination provides parallel rays of light, the fundamental principle of illuminating objects is to cast shadows and depict surfaces using a simplified method of shadowing based upon solar illumination. This toaster oven image is used to demonstrate how the shadow below the form would be cast using parallel rays of light.

TIP - Simplify shadows. The purpose of the shadow in conceptual drawing is to offset or present the object to the viewer—to make it seem three-dimensional. ■

Figure 4-6
(Joseph Koncelik: from original demonstrations by R. Preston Bruning)
Each drawing illustrates the effect of illumination on specific objects. A convex-shaped box is lighted from the front with a dark upper plane and a semi-reflective side capturing light along the side.

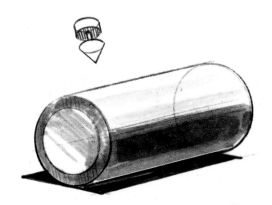

Figure 4-7
(Joseph Koncelik)
A cylindrical shape with an indentation on the front circular surface is shown with an overhead light source. Note the highlight line at the base of the cylinder defining the distinction between shape and shadow.

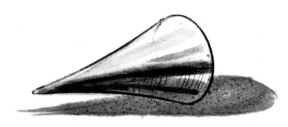

Figure 4-8
(Joseph Koncelik)
A conical shape is illuminated from the front and slightly elevated over the object. The surface shown is a "brushed" finish giving off a degree of reflectivity.

in precise construction of shadows, John Montague's book, *Basic Perspective Drawing* (2005), is an excellent resource that has detailed guidelines for the construction of shadows in perspective.

Object positioning—It is typical in novice design student drawings that their sense of perspective results in the placement of one corner of the object directly on the centerline of the viewer's eye point. (See Chapter 2.) The resulting drawing has two sides in view that are of equal emphasis with the top and bottom edges converging at equally spaced vanishing points. A method an instructor can use—and should certainly be recommended for students of design—is to acquire an electronics trade magazine, newspaper advertisements, or other sources and study how these items are photographed. It will become evident that the placement of an object for viewing usually results in a full view of one front face with one other side diminishing to a vanishing point relatively close in to the object. (See Chapter 2.) This convention employs a two-point perspective with the object placed close to the horizon line. Little top surface will be showing. It is easier to understand this concept by looking at the examples provided in Chapter 2 than to try to describe it in words.

Another important aspect of positioning an object in this way is that the drawing time to represent the object is greatly decreased. More time will be used to represent that object with two equally dominant sides in view. In addition, lifting the object closer to eye-point reduces the visible top side and again cuts down the time of drawing—and increases the level of communication of the object.

Light and dark—The accuracy of a shadow in conceptual drawing is less important than how it sets off the object on the page. Shadows may be simplified or abstracted to set off the object without the designer becoming fussy about the specific detail of the shadow image cast by the light source. It is wise to place shadow in middle tone grays rather than jet black. Such stark shadows frequently press forward of the object visually or they tend to make the lighting effect similar to that of a flash bulb being used to illuminate the object. Shaded surfaces are away from the light source. Lighted surfaces catch the light from the source or face the light source.

While the following convention can be reversed with success, generally the side of the object that should convey the critical visual information about the object should be in light. Sides of objects in shadow are generally those sides that have less of the information necessary to represent the object. "Visual information" representing the object is that configuration of surface detail that informs the viewer what the object is and how it is used. For example, a desktop computer has a forward surface with controls and displays, slots for discs, panels for connections of peripherals, etc. that convey what the object is and where the important operational devices are located. Most electronic devices have what is frequently called a "fascia" or faceplate where critical controls and display are located. Other product appliances have what is termed a "backsplash" that also houses controls and displays. The location of this critical information determines how the object should be positioned and drawn to communicate design intent. While the rear of the computer is critical with multiple attachments for

Figure 4-9
(Joseph Koncelik)
A cylinder is illuminated directly from the front left, showing a shadow extending to the rear.

Figure 4-10
(Joseph Koncelik)
A similar cylinder is illuminated from the backside of the object, showing a shadow extending to the front. While this depiction of shadow is accurate, the shadow becomes a dominant shape over the object and may detract from the communication of the object intended by the designer.

Figure 4-11
(Joseph Koncelik)
In this ink line drawing, there is no apparent source of illumination—with the exception of the simulation of a shadow below the bedside table. Using contrast creates the drawing's impact.

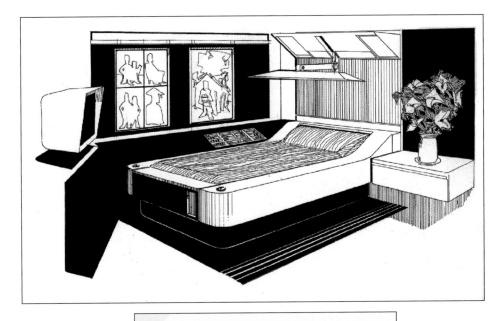

TIP - Create contrast using black and white to develop a strong image. ■

Figure 4-12a
Figure 4-12b
(Joseph Koncelik)
Similar to the preceding image,
Figure 4-11, the two conceptual
drawings at right utilize contrast or light
and dark to create impact. In the upper
drawing, shadow is cast across the face
of the woman in the wheelchair as if
there were a light source to the upper
left. In the lower drawing, the task
lighting above the workspace provides a
simulation of lighting.

TIP - Lines in close proximity
create effective shadows and
surface treatments. ■

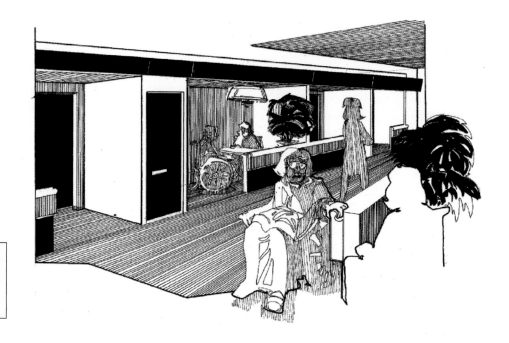

power cords, peripheral cables, and telephone line connections, it is the "control and display" information that is the primary concern and requires initial attention of the designer—and usually the most attention with respect to form giving.

Shadow—To distinguish shadow from shading, be aware that shadow is a definitive drawn shape resulting from an absence of light on a surface. Shading is properly seen as that aspect of light and dark on the surface of an object. Shadow is typically seen on a surface other than that of the

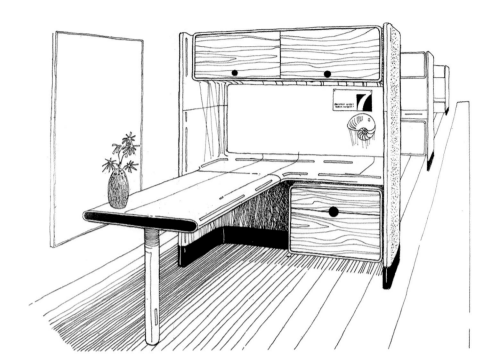

Figure 4-13a
Figure 4-13b
(David Tompkins)
Line work and use of black tone can be an effective way to communicate surface textures and light and dark shadow. The two drawings by Tompkins in this sequence of drawings use differing line weights and combinations of line—similar to the way Bruning has used line—to convey the concept of an assembly of office systems furnishings.

> **TIP** - Text must be carefully placed to enhance composition. ■

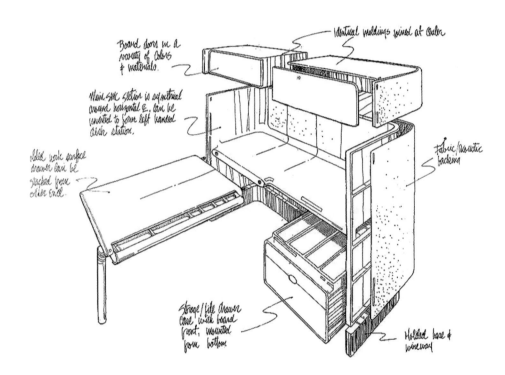

object itself. There are exceptions, but first it is important to convey the basic development of shadow. In most conceptual drawings, shadows are cast on a ground or floor plane. Since most tabletop electronic devices and appliances have "feet" to stabilize them on uneven surfaces, these objects are lifted slightly from the ground, table surface, or floor plane and a shadow results underneath the object.

Figure 4-14a
Figure 4-14b
(David Tompkins)
The final two drawings in the sequence of four convey ceiling treatments as well as the details involved in the design of the lighting systems. In the uppermost drawing, the panel system is emphasized through the line work shadow of the rear wall, the overlap of systems panels, and the black tone of the overhead storage system doors. The concept is given added weight through the attention to thoughtful detail and the notations in a personalized style of script. (See Chapter 7.)

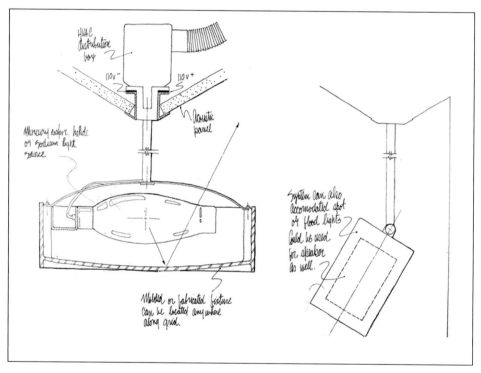

With the representation of objects such as furniture, the shadows will be more extended and resemble the shape of the object on the floor— and wall—surfaces where light is not falling. In well-defined mechanical perspectives, shadows are defined by constructing the shadow by running lines from the light source to the edges of the object and then to the floor plane. The closer the light source is to the object, the more exaggerated and darker the shadow. The farther away the light source from the object, the less exaggerated, more diffuse, or fuzzy the edges and lighter the shadow. Delineating exaggerated shadows from objects detracts from the overall communication of that object to the viewer. *Shadows should not be larger than the object* as a general rule of thumb and should offset the object from the surface on which they are "grounded."

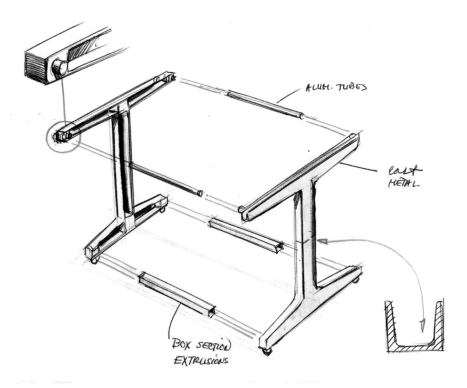

ALUM. TUBES

CAST METAL

BOX SECTION EXTRUSIONS

Figure 4-15a
Figure 4-15b
(R. Preston Bruning)
In the quick sketching mode, simple light and dark areas are carefully chosen to enhance the drawing and create impact. Note the interior shading of the table structure on the upper left and the simulations of shadow on the interior of the containers in the lower drawing.

TIP - Shadow should be used to inform the viewer about the design idea. ■

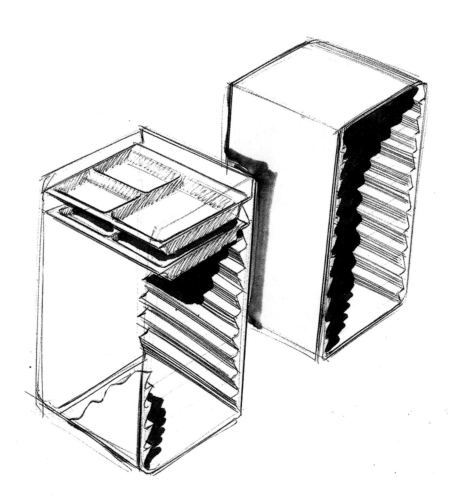

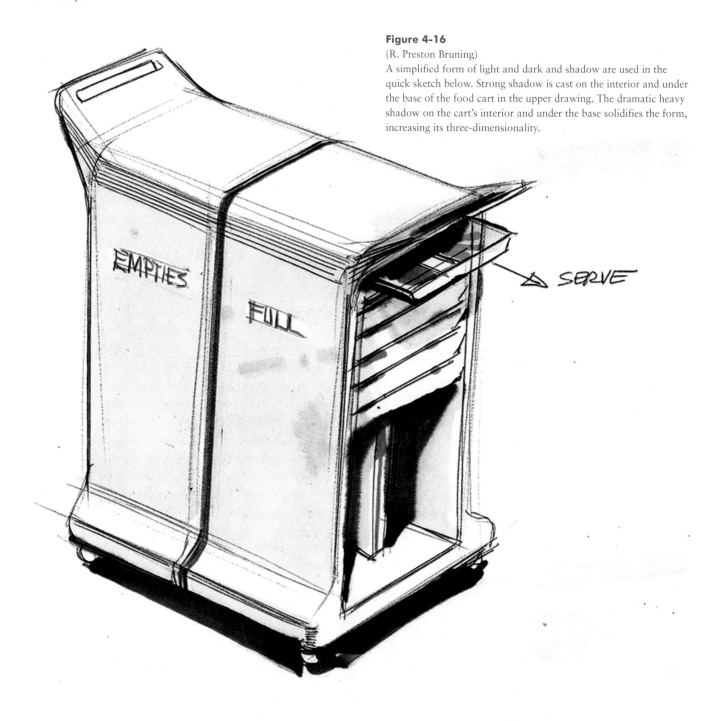

Figure 4-16
(R. Preston Bruning)
A simplified form of light and dark and shadow are used in the quick sketch below. Strong shadow is cast on the interior and under the base of the food cart in the upper drawing. The dramatic heavy shadow on the cart's interior and under the base solidifies the form, increasing its three-dimensionality.

As a useful convention in conceptual drawing, shadows should be simplified or even abstracted so as not to confuse the viewer about design intent and content. In addition, it is useful to view light sources as being as distant as the sun from the earth so that shadows are not terribly exaggerated and detract from the object being represented. This convention means that all "rays" of light run virtually parallel to one another. Artificial light sources that are placed close to an object radiate from the light's point of origin and present more complex shadows—to be avoided in conceptual drawing.

Backgrounds—One of the most frequently used conventions in product drawing is a background that is a plane of gray or black, as well as color. Background shapes may or may not have any relationship to the light source or the shape of the object other than placement away from the object's lighted surface. Some of these

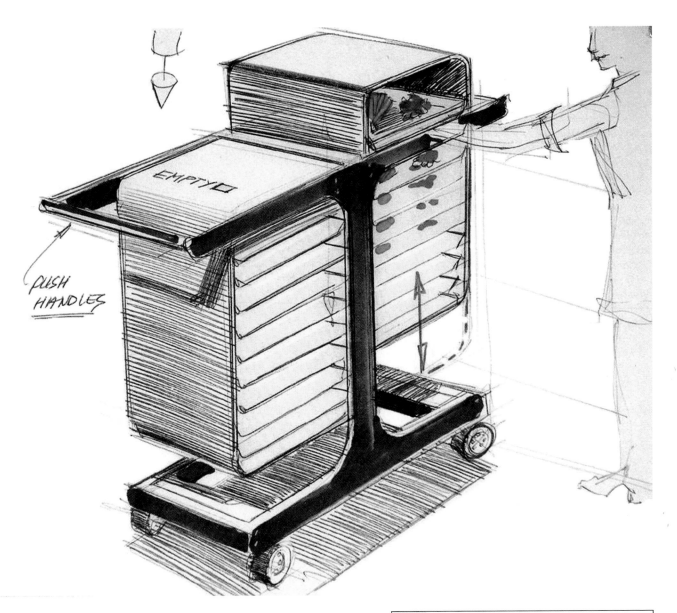

PUSH HANDLES

Figure 4-17
(R. Preston Bruning)
This drawing emphasizes the structural member using dark line work—and additional shadowing with line below the cart. In spite of the quickness of the sketch, placing a shadow cast from the arm across the container section increases the sense of spatiality.

> **TIP** - Keep turning the paper to control line work—using the "power stroke." ∎

planes drawn by designers are basic rectilinear forms, while others are more amorphous. Again, this convention seemingly separates the object from the page.

A cautionary note must be sounded about the use of intense colors—typically the colors most markers produce—as backgrounds. Backgrounds should not overpower the object that is the central idea to be communicated to the observer. The novice designer will be tempted to utilize bold color or black backgrounds after seeing the effect of such backgrounds on the impact of a conceptual drawing. This can result in the background overpowering the communication of the design intent. In the initial stages of developing conceptual drawing skill, it is best to keep the application of backgrounds relatively simple—without extreme use of color or use of overpowering dark shades or marker or mixes of pastel.

Figure 4-18a
Figure 4-18b
(R. Preston Bruning)
Bruning generated these images and those that follow in this sequence of drawings to explain the construction of a full-sized mock-up of a "people mover" using construction materials that would give the look and feel of such a device set up in a studio space. These drawings clearly communicate how each component would be fabricated—including the materials chosen. Notice the use of light and dark on the drawing at right to emphasize the distinction between components and the strong shadows (below) to convey the mock-up's three-dimensionality.

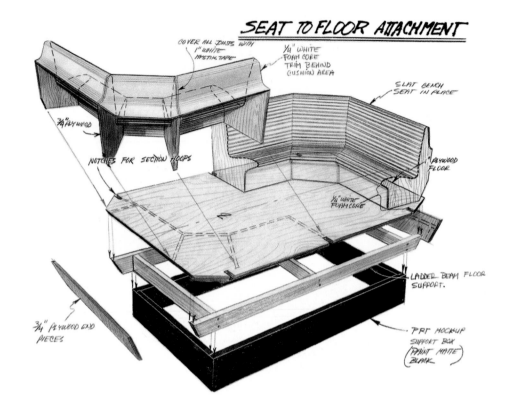

SEAT TO FLOOR ATTACHMENT

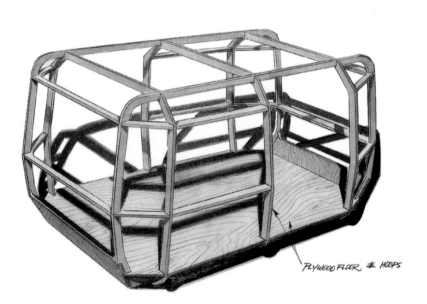

FRAME WORK & FLOOR

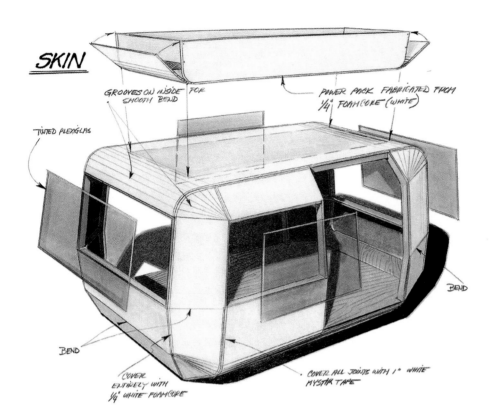

SKIN

TINTED PLEXIGLAS

GROOVES ON INSIDE FOR
SMOOTH BEND

POWER PACK FABRICATED FROM
1/4" FOAMCORE (WHITE)

BEND

BEND

COVER
ENTIRELY WITH
1/4" WHITE FOAMCORE

COVER ALL JOINTS WITH 1" WHITE
MYSTIK TAPE

Figure 4-19a
Figure 4-19b
(R. Preston Bruning)
All four drawings clearly explain how
the mock-up should be constructed
and in what sequence each of the
parts would be assembled. Note how
the shadowing is clear but simplified.
Also, note that the perspective views
are chosen to provide the maximum
information for model-makers
handling the assembly. These four
drawings are freehand with tools
such as straight edges used to
"true-up" line work where necessary.

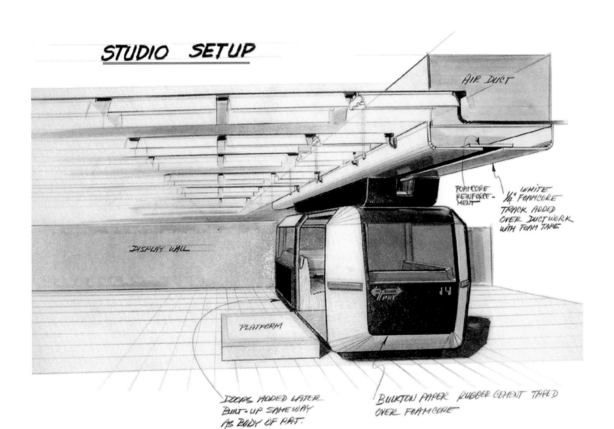

STUDIO SETUP

AIR DUCT

FOAMCORE
REINFORCE-
MENT

WHITE
1/16" FOAMCORE
TRACK ADDED
OVER DUCTWORK
WITH FOAM TAPE

DISPLAY WALL

PLATFORM

DOORS ADDED LATER
BUILT-UP SAME WAY
AS BODY OF P.R.T.

BULKTON PAPER RUBBER CEMENT TAPED
OVER FOAMCORE

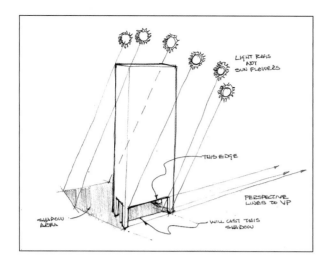

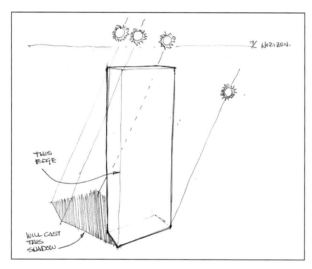

Figure 4-20a, Figure 4-20b
(Kevin Reeder)
Two simplified drawings show the fundamental principle of using shadow in conceptual drawing: sources of illumination are envisioned with rays of light running in parallel to create shadows—avoiding the complexities of non-parallel rays of light from artificial illumination.

Reflections—Reflections, and the specular form of reflection called "highlights," are actually a form of "glare" reflected off a surface. The eye perceives three types of glare: direct, indirect, and specular. Indirect and specular glare are forms of reflected light that define the reflectivity of a surface and become important conventions to represent surfaces. A highlight on the surface of any object is related to the physics of lighting and results in a reflected "specular illumination." The collected illumination off the surface of glass

from an automobile is specular illumination and, as such, a form of highlight. Highlights in drawing are frequently used to give the drawing a dazzling effect or "sparkle." Designers refer to this form of specular illumination as a "starburst" effect. While this device in drawing—and in rendering—has largely gone out of fashion, it is what most novice designers think of when highlights are discussed. There is, of course, a great deal more to the use of highlights in a more serious understanding of light on surfaces.

Highlights are the most intense gathering of light on a surface. Of greater importance than giving drawings sparkle, highlighting is also a device to convey edges and so-called "cut-lines" on the surface of fabricated objects. Designers who are adept at conceptual drawing can convey in their drawings how the object was produced, a communication of materials, and processes. This means that there should be attention to radii at edges, breaks in surfaces where two molded forms close on one another, cut-lines for doors housing batteries, removable components, hatches, and other combinations of components that make up the world of products.

All quantity-produced (sometimes referred to as mass-produced) products and objects have edges—but virtually none have a knife-edge either at the junction of two surfaces or where one part fits against another. There will always be a radius, no matter how small, at the edge of a fabricated product surface. In delineating one edge from another, there will be a slight gathering of light on a line that is just below the dark line indicating the separation between surfaces or edges. This type of highlighting is far more critical to communicate object surface than the starburst meant for the purposes of dazzle.

Another important aspect of highlighting in a drawing is communicating reflected light on a surface—depending on the material used for the fabrication of that surface. This is the crossover point between surface treatment or representation and the conventions employed to delineate light dark and shadow. Again, surface representation in conceptual drawing requires a simplification of the uses of media to convey surface rather than complex color mixing. Almost everything useful

Figure 4-21

(Joseph Koncelik)

In this developed mixed media drawing, the sun lights the subject matter directly overhead and slightly to the rear. The cap and shadow on the face indicate the direction of the light source—as does the heavy shadowing of the lawn tractor below the primary subject matter. The shadowing offsets the subject matter—especially the motorized hitch to the rear below the seat platform.

This drawing brings out virtually every aspect of this chapter—light and dark, shadow, object positioning, reflection, and surface representation. Object positioning relative to the light source has already been mentioned, along with the delineation of shadow—simplified and exaggerated to offset the primary subject matter. Materials and surface treatment are exemplified in the drawing of highly polished, likely cast aluminum, wheels as well as the mechanical structure of the hitch to the rear of the tractor.

Such a drawing was probably executed as an overlay on a drawing that had much more developed line work—including the development of freehand perspective. Further development of the ideas presented conceptually would require additional overlays and changes to surface, structure, and materials.

Figure representation, along with the initial problem of delineation of ellipses, is perhaps the most difficult aspect of conceptual drawing facing the novice design student. As will be explored in greater depth in Chapter 5, the issue of "human scale" can be an essential part of the representation of products—especially to provide a relative visualization of size as well as operationality. In this drawing, it was imperative to provide the scale of this tractor as a riding lawn tractor as opposed to a larger vehicle that would be used for heavy-duty farm and commercial work.

Initially, students are advised to "trace" man-machine visualizations or photographs to do overlays that will show relative scale. As skill in conceptual drawing advances, it will be possible to sketch the human figure in such a way as to be consistent with the designer's personal drawing style.

> **TIP** - In a line drawing, depict the ground shadow as a group of loose vertical lines. This visually separates the shadow from the object. ■

Figure 4-22a, Figure 4-22b
(Joseph Koncelik)
Two quick sketches of cooperative play object ideas. Only seconds were used to generate these notions of inflatable double-walled toys. Shadowing creates the ground plane in both.

Figure 4-23a
Figure 4-23b
(Kevin Reeder)
These two drawings have greater refinement—but where shadowing is important to the description of the forms and offsetting the forms from the page. The appropriate use of media is indicated to communicate the formed plastic materials used and the drawings of children help engender a sense of human scale. (See Chapter 5.)

> **TIP** - If it is rounded, use a simple core line to show the curve. ■

Figure 4-24
(R. Preston Bruning)
This quick freehand drawing illustrates how background can be effective in demonstrating the curvature and overall shape of glass objects. Note the shadow used to bring the wine glass forward and the simplicity of a gray shadow on the cylindrical glass.

to communicate surface, texture, and sense of material can be achieved with careful application of line-work in mixed media without delving into the sophistication of rendering and color mixing. (See surface treatment examples in Figures 4-32 a and b as well as 4-33a & b drawn by R. Preston Bruning.)

Surface Representation

As stated previously about conceptual drawing, *all lines are designed*—including the line work that depicts a surface representing specific geometry, material, color, and texture in light, dark, and shadow. A lack of careful attention to the weight, direction, and control of a marker line or pencil line that is used to depict a surface will result in a poor representation. It is not possible to draw the outline of an object carefully and then develop

the interior surface treatment with less care. Students of drawing should keep these rules of thumb in mind regarding attempting complex surface representation as well as improving their drawing in general:

1. A carefully executed drawing with excellent line control is essential in all design drawing. Pushing the drawing beyond a level of adequacy is, many times, unnecessary and undesirable because of the extra time involved. It is always important to keep in mind that ideas require sufficient visualization to communicate intent and content.

2. Work with an expert. Watch the way surface representation is accomplished in a step-by-step manner. Emulate or copy the methods of those designers who have superior technique to your own. In time, with practice, individuals develop

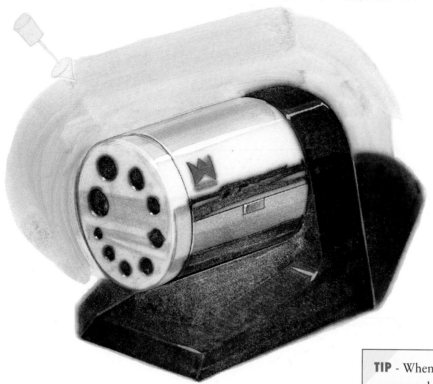

> **TIP** - When the viewer can see both sides of a corner, a thin white line depicts a highlight. If one side of the corner is shown, use a slightly heavier line to depict shadow. ▪

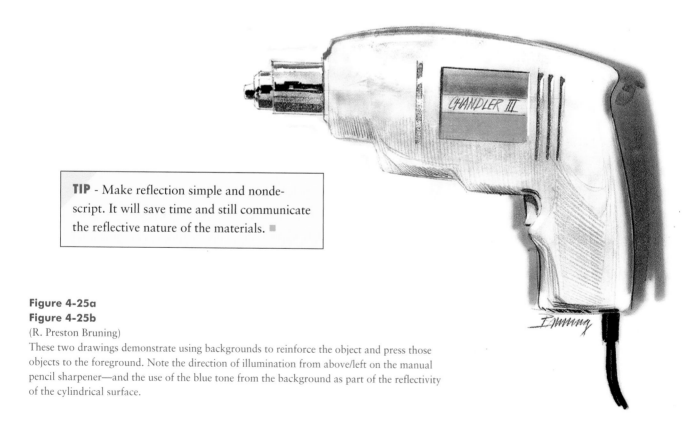

> **TIP** - Make reflection simple and nondescript. It will save time and still communicate the reflective nature of the materials. ▪

Figure 4-25a
Figure 4-25b
(R. Preston Bruning)
These two drawings demonstrate using backgrounds to reinforce the object and press those objects to the foreground. Note the direction of illumination from above/left on the manual pencil sharpener—and the use of the blue tone from the background as part of the reflectivity of the cylindrical surface.

Figure 4-26a
Figure 4-26b
(Kevin Reeder)
Two drawings by Kevin Reeder demonstrate using a simplified background of dark marker in a rectilinear form to offset the product to be "highlighted." Again, children give scale and the materials are indicated. Also note the highlighted edge on the pull-toy (lower) deftly indicating the parting line between the upper and lower components.

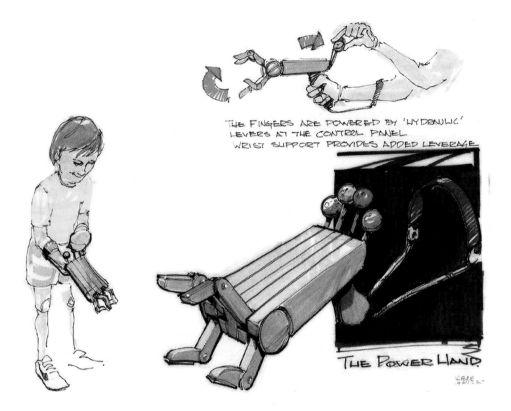

THE FINGERS ARE POWERED BY 'HYDRAULIC'
LEVERS AT THE CONTROL PANEL
WRIST SUPPORT PROVIDES ADDED LEVERAGE

THE POWER HAND

TIP - Avoid drawing backgrounds larger than the object itself. Also avoid the use of strong colors as a background because they visually press forward of the object. ■

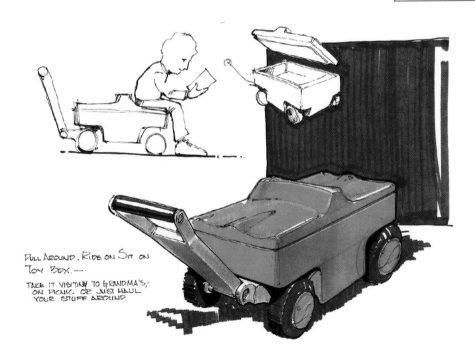

PULL AROUND, RIDE ON, SIT ON
TOY BOX. —

TAKE IT VISITING TO GRANDMA'S,
ON PICNIC, OR JUST HAUL
YOUR STUFF AROUND.

Figure 4-27
(R. Preston Bruning)
This advanced drawing pushes toward full rendering. Nevertheless, reflection is depicted not only in the product but also in the use of ground reflection that depicts a wet surface reflecting the bus. The directionality of the background indicates motion through inclement weather.

their own independent style of drawing. Students are advised to learn from one another—especially from those who seem to move quickly through the subject matter of conceptual drawing.

3. Again, related to practice, draw those objects, spaces, buildings, and graphic ideas that are appealing and make drawing practice enjoyable. The concepts that are learned using one subject can be translated to other subjects with time and practice. No drawing is a waste of time. Learning how to convey surfaces takes practice and, in the end, will literally become a subconscious act executed without excessive deliberation.

4. As a rule of thumb, conceptual drawings are complete when the designer pauses and is deciding where to place the next line. It is wise to stop when the idea is complete and not over-draw the subject. In addition, some information is best conveyed visually, while other information should be conveyed through text.

Conclusions about Light and Surfaces

Students of drawing are alternatively awed, sometimes perplexed, and frequently stymied by

the way the surfaces of objects are depicted or rendered by the skilled designer. Understanding surface rendering is a matter of being able to translate the fundamentals of light reflection as it is represented by a variety of colors seen in reflection on a surface. As a general rule, a surface given a high degree of texture reflects a lower amount of light back in the same direction. A mirror theoretically reflects all light back in an equal angle from the direction of the light source. A surface with higher texture, such as a fabric, will seemingly absorb light regardless of the direction. In fact, the surface of fabric refracts and reflects light at many angles different from the source direction. Surface sheen on a fabric results from the reflectivity of the fabric and the fineness of the weave. Silk is very reflective, but woolen fabrics absorb light. Representation of material, texture, and color of the surface of an object depends on four components:

1. Light source—(Refer to the previous segment on establishing the light source in a drawing.) The direction of the light source establishes how the light is reflected from the surface of the

Figure 4-28a
Figure 4-28b
(R. Preston Bruning)
In these two drawings, reflection characterizes specific materials. The upper drawing uses a ground line through the side window glass and color change on the front end to give a clear idea of materials used. Below, the conceptual drawing of a bed liner again provides indications of material choices as well as structural and fastening componentry.

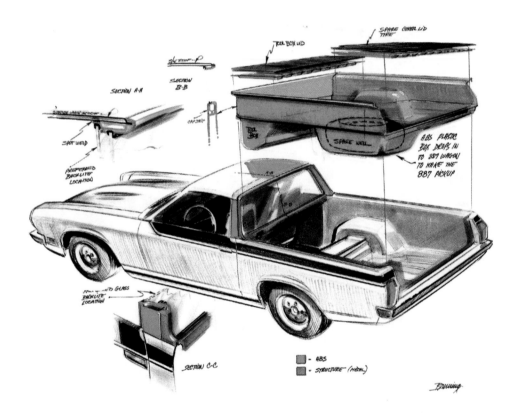

object. Again, and emphasizing simplicity, single light sources with all light flowing in one direction establish how the surface of the object will be seen.

2. Surface shape—How light is received by an object determines the way it is reflected back to the eye point of the viewer. Diagrams provided in this section illustrate how reflections change as surface shape changes. Understanding how illumination alters as it is reflected off surfaces of

varying shape is central to representing a reflective surface appropriately.

3. Surface reflectivity—Surfaces such as chrome return all light and essentially become a mirror. If the object curves, its surface reflects its surroundings depending on the degree of curvature of that object (See diagrammatic drawings, Figures 4-35 through 4-40.)

4. Surface color—All the principles of reflectivity remain the same, but are altered by the color

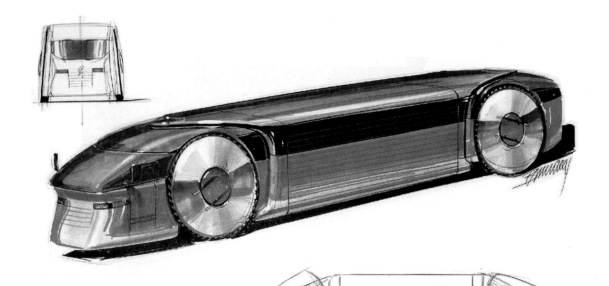

Figure 4-29a, Figure 4-29b
(R. Preston Bruning)
Two relatively quick freehand drawings of conceptual vehicles that utilize reflection in the wheel materials (upper) and then use the background to reflect into the top of the trailer (below). As can be seen, both drawings indicate articulation in the structure of the vehicles.

of the surface. Technically, all light is absorbed by the object except the color of light that is represented on the surface of the object.

Just as line control cannot be achieved without practice, understanding how surfaces appear to reflect light cannot be accomplished by understanding the theory alone. Students of drawing must make several attempts to represent surfaces by using underlay and overlay drawings to develop surface treatments properly. All too frequently, students tend to make artificial separations between sketching and finished drawing—as if they were different acts. One overriding principle applies in all design drawing;

it is a part of conceptual thinking or visualizing so that it communicates ideas to others.

Techniques for surface representation can be applied to quick sketching so that the concept is more fully explained to the viewer. Preston Bruning's drawings in this chapter provide visual studies of various objects more fully articulated with regard to surface. Yet the transition from the so-called thumbnail sketch to the finished drawing is seamless—there really is no loss of technical ability between levels.

At the beginning of the era of automotive design in the 1930s, one person usually directed a small group of people who designed most of

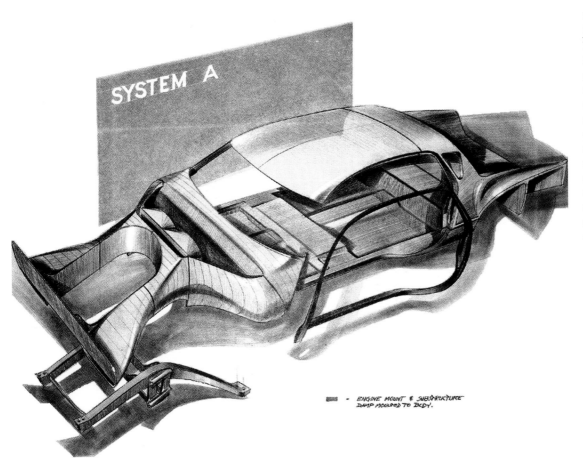

Figure 4-30
(R. Preston Bruning)
This advanced
freehand drawing
provides information
about the
development of a
semi-monocoque
automobile body
concept that uses
reflection in the
surfaces as well as
relatively simplified
shadow to convey the
separation of
components.

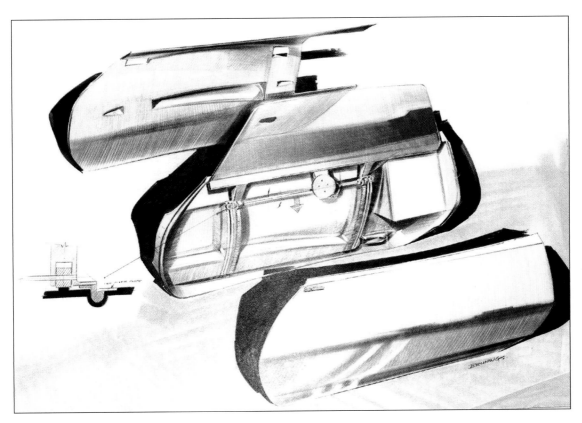

Figure 4-31
(R. Preston Bruning)
As with the previous
drawing – Figure 4-30
– this freehand drawing
expertly uses dark
shadowing to reveal
the components of this
automotive door
structure. The
shadowing is really a
form of background.
The reflection in
surfaces conveys the
glossy metallic surfaces
of the outer door panel
and the glazing.

Figure 4-32a, Figure 4-32b
(R. Preston Bruning)
These rectilinear cube forms capture the fundamentals of reflectivity in that the first (on the left) is a highly polished surface and the cube on the right is rusty! Note the attention to direction of illumination.

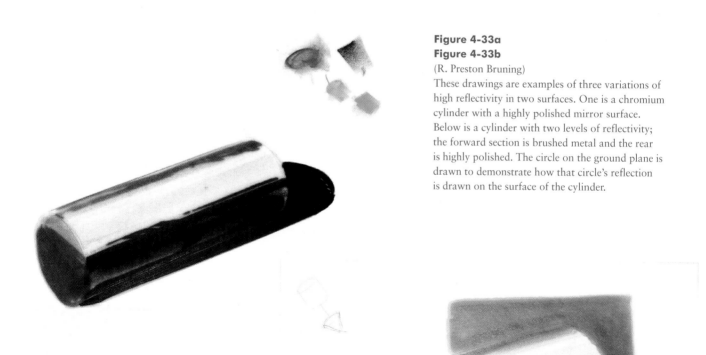

Figure 4-33a
Figure 4-33b
(R. Preston Bruning)
These drawings are examples of three variations of high reflectivity in two surfaces. One is a chromium cylinder with a highly polished mirror surface. Below is a cylinder with two levels of reflectivity; the forward section is brushed metal and the rear is highly polished. The circle on the ground plane is drawn to demonstrate how that circle's reflection is drawn on the surface of the cylinder.

TIP - The sharper the core line, the more reflective the material. ■

Figure 4-34
(Joseph Koncelik, R. Preston Bruning)
To the left, the effect of illumination on three metallic surfaces with simple geometric shapes, the football, cone, and sphere. The fourth is a "bread loaf." All have light directed from the front left and above with shadows falling to the right.

the classic automobiles from the pistons outward to the fenders. Buggati designed all of his cars personally from the engines to the exterior body designs. That all changed when General Motors first moved from its "Art and Color Studio" that evolved into "Styling" under the leadership of Harley J. Earle and, later, William Mitchell. Today that division of the corporation is called General Motors Design. Outer body surface design was divorced from the mechanical enterprise of engineering. The slippery shapes associates with speed and glamour were all developed in the studios of Styling and later Design and there is little difference between how General Motors develops exterior and interior automotive design and how Ford, Daimler-Chrysler,

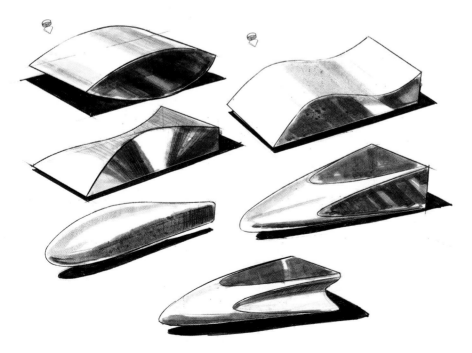

Figure 4-35
(Joseph Koncelik, R. Preston Bruning)
Complex forms with illumination from the left front. Again, each shape is a metallic form with variations in the surface from concavity to convexity.

Figure 4-36
(Joseph Koncelik,
R. Preston Bruning)
Each of the six surfaces
demonstrates the effect of
reflection on different surfaces. It
seems that the ground to be
reflected is a sunrise over a
hilltop with a tree and ground.
Note the differences for each of
the surfaces: A flat reflective
surface in a reflective metal finish
gives the least distortion to the
image visible. A convex surface
compresses the image and
intensifies the "core" ground that
would be the hilltop. A concave
surface reverses the image top to
bottom and compresses the core
in the same way as the convexity.
A concave football-shaped
surface produces distortion
according to the shape of the
object. A convex football-shaped
surface maintains the relationship
of sky to ground as they appear,
but they are compressed at the
ends of the shape. A conical
surface extends the reflection
along the lines of the surface
from the point to the circular
section at the rear with greater
compression at the front.

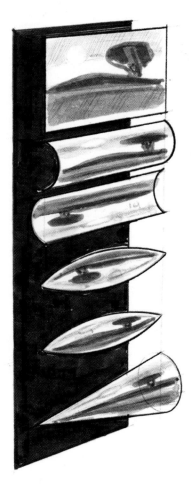

Figure 4-37
(Joseph Koncelik,
R. Preston Bruning)
With the use of light
gray warm markers,
Bruning illustrates the
differences in the
reflected sun, hilltop,
tree, and ground in a
cylindrical shape in
both convex and
concave form (upper
drawings) with a metal
form having two
concave surfaces joined
at a peak line. Note
that no such break in
a surface is ever a sharp
line but has a very
tight radius.

Nissan, Toyota, or any automotive company develops this work.

Automotive design was born from the need to sell cars in saturated markets during the 1930s. Industrial design as a profession had the same mother—advertising and sales. There is certainly more to developing design then the need to sell, but the roots of the profession are undeniably clear in this respect—and provide the legacy from which conceptual drawing and all of design visualization have evolved. Selling the idea became as important within design groups as it was to selling the public on the need for—or the desire for—the product. The skill of representing designs reached its highest point in the automotive industry in the internally competitive environment of corporate design. Some of the most talented designers who have developed a high

level of skill in communicating surface are part of the automobile industry. They all love to draw and their example benefits the student of conceptual drawing.

Bruning's drawings are rooted in the automotive design experience, but have a character all their own. His studies are quick drawings that utilize surface representational techniques rather than drawings developed as full renderings. As can be seen in the ideal examples of drawings in this section of the text, surface treatments on the engine walls are denoted with quick marker technique to depict a hammertone finish or other simulation of the metal surface. Also note the geometric construction of the engines in the modified two-point perspective—chosen because it would permit the fastest method to represent the engines. Note also the treatment of cylindrical forms as if they were receiving light from a specific direction. Ground lines and highlighted areas are clearly drawn. Valve covers and other modified geometric forms receive the same light source and light and shade treatment.

In this chapter, discussion centered on developing form in light, dark, and shadow as well as representation of surfaces. As stated, these two aspects of conceptual drawing are linked. Light reflected from the surface of an object—or from within a space—determines perception of surface. The discussion began with six aspects of developing objects and spaces in light:

1. Positioning of a light source
2. Positioning of the object relative to that light source
3. Use of light and dark on the surfaces of objects
4. Placements of shadow
5. Appropriate use of backgrounds
6. Use of highlights

The distinction was drawn between *surface representation* and *rendering*. Rendering is a broad deep subject that takes design visualization into the realm of the illustrative—not the conceptual. Other texts cover rendering far more adequately than is possible in this text. The term "representation" was chosen because it is necessary to develop ideas in conceptual drawing that convey intent about materials, color, and surface texture. However, all surface representation can be developed extending the control of line and quality of line that has been a central theme throughout this text. Rendering requires color mixing—surface representation achieves similar results through careful placement of line in marker and pastel with each component of mixed media chosen for a specific visual effect. The eye perceives these applications of the various media as mixed by virtue of their proximity. A number of conceptual drawings and demonstration drawings were selected for this chapter that illustrate in visual terms the concepts discussed in the text. Students of design are encouraged to emulate the examples provided as part of their practice regimen.

TIP - Keep reflections in materials simplified. ▪

Figure 4-38
(Joseph Koncelik, R. Preston Bruning)
This collection of eight drawings illustrates the same reflected shapes in a concave arrow form, two different reverse-curved surfaces, and five differing spherical section surfaces from the convex "moon" type surface to variations of concavity and convexity as well as conical convex/concave shapes.

Finally, and to iterate a point, the roots of exemplary design drawing and object representation can be traced to the genesis of the automotive industry and the development of automotive styling—as a separate activity from automotive engineering. The purpose of developing such a high level of surface representation in automotive design as well as in other areas of corporate and consultative design has been and continues to be

Figure 4-39
(Joseph Koncelik, R. Preston Bruning)
Plastics and metals can have varying
surfaces in terms of the radius of
curvature that defines edges. Bruning's
drawings provide visual guidelines as to
how the reflectivity of these surfaces is to
be treated. In these two drawings, there is
a relatively hard surface break with a
small radius resulting in a highlighted
edge. The drawing below has a more
generous radius and then a reverse radius
on the lower portion. The highlighted
section above is broader and the
reflection of "ground" is captured in the
concave surface of the lower section.

Figure 4-40
(Joseph Koncelik, R. Preston Bruning)
The upper-right drawing has a generous
radius that is continuous and a resulting
broad highlighted section with a reflection
of ground in the lower area. The drawing
below shows the concave surface on
the upper section and a tighter radius
that reflects the highlight with the ground
reflected below it.

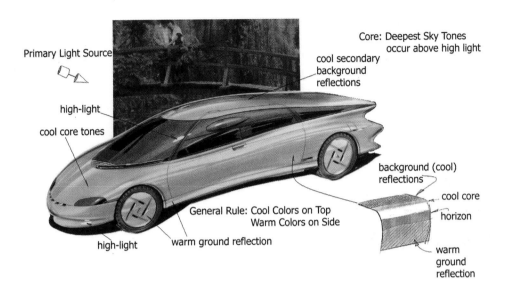

Primary Light Source

high-light

cool core tones

high-light

warm ground reflection

Core: Deepest Sky Tones occur above high light

cool secondary background reflections

background (cool) reflections

cool core

horizon

warm ground reflection

General Rule: Cool Colors on Top Warm Colors on Side

Figure 4-41
(R. Preston Bruning)
In the drawing at left, R. Preston Bruning demonstrates the treatment of surfaces on a conceptual vehicle drawing. Note that the section of material to the right of the image provides the basic information for the development of reflectivity in the overall form of the vehicle. Bruning conveys how to produce an effective reflected surface using marker and pen lines. The light source is high and to the left (as shown by the directional arrow). He refers to the "gathering" of reflection as a "core" and starburst highlights are used sparingly—only one appears on the upper part of the reflection in the dark glass of the canopy.

Figure 4-42
(R. Preston Bruning)
The vehicle in the drawing above uses a convex wheel cover, to the left is a variation of such a covering that is both concave and convex. Note that the light reflection is gathered below and the ground reflection in the upper part of the concave shape and is just the opposite in the convex part of the shape.

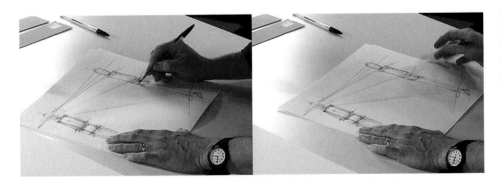

Figure 4-43
(Michael Butcher)
Drawing the figure in perspective requires an understanding of human proportion—as demonstrated in Segment 4, Human Figure in Context, of the DVD.

See DVD Segment 4, Human Figure in Context, for detailed information on drawing the human figure in perspective.

Figure 4-44
(Michael Butcher)
An understanding of the human figure helps establish the context for simple and complex products. Again, this sequence is part of the DVD demonstrations.

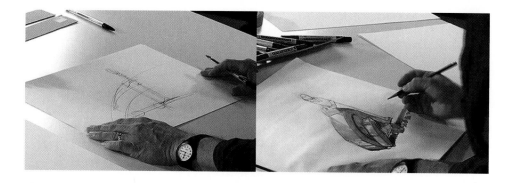

 See DVD Segment 4, Human Figure in Context, for additional information regarding using mixed media and products with drawing the human figure.

competition. Competition has been internalized within the corporate settings for designers and also is part of the legacy of advertising and sales from which design professions emerged in the 1930s. Design professions may have developed a more sophisticated range of activities and responsibilities at this juncture in their evolution, but the roots of all design visualization are directly attributable to its earlier primary objectives.

Figure 4-45
(Kevin Reeder)
Reeder demonstrates the "fit" of a product to a human figure in perspective using mixed media drawing techniques.

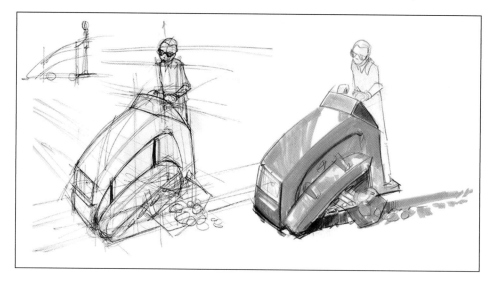

Figure 4-46
(Kevin Reeder)
The quick sketch generated on opaque drawing paper is the underlay for a tracing that allows for corrections and the addition of product details such as the roll bar.

5

Human Scale and Context

Objects in Relation to People and Places

All objects exist in an environment and virtually all products or man-made objects are used by people—except for a few adventures in technology that have sunk into the depths of the ocean or have been blasted into outer space without the accompaniment of a human being. The consumer-oriented and commercial products, furnishings, or machines used by people sit on a surfaces or a floor, are held in the hand, are mounted to walls, or establish some other relationship between their mass, dimensionality, and a surrounding. This is the *context* for man-made objects and that context establishes a sense of size and scale, relationship to use, and also relationship to space and the presence of other objects nearby.

Contemporary designers use a term called "interface," a connection between the machine and the human user. Interface refers to the ability to use, operate, or interact with a product or environment. It is established in conceptual drawing by incorporating the human figure as if it were using, wearing, driving, or otherwise interacting with a product. Products do not exist in a vacuum. Commercial photography usually places products against a white background without any horizon visible, but when drawing an object, it will be better understood if a person is near it, holding it, grasping it, sitting on it, or riding in it.

Clients and others participating in the design process may be confused by a lack of context when they are shown conceptual drawings that have no relationship to users or environment. Products depicted in such drawings will seem out of place and lack scale when no context is incorporated. While questions about use and scale might not be asked, it will be difficult to understand the product's relationship to human use and scale. Another way to understand this confusion is to envision how cleverly a toy car or ship appears as though it were an object at full scale when cleverly photographed. Designers are adept at fooling the mind's eye and, if used carelessly or unconsciously, this misuse of presentation may fool others unintentionally.

Another important context in conceptualization is to incorporate anthropometry, or body measurement, in the conceptual drawing process. Designing for "others" requires exploration of the differences among people in terms of their body dimensions. For example, if a design for a wall-mounted thermostat appears in context, that surrounding should include some indication of its relationship to the smallest and the largest

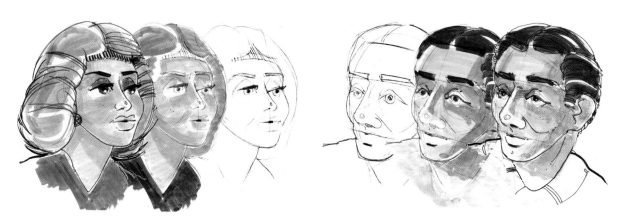

Figure 5-1a
Figure 5-1b
(Joseph Koncelik)

One of the hardest requirements for design students is drawing a man's or woman's face—and the human form for that matter. A face without guidelines will have eyes, mouth and features in general, seeming arbitrary in their placement on an unstructured form. In this chapter, there will be substantial coverage of "conventions" that will permit students the ability to develop reasonable drawings of the human form. The sketching method shown above is fast and has only three steps: 1) a line drawing in Verithin pencil; 2) quick use of marker to describe the structure of the face; and 3) the final detailing that is an emphasis of line to describe the face and accentuate detail.

intended user of the product. When wearing a product is part of its intended use, it is impossible to escape the need for demonstrating how the product accommodates diversity among users at the beginning of the conceptual process. Clearly, incorporating the use of context requires a good deal of advancement in the development of conceptual drawing capabilities.

Of all the problems confronting the novice designer in design classes, drawing the human figure is perhaps the most challenging. The task of learning to draw the human figure is daunting—especially because so much of the curriculum in contemporary design programs is devoid of any figure drawing and such drawing has no emphasis in design studio courses. Nevertheless, the accomplished designer has established a means to communicate the presence of people in drawings. The need to show scale compels drawing a handheld product or a simulation of an operating product in context with the human hand or human figure. Thus, the most important context to establish is that of human scale and conventions for drawing the human figure.

Conventions for the Human Form

Drawing the human figure is one of the greatest challenges for any designer and student of design. It is, however, a useful way to learn about drawing in general. Figure-drawing classes are important as electives or post-study courses beyond the design curriculum requirements. Because this is a book about fundamentals, figure drawing limits the subject's complexity and depth so that the simplified methods of drawing human form can indicate scale to other objects and spaces. Drawing the human figure is perhaps the best way to develop a sense of form and structure. The human form presents virtually every complex drawing problem and every manner of challenge to the designer and to the artist. No person who enjoys drawing can ever "wear out" the infinite number of possibilities that the figure presents as a drawing problem. The one piece of advice any drawing teacher should give to the student of drawing is to take a figure drawing class.

Figure 5-2a, Figure 5-2b
(Joseph Koncelik)
Depending on the level of sketch and the degree of detail invested in the drawing, there will be several levels of approximation of reality appropriate to the drawing. These two sketches depict two ends of the spectrum, from a figure that gives scale and little else to a human form that conveys a greater level of detail and character.

The following collection of drawings and diagrams provides simplified information about structuring and constructing human figures that will "look" natural. Many beginning students do not understand the conventions that really differentiate between women and men. Problems drawing the face relate back to earlier instructions regarding the geometry and structure of a form. Many of the conventions of drawing have evolved from those developed over the centuries in Western art. Those who draw the figure well understand there is a difference between capturing reality and what seems to "look right" on the page. In fashion drawing, linear figures are the commonplace with extended leg lengths. Upper torso lengths are much shorter than the length of lower extremities.

In addition, the general convention in drawing the human figure is that the standing height of the figure is seven heads high or the vertical distance of seven heads stacked one on top of the other. However, in fashion illustration and other forms of advertising art, human figure drawings may be

Figure 5-3a
Figure 5-3b
(Joseph Koncelik)
Two face sketches are used to display two very different concepts for eyewear. The drawings show the three-step process of initial rough line work, use of broad tipped markers, and finish using fine-line pens and Prismacolor pencils. Use a Verithin pencil to sketch a line drawing on tracing paper quickly. After this step, use a marker to delineate the structure of the face in light and shadow. After this step, draw line details in place to finish the drawing—at a level appropriate to a sketch consuming a few minutes.

well over seven heads high—with most of the height in the legs. It is not productive to discuss the philosophic aspect of Western imagery here, but there is no doubt that our self concept has been much affected by the linear, ultra-thin figurative conventions used in the fashion and advertising world—even though most people are nothing like the images portrayed, nor can they be.

The human figure can be an important aspect of design drawing for several reasons. First, the human figure gives scale to interior drawing and to many forms of product design development. Second, numerous body products inundate our culture: the ubiquitous I-Pod, bicycle helmets, glasses and goggles; handheld tools are a few. Third, many commercial products such as lift

Figure 5-4

(Joseph Koncelik)

This series of variations uses computer enhancement of a scanned line sketch to show the steps in the process. The process involves scanning the line drawing into Adobe Photoshop and then transferring the image to a paint program to achieve a composite drawing. The image uses "custom colors" for a skin-tone palette appropriate to the subject matter. The image uses the application of the area inlay function of the paint program for the application of flat colors. This drawing shows all of the original construction lines for the face because the area inlay function cannot cover those areas. The third drawing from the right, top row, has been augmented through the use of "paint" functions to properly reduce the effect of the white structure lines. Other functions of the program have been used to amplify areas of shadow and skin tone and reflectivity.

The remaining variations import the scanned image back into Photoshop. The upper-left image and all four images below the top row have been "manipulated" in Photoshop. For those students and designers familiar with the multiple functions of Photoshop, there are literally thousands of variations that use the digitizing functions of this program. These include simulations of pencil and brush strokes, area blending and highlighting, as well as color manipulation (the second drawing from the right, bottom row, shows a variation in color from the other images). Each of these images were developed in a matter of minutes— allowing the designer to explore several alternative variations to select a process appropriate to the design task's subject matter.

So-called "hybrid" drawings proliferate on the World Wide Web. Hybrids begin with manually developed line drawings on paper. One of the reasons for creating images this way is that pencil and paper drawings allow the development of a perspective image and other subjects more quickly than developing them as computer renderings. Since all of the images of this book are digital, they are all—in a sense—hybrids. However, the computer captures images for reproduction it is not used to alter the drawings or develop the images. The final chapter of this book contains several examples of hybrid drawings that are far more complex manipulations of images than those shown here. In some instances, image capture, uses of scanning to convert manually generated images into digital form, and generation of the finished conceptual images, uses three or more software programs such as Adobe Photoshop, Microsoft Paint, and Adobe Illustrator – among several available.

There are some specific design challenges that necessitate using computer enhancements. After scanning line drawings, developing complex images is far easier using computer technology than developing manual renderings.

trucks, commercial cleaning equipment, and large Xerox copying machines have no scale unless seen with a human figure. Finally, products form their own environment of use, commonly called workstations. These complex microenvironments include control and display devices, seating, storage, communications systems, and work surfaces—all based on proximity to a human user. Drawing such arrangements without the human figure frequently leaves the viewer unconvinced about scale and relationships of use.

Some of the more important conventions that the beginning student must observe to depict the human figure properly are as follows:

1. Drawings of men generally have shoulders wider than their hips and the upper torso shorter than the lower extremities. The convention of facial features is larger for a man than for a

Figure 5-5a
Figure 5-5b
Figure 5-5c
(Kevin Reeder)
Several drawing and design assignments will require an understanding of the human form and the face, otherwise the design becomes impossible to conceptualize. In these line drawings, face images with character and humor are a "context" for the development of goggles.

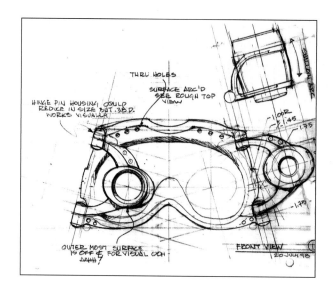

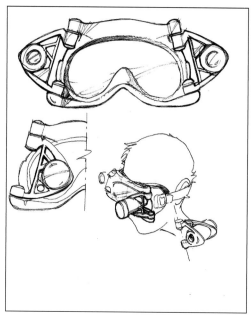

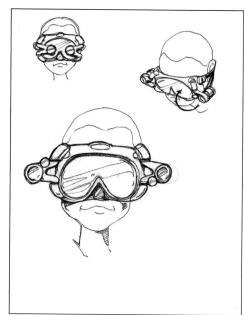

woman. Men's faces generally have a larger chin and more pronounced jawline. A man's eyes, nose, and mouth use more area of the face than a woman's.

2. The convention for drawing women is to draw the shoulders narrower than the hips. The defining convention that differentiates men from women in drawing is hip width—not breast development or size. Large breasts on a big-shouldered figure may make the figure seem like a football lineman gone wrong. Female conventions in drawing include drawing smaller faces with smaller chins—but larger eyes. Hair mass conventions have changed and no longer define

sex. Again, upper torso length will be shorter than lower extremity length.

3. A critical error that shows up in the drawing of most beginning students of drawing is that they set the head vertically above the shoulders on a straight line from the backbone. The backbone is curved in an S form and the head is generally thrust forward of the shoulders.

4. The convention for drawing upper-arm length and upper-leg length is that both are shorter in length than the lower arm and leg. It is wise to view the torso on an armature and then strike off the leg and arm lengths before drawing in the detail.

5. The human figure is a structure as if it were a highrise building hung on steel posts and beams. Many beginning drawing students attempt to draw the human figure by drawing an outline and then filling in that outline with unstructured detail. This method does not work well—especially for the uninitiated.

6. The figure requires the same approach any good designer would use in architecture, interior design, or product design; namely, one draws the subject from the inside out—beginning with the frame, hanging on the geometry of the human form, and completing the drawing with sufficient detail to make the figure a human being instead of some mutant from another galaxy. Study—even copy—the drawings shown in this section. With some practice, conventions and abstracted figure forms give objects and spaces human scale.

The Human Figure As Context

Design drawing often defines the context of its surroundings. For example, a kitchen appliance should not always be shown isolated as if it were a piece of sculpture rather than a functional object. Therefore, one aspect of context for a product is the setting in which it will be found. Another aspect of context is use. Industrial designers are responsible for creating the association between product and person, an "interface" that provides a visual indication of operationality. In addition, a product requires a sense of scale.

The viewer expects to understand just how large or small something is and, seeing objects in isolation, the viewer has difficulty getting any sense of scale. The addition of human figures is essential to the viewer in providing that sense of scale and context. A question that arises regarding context is: How detailed should the figure be in relationship to the drawing of the product? The answer, usually, is that the figure should be subordinate in its level of drawing detail. Frequently, figures in design drawings are merely outlines that indicate the presence of a human scale. In other drawings, figures will vignette or fade away from the object with detail drawing given to part of the figure, but not to the entire figure.

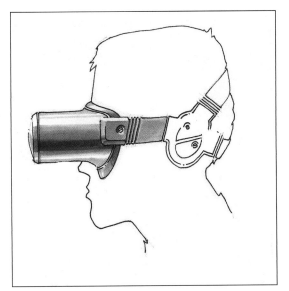

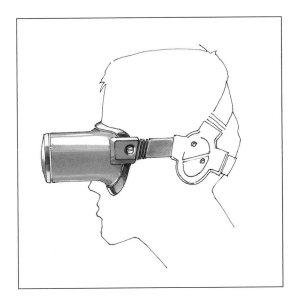

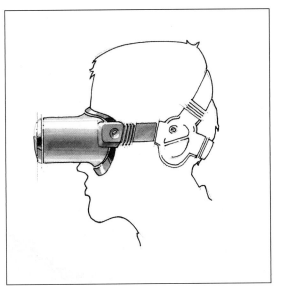

Figure 5-6a
Figure 5-6b
Figure 5-6c
(Kevin Reeder)
The designer uses a common underlay for images incorporating the human face as "context" for the development of face wear; in this case, special field goggles for children's play. Overlays, as well as scans and Xerox copying, are effective demonstrations of a range of color variations.

Figure 5-7

(Joseph Koncelik)

Defining "male" and "female" requires knowledge of anatomy and the use of drawing conventions such as the relationship of hip to shoulder breadth. The male figure will appear like a male if the shoulders are wider than the hips.

TIP - The human figure presents the best indicator of scale—size of the object or space. ■

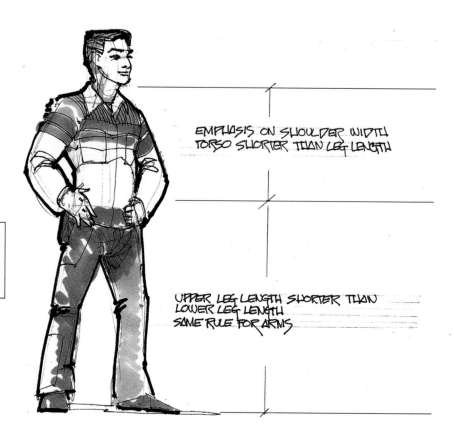

EMPHASIS ON SHOULDER WIDTH
TORSO SHORTER THAN LEG LENGTH

UPPER LEG LENGTH SHORTER THAN
LOWER LEG LENGTH
SAME RULE FOR ARMS

Figure 5-8

(Joseph Koncelik)

The female form should follow a different convention from the male in that the shoulder width should be smaller than the hip width. Regardless of the differences among men and women—and the reversals of the conventions that naturally occur—these drawing conventions convey distinctions that are workable in developing context.

SKETCHING CONVENTIONS FOR THE
FEMALE FIGURE EMPHASIZE HIP WIDTH
OVER SHOULDER WIDTH ... ALSO
EMPHASIZE LEG LENGTH

TURN KNEE INWARD ON FEMALE
FIGURE ... OUTWARD ON MALE

AS A GENERAL RULE OF THUMB, BODY HEIGHT IS A PROPORTION OF "7 HEADS HIGH."

THE SHOULDER TO HIPS IS LESS DISTANCE THAN THE HIPS TO THE GROUND PLANE

UPPER ARM TO SHOULDER IS LESS THAN THE DISTANCE FROM THE ELBOW TO THE HAND

STRIKE THE LINE FOR THE HIPS JUST AFTER DETERMINING THE "ARMATURE LINE" TO DETERMINE THE OTHER PROPORTIONS OF THE HUMAN TORSO

UPPER LEG LENGTH IS SHORTER THAN THE LENGTH OF THE LOWER LEG

THE ANKLE LINE DETERMINES WHERE THE TRANSITION OF CURVES OCCURS BETWEEN LOWER LEG AND FOOT

A VERTICLE "ARMATURE LINE" POSITIONS THE BODY AND SHOULD BE STRUCK JUST AFTER DETERMINING THE GROUND PLANE

THE GROUND LINE SHOULD BE THE FIRST LINE STRUCK FOLLOWED BY THE ARMATURE LINE THEN THE HIP LINE

Figure 5-9
(Joseph Koncelik)
One way to develop a simple, structurally sound image of the human form is to envision that form on an armature fixed in space to the ground. A vertical line is drawn and the proportions of the figure "measured" off as the eyes see it.

TIP - Draw the figure first and the product second, not the other way around. ▪

Figure 5-10a, Figure 5-10b
(Joseph Koncelik)
The old axiom of a figure being "seven heads high" is a valuable guideline that will help students avoid awkward proportions when heads seem either too large or too small. In this series of drawings, a male form becomes the context for the development of power-washing equipment for commercial applications.

TIP - The conventional way to gauge the height and proportion of a figure is that the human body is seven heads high from the ground to the top of the head. ▪

Figure 5-11
(Joseph Koncelik)
Note that the finished sketch conveys some action, but the gestures have no exaggeration as they might have in cartoon imagery. While the study of animé and other cartoon forms is helpful, the figures can become dominant when they should only provide context.

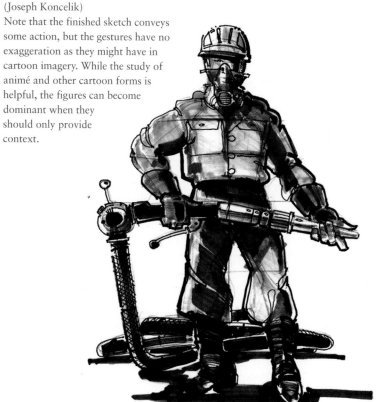

TIP - Do not draw the figure as a superhero. Remember that the sketch is nothing but a sketch, a communication of an idea. Any conceptual drawing has no value until it is time for evaluation. ▪

Drawing the Human Face in a Product Context

Product designers confront the necessity of drawing the human face to provide context for product developments such as hats, helmets, eyeglasses and goggles, communications devices, and many other items of technology and outerwear. Drawing the face poses problems of understanding human anatomy and the fundamental structural aspects of the skull and muscles. The uninitiated drafter/designer tends to see the face as a mushy construct of a head form with arbitrary placement of eyes, nose, and a mouth. Unfortunately, this usually results in a face that is neither useful as a context for the product to be portrayed nor does it have a semblance of reality

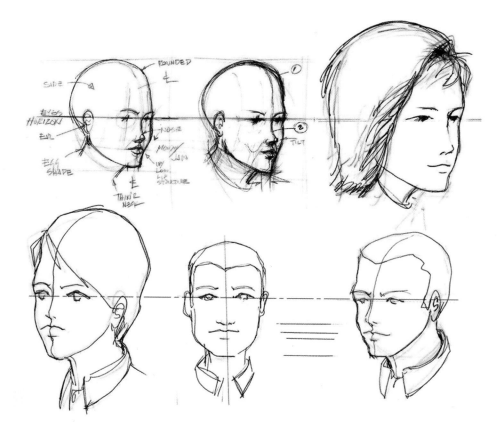

Figure 5-12a
Figure 5-12b
(Kevin Reeder)
This series of two drawings illustrates the development of head forms with knowledge of anatomy and geometry. The resulting images are simple line drawings but convey significant differences in facial characteristics.

FEATURES ARE LARGE, EMPHUSIZE JAW LINE
NECK SLANTS FORWARD TO HEAD

TIP OF NOSE IN FRONT OF TIP OF CHIN
EAR DEFINED BY LINE FROM BROW AND NOSE

Figure 5-13
(Joseph Koncelik)
Conventions for the male face include a
strong jawline and more pronounced
features such as the nose and chin. Eyes are
generally drawn smaller and closer
together than for the female head and face.

sufficiently convincing as a drawing of human
characteristics. Others will frequently trace a face
from a photographic source. Using a photographic source can be successful if the designer
sees and understands the underlying structure of
the face. The novice sketching designs for products that most conform to a face or head form
frequently will not depict that underlying structure, and the match between product and human
context will seem awkward.

FEATURES ARE SMALLER WITH
EXCEPTION OF EYES AND MOUTH

SOFTEN HAIR AND FEATURES
GENERALLY.... LENGTHEN NECK

Figure 5-14
(Joseph Koncelik)
The female face convention is for the chin
to be smaller, lips to be drawn fuller, and
the eyes larger and set farther apart than
for the male.

TIP - Do not have the figure in the drawing
looking at the viewer. ∎

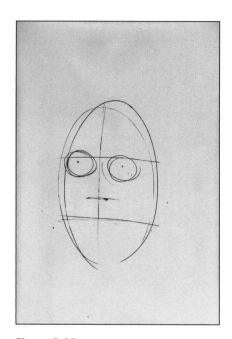

Figure 5-15
(Joseph Koncelik)
Step 1 in the development of this sketch is the placement of an ovaloid form depicting the placement of a three-quarter-view face at eye-level, appearing to look to the right. All of the line work uses a thin-tipped marker and empathic drawing fundamentals are observed regarding control and quality of line. (Note: All newsprint drawings have no corrections or erasures.)

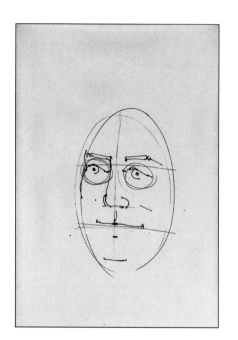

Figure 5-16
(Joseph Koncelik)
Step 2 provides a few more cues regarding the development of facial characteristics that will permit development of a face mask and eye protection. This step also includes a "marker" for the limit of the face at the chin line and additional cues for the mouth and nose. It is necessary to observe care in the placement of eyes recessed in relation to the forehead.

Figure 5-17
(Joseph Koncelik)
Step 3 demonstrates the provision of additional details about the shape of the face and head, the placement of the ear of the left side of the face at a location equidistant from the line of the top of the eye and the base of the nose. Note the convention for depicting the complexity of the ear using one line to describe the outer shape and another to delineate the shaping of the ear's inside characteristics. This face is obviously male, owing to the heaviness of the chin and delineation of the side of the face as having definable facial muscles and much thinner lips than those used in the conventions for a female face.

In the following sequence of drawings (Figure 5–24 through Figure 5–35), a simplified method for drawing a head is given that begins with the simple generation of an egg form with the pointed end in the down direction. After describing the egg form, a vertical line divides the surface that depicts the curving surface of the form. Horizontal lines are placed on the surface to delineate the placement of eyes and the mouth. Orbs depicting the full eyeball appear below the brow and the mouth after the projection of a triangular nose form. It is important to keep in mind the following issues of constructing the human face:

1. The chin should not project beyond the line of the nose.

2. Eyes are set behind the brow—not forward of the brow or on a vertical plane dropped from the forehead.

3. The line of setback from the tip of the nose to the chin is roughly equivalent to the line of setback of the eye rearward of the brow.

4. The top lip will be seen in shadow with the bottom lip seen in light—they will not be equal in their color or value.

5. The face, and the skull beneath, is not a round ball, but a structure with rather defined ridges where the brow meets the side of the skull—giving the face its definition in shadow.

6. Larger chins and jawlines may characterize men's faces. Eyes will be less defined and somewhat smaller than a woman's. Lips have less definition.

Figure 5-18

(Joseph Koncelik)

Step 4 shows the development of facial position in relationship to the upper torso (shoulders) and the neck. In addition, the face uses delineation of geometry of the product characteristics to follow. Sketched ovaloid shapes provide for the location of eye protection. Vertical lines locate the boundaries of the face mask that will provide nose and mouth protection. A brow line illustrates the placement for the lower brim of the helmet. In addition, there is line work to illustrate the collar of a protective suit that will be integral with the lower part of the face mask. At this juncture in sketch development, only a few seconds have passed.

Figure 5-19

(Joseph Koncelik)

Step 5 shows the process extended to include the rough geometries of the face mask, ear protection, and rough outline of the top of the helmet. Specific ideas about the position of the filters on the surface of the mask as well as a front piece at the forward part of the nose of the mask indicate the position for a two-way radio. Again, all of the line work remains in plain sight and remains through to the finalization of the drawing.

Figure 5-20

(Joseph Koncelik)

Step 6 is the first one to show differentiating use of line and marker. Heavy black ink line delineates the shape of the eye protection and convex form of the goggle section of the mask. Note that marker is used to delineate the flesh tones that will be visible behind the mask and that eyes, eyelids, and the shape of the eye are indicated. Backing up, the face drawing is critical to shaping the mask itself. Without the face, there is little relationship to human form—critical to the development of this specific product. It is possible that a marker on newsprint drawing (such as this one) becomes an underlay for a more detailed study of the design idea. The emphasis here, however, is moving a sketch to a level of completion without removing any of the line work, expediting the time required to develop and complete the drawing.

7. Smaller chins and less severe jawlines, larger eyes, and fuller lips may characterize women's faces.

8. Use of a light source should appear from one direction and usually from above.

9. Start by constructing the head as described previously. A tapered block or oval shape serves the purpose of defining the head form. Note that, proportionally, the head is nearly the same in height and depth and is about 70 percent as wide.

10. Mark a horizontal line halfway down to locate the eyes.

Note: In both proportion and anthropometric constructions, the eyes are approximately halfway down the head and halfway to the side. Depicting the eye as a line with a parallel dash placed below it, is a simple, effective technique. Simplifying the skin structure around the eye to a couple lines is quicker and less prone to error than more rendered techniques.

11. Mark another horizontal line short of three-fourths of the way down to locate the bottom of the nose. Indicating the nose with a short horizontal line approximates the shadow cast by an overhead light source and is quick and effective.

Figure 5-21

(Joseph Koncelik)

Step 7 shows the first use of marker to delineate the shape of the mask using a number 6 cool gray design marker. Again, the fundamentals hold true here in that the marker stroke flows in the direction of the curvature of the mask to reinforce its shape. Note that there are areas of "white" or page color showing through, helping to define the shape of the mask and also allowing for some of the "bleeding" of marker color that will occur using a porous medium such as newsprint.

Figure 5-22

(Joseph Koncelik)

Step 8 shows more development of the helmet—a shape that was initially too flat for the size of the head—the accommodation of straps beneath the helmet as well as the positioning of a light on the front surface of the helmet. The indication of an earpiece on the left side of the helmet exists in outline on the right side. Another important component of the drawing is that the heaviest line work will be on the right side away from an implied light source coming in from the left overhead. The areas left without marker indicate the presence of that light source. In both of these areas, some specific treatment of the earpiece indicates the possibility of this fully contained unit having two-way communications. This sketch might benefit from text to amplify such ideas.

Figure 5-23

(Joseph Koncelik)

Step 9 shows the provision of surface color to the helmet and the protective garment that are an integral protective covering. The removable filters at the sides of the mask use a lighter green marker. Notice that the marker color stops short of the outline of the helmet shape because, again, there is likely to be bleeding of the marker color, and the paper color or "white" of the page helps indicate a highlight and the convex curving shape of the helmet. At this point, the designer has committed eight to ten minutes to the drawing. This is because the designer is not spending time in correction, but is overdrawing lines and using markers to cover some of the line work that fades as the drawing develops. Note that the facial features such as mouth, ears, nose, and chin have been important guides to develop the protection gear, but are now only faintly visible behind the surface marker colors.

12. Mark another horizontal line down three-fourths from the top of the head to locate the mouth. Note that a broad, inverted, V-shaped line within the vertical centers for the eyes will describe the mouth. A shadow line cast by the lower lip is located about a third of the way to the chin.

13. If it serves the drawing's goals, draw the ears as a simple oval shape. Note that ears are approximately as long as the nose and are placed slightly past the halfway mark on the side of the

head with one-third of each ear's length above the horizontal centerline for the eyes.

This sketch following this body of text begins a sequence of twelve images, a step-by-step conceptual drawing on newsprint. It is one idea for the complete protection of head, face, eyes, mouth, and nose for a person working in a hazardous environment. It illustrates the process through which the components' product development originates from the context of the human face itself. All the line work uses hard-tipped felt-tip

Figure 5-24
(Joseph Koncelik)
Step 10 shows the shaping of the helmet-mounted light as well as the first indication of the color of the lenses in the eye protection. This will be the only instance of markers blending with one another. Note the highlighted area on the left eyepiece (right side) indicating a transparent surface of the mask.

Figure 5-25
(Joseph Koncelik)
Step 11 shows further delineation of the earpiece as well as the helmet-mounted light. Areas of the drawing—around the collar and around the junction of the mask and filter shapes—have been delineated in line to avoid overemphasizing the white areas that separate one facet of the mask from another. In such a conceptual drawing, the product visualization begs visual questions, such as: Are the earpieces integral to the mask or the helmet? What is the strapping design that "nests" with the support of the helmet on the head? These and several other questions will require additional conceptual drawings and detail drawings to illustrate how these functional aspects of the design will be developed—and visualized.

Figure 5-26
(Joseph Koncelik)
Step 12 represents the finished freehand conceptual sketch. Total time committed to the drawing is not in excess of twenty-five minutes. In a two- or three-hour session, four to six drawings could be generated to explore alternative design ideas for this system of integrated products. In addition, this step in the drawing process conveys finish through the use of a background—an abstracted environment in gray behind the figure further defining the figure and product and context. Additional lines define the surface of the mask and the curvature of the protective covering and the reflection of the lens.

pens and design markers. None of the line work has been removed or erased to develop this sketch, which is done quickly to move on to the next idea without fussiness or heavy investment in an idea that might not be viable.

Drawing Hands and Feet

The hands and feet are complex forms that depend on shade and shadow for description. Describing these features in the sketch is a function of the requirements of the drawing and the time allotted for the task. As such, a simple approach is most appropriate and described in the following text. More refined drawings frequently require the use of photographic or digitally scanned images. They supply the necessary level of detail and quicken the drawing process. Like the head, the hands and feet are complex forms that can appear as simple geometric solids. Three rules of thumb should guide the development of hand and feet:

1. The hand can be drawn as a mitten with the thumb constructed on the inside corner and its width as half its length. The hands can show fingers and knuckle joints, but these need to be less detailed than the object. In this manner, the visual emphasis stays appropriately focused on the object and not the hand.

Figure 5-27
(Joseph Koncelik)
The separation between fingers is
not arbitrary with the index finger
capable of greater separation from
the middle finger.

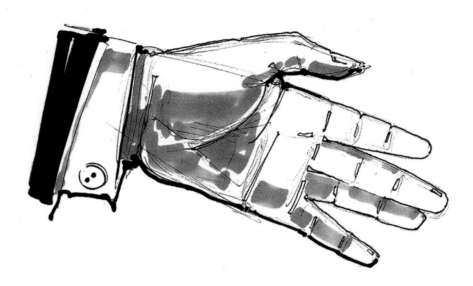

MIND PALM LENGTH TO FINGER LENGTH.
REMEMBER... FINGERS ARE DIFFERENT LENGTHS.

2. The feet can be drawn as elongated pyramids
both in the front and side views. The foot length
is about the length of the forearm and its width is
slightly wider than the hand.

3. It is worthwhile to remember that the fingers
and toes from the center out create a curve and
that the forms are always flat on the top for the
nail and rounded on the bottom.

These simple notes help to depict the digits in a
clear simple fashion.

Matching Objects to the Human Figure

Designing products may entail matching those
products to the human figure—or developing a
relationship between separated products that
indicates cohesiveness in design. The human body
helps the designer to relate products to use in
many ways.

Another important issue resolved by the
human figure is that of wearable products. The

Figure 5-28
(Kevin Reeder)
Generally, the "convention" for digit length of the
human hand will have the three sections of the
fingers roughly one-third shorter in each section
from the palm to the end of the digit. Palm length
is roughly the same proportion as the middle
finger.

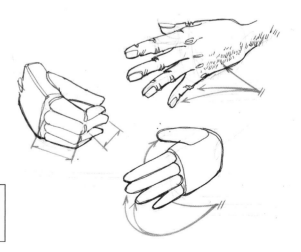

TIP - Fingers are always round on one side
and flat on the other. ■

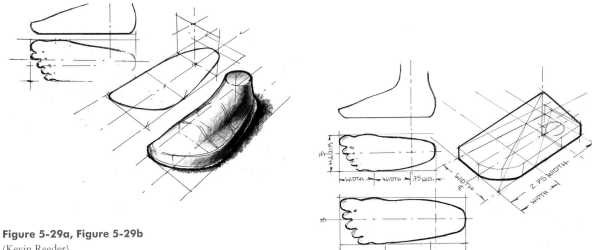

Figure 5-29a, Figure 5-29b
(Kevin Reeder)
Generally, the "convention" for the foot is a length to width ratio of one to three. Note the rather flat slight curve to the inside of the foot and the more pronounced curve to the outside of the foot.

trend in wearable telephone/radio/computer-gaming devices is a good example of products that appear in relationship to the figure and the human head form. Divorced from "fit" to the human body, such products are difficult to see in scale and conceptualization without the human form is insufficient.

Yet another aspect of use of the human figure is that of wearable products that relate

to the user and where the conceptual drawing must indicate how the products are operated. Items worn by a hockey player or football player demonstrate this point. However, there are many

recreational and utilitarian products that are part of this interrelatedness with the human body. It would be difficult to see the value of a windsurfing ensemble without the setting and the figure straining against the pull of the wind.

The steps involved in the development of a concept sketch showing such product relationships are logical and should follow these guidelines:

1. Decide what type of figure and pose of body is necessary to best characterize the wearing of products.

2. Sketch the basic axis arrangement of the figure—its gesture line—on the page.

Figure 5-30a, Figure 5-30b
(Kevin Reeder)
The running shoe has become a subject for intensive design variation and is sold largely on the basis of aesthetics. Design students interested in this direction for a career path must pay attention to the conventions for foot drawing—as shown.

3. Sketch the skin and bones—the structure of the body parts—over the outline gesture line.

4. Sketch in place the structure of the face, position of the hands and feet, and possible break lines for pieces of clothing.

5. Sketch products over the three-dimensional drawing of the body or body part to achieve the proper relationship in position.

6. Place the emphasis of modeling on the product to demonstrate that the product is the actual focus of attention rather than the overall figure drawing. However, rendering of the figure and products must be consistent.

Ideas that take three-dimensional form or interior space are ideas requiring visualization. With the advent of computer technology, there is an argument regarding the necessity of the practice of manually drawing concepts using pencils, pens, or other media. Is this practice useful, efficient, or necessary? Is the computer a tool that

Figure 5-31a
Figure 5-31b
Figure 5-31c
Figure 5-31d
(Kevin Reeder)
With the advent of so many wearable products, the context of the human form becomes all the more important as an asset in conceptual drawing. The conceptual drawings at right represent ideas for a "data glove" that requires a reasonable conception of the human hand to provide a visual context for the product.

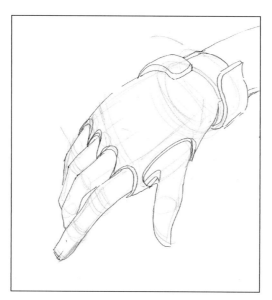

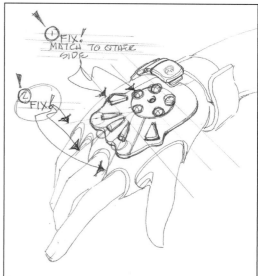

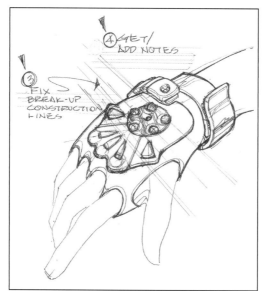

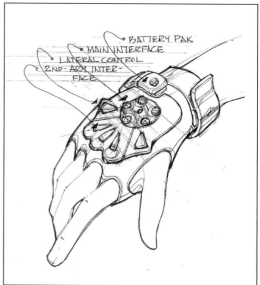

TIP - It is okay to trace from a photograph of a hand or foot versus trying to draw them in detail from memory. ∎

Figure 5-32
(Joseph Koncelik)
This conceptual drawing depicts the development of a pool closure and locking system that prohibits small children from entering what could be a dangerous environment.

can replace the drafter/designer and speed up the process of visualization? These questions are representative of the argument and arise regarding the continued usefulness of learning to draw in an age of powerful computer visual technology.

Design educators generally accept the idea that developing manual drawing skills precedes the use of computer technology as a visualizing tool. The computer user should know how to draw before attempting to make or manipulate images using the computer. Understanding perspective is necessary before attempting to create perspectives on a computer, or the machine frequently makes the choices and those choices might be inaccurate or inappropriate. The potential of the machine is tremendous and will have a growing impact on all design professions. In the hands of a skilled designer, the computer is a technology of great promise; in the hands of the uninitiated, the output can be as bad as any manually produced poor drawing—and much more expensive to produce.

Figure 5-33
(Joseph Koncelik)
The design of the system requires a lifting motion of the top release and a simultaneous release using the foot on a pedal at the base. Small children would not be able to operate such a release device.

Figure 5-34
(Joseph Koncelik)
This three-stage image is a conceptual drawing for the design of an exoskeleton robotic assisting "tool." It is designed to lift and carry heavy objects—beyond the capacity of most men or women. Devices of this kind have appeared in science fiction films, but are not that far removed from reality.

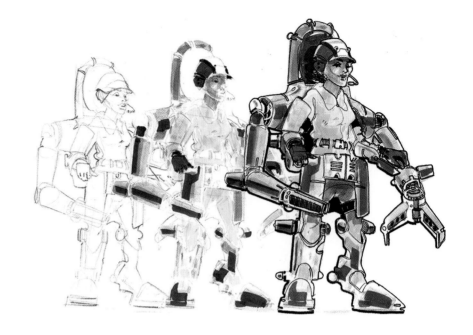

Figure 5-35
(Joseph Koncelik)
This progression is a conceptual drawing for the design of a motorized work dolly. The dolly allows the performance of many tasks by a diverse population with varying levels of physical capabilities.

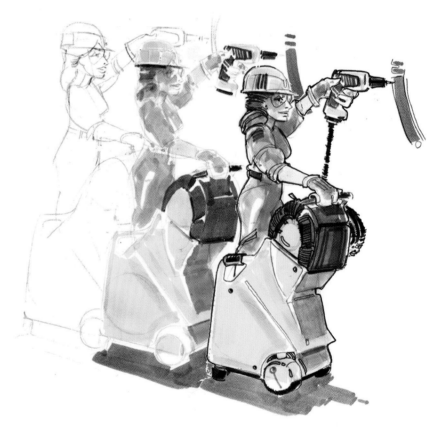

The Dynamic Figure

Some product concepts communicate best by including a figure that is actively involved with the object. In this instance, the figure not only adds scale and function to the concept, but a great deal of visual energy. Using "dynamic figures" is most appropriate when visualizing products that are associated with action and sport. In designing a snow sled for example, it is an advantage to communicate the exhilaration of moving quickly down a snowy hill on a wintry day with cold air sweeping across the face of a young person. The figurative image appears simply and the action includes appropriate clothing

Figure 5-36
(Joseph Koncelik)
The computer gyroscopically balanced mobility device opens new opportunities to move items over extended distances. Note that all of the drawings use blue pencil, marker, and ink lines and all the three-step sequence images use the same media.

HAND WASHING

FACE WASHING

WARM MIST SPRAY

TEETH & GUM CARE

Figure 5-37a
Figure 5-37b
Figure 5-37c
Figure 5-37d
(Joseph Koncelik)
Conceptual drawings illustrate the idea of using the bathroom sink as a support for arms for frail older adults. The concepts also explore added features to the sink—such as a warm misting feature—that would enhance usability, functionality, and potential marketability.

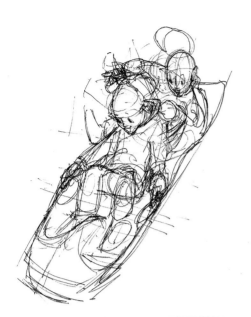

Figure 5-38
(Joseph Koncelik)
In this conceptual drawing, the hand is a crucial part of establishing context. In this series, conceptual drawings depict a bathing machine for home caregiver use—an extrapolation of a device once proposed for the orbiting space station. The device allows for the application of water, a body-cleansing agent, and a rinse. After these applications, a vacuum extracts the water, avoiding saturated bedding.

such as a hat and scarf. In this way, the drawing retains focus on the sled; the figure with appropriate attire adds to the visual impact of the overall drawing.

Drawing dynamic figures is not the same as drawing so-called "action figures." Action figures are the cartoon images of hyper-muscled males and females in wildly exaggerated poses—usually in a costume. This form of cartooning is inappropriate as context because the figure is the focus of visual attention—not the design of the product. Another form of the same visual deception is

Figure 5-39a, Figure 5-39b
(Kevin Reeder)
These drawings are quick concepts of sleds and other snow toys for children and utilize simple line drawings of the object and the child.

Figure 5-40a
Figure 5-40b
(Kevin Reeder)
These conceptual drawings of
sleds with child and adult
figures convey the sense of fun
implied by these product
designs. Note that the rough
line work in the drawing at
left is transferred to an
overlay for the drawing
at right.

placing a scantily clad female figure draped
across the hood of a car or posed on the prow of
a boat. The message about product becomes
ambiguous, if not questionable.

Animé cartoon art has become very popular
among students in design. However, transferring
these highly stylized figures into context to por-
tray product and technology sends a message of
visualization of aesthetics that delimits the product's appeal as well as its appropriateness.
Students should observe and absorb as much

visual information for drawing the human figure
as possible. All of it will be helpful, but all of it
also requires an appropriate translation as a context for object and interior development. Cartoon
art rarely depicts older adults—anyone older than
eighteen—in any other role than wizard, mad sci-
entist (usually with goatee), or witch. The
designer must develop sensitivity to the diversity
among all people and provide images of the
human form appropriate as context.

Figure 5-41a, Figure 5-41b
(Kevin Reeder)
These additional conceptual drawings of sleds with child and adult figures are modifications of the original rough drawings
that were underlays. Using both children and adult figures provides an idea that families playing together use these
recreational products.

Figure 5-42
(Joseph Koncelik)
1. This drawing is broken into four steps and is not unlike the twelve-step drawing of the human head form and protective equipment demonstrated earlier. The drawing is mixed media on newsprint. Mixed media in this drawing includes Verithin pencils, Prismacolor pencils, fine-, medium-, and bold-tip black marker pens, and colored design markers. The drawing begins with the proportional division of figure and object—including developing a ground plane from which the stick and user are bouncing. As with all conceptual drawing, the idea emerges from the drawing process itself; the drawing was not predetermined. There were no erasures and all line work remains in place.

Figure 5-43
(Joseph Koncelik)
2. After light-line Verithin pencils were used to generally sketch the figure and product, color markers describe the overall massing of the figure. When using markers on newsprint, it is wise to allow a good deal of "white space" (as shown below) to allow for marker ink bleeding in the paper. Details begin to emerge and materials— separations between the clothing and the sheen of the metallic parts of the pogo stick—are in place.

Figure 5-44
(Joseph Koncelik)
3. After applying color marker, the fine-line and medium-weight marker pens further enhance the two related forms in the drawing. The face and the expression on the face, the unruliness of the hair, and the looseness of the clothing are all further delineated using the pen lines. In each step of the drawing, the conceptual development is a continuing process. A general idea at the beginning begins to become more specific as the drawing is shaped and refined.

Figure 5-45
(Joseph Koncelik)
4. Finalizing the drawing requires further defining the shape of the pogo stick and its components. Final touches include adding the wire-harness to the two cylinder heads and further describing the components of the machine. The figure is important in establishing the user context, but the object itself must have dominance, as it is the objective of the design process.

Apparel and Body Coverings

If the drawing requires a higher level of detail, apply clothing to the figure by overlaying the drawing with a new sheet of paper and tracing the figure. Tracing the outline of the figure is a simple way to draw shirts, with collars and long sleeves, pants with a waistband or belt, and shoes. Include wrinkle lines at the elbows and knees and ellipses at the wrists for the shirt and ankles for the pants to aid the visual description of the figure. Tracing with a consistently lighter line will leave the figure in a supportive subdominant relationship to the drawing. With clothing, the figure provides even greater context and the drawing will appear more finished.

Concept drawings communicate objects/ideas to all participants in the design process. As such, the purpose for including a figure in the drawing is to

Figure 5-46
(Joseph Koncelik)
A three-sequence step-by-step drawing of a boy on a motorized scooter shows the application of basic colors—prior to the application of tone and line work to define the product and the user. A Verithin Prismacolor pencil outlines the drawing before marker is applied. Each sequential scan was placed as an overlay from left to right providing a close visual comparison of the level of finish ascribed to each step. As with drawings generated on the first page of this chapter, there are three fundamental steps in this quick-sketching process: 1) layout with pen or pencil line (in this instance a rough approximation of color was also drawn in place); 2) development of the marker color; and 3) final detail with fine-line markers and fine-tipped color markers. Note: Draw all marker colors in place and do not "color in" between line work as if the conceptual drawing is a coloring book. One theme bears repeating: design all lines in conceptual drawing.

provide more information about the object's size and its functional relationship to people. Visual emphasis on the object reinforces communication of the object in context. Conceptualization then has additional clarity and effectively supports the objectives of the drawing and design intent.

Conclusion: Context in Conceptual Drawing

Including the human form in the conceptual development of objects and environment provides a sense of human scale. Without the human figure in place, there is usually no sense of the size of an object or the dimensions of a space. Drawing the human figure is one of the most difficult drawing requirements—especially for the novice design student with little to no figure drawing experience. Nevertheless, the conventions and guidelines of this chapter expedite skill development in drawing the human form.

There are serious issues regarding the future of design professions and design as content regarding

Figure 5-47
(Kevin Reeder)
This is a line drawing of mother and child in winter clothing. Note the simplicity of delineation of the type of clothing. In addition, describing differences between adults and children can be difficult. A major visual distinction is the "head size" in relation to torso. Children have a larger head size in proportion to the torso or body size than adults.

TIP - Use the edges and seams in clothing to help communicate which way an arm or leg is situated. ■

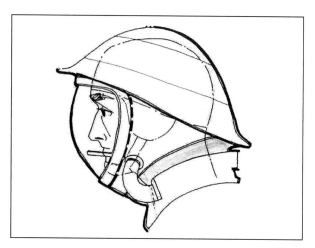

Figure 5-48a, Figure 5-48b, Figure 5-48c, Figure 5-48d
(Joseph Koncelik)
Functional clothing is the type of garments worn for specific tasks such as for hazardous duty (see the above two d rawings), sports, and job-related tasks. The images represent a project for developing responses to unusual hazards. At the time, the vision was to equip firefighters as reconnaissance teams after tornadoes had struck. The project now resonates with the special duties required of first responders after terrorist attacks. The drawings above represent potential advancements in the clothing and equipment worn by advance scouting teams after a natural disaster. Protective clothing concepts have functional requirements for the development of prototypes. Note that each of the drawings uses mixed media including pencil, line markers, color markers, and Prismacolor pastels and pencils. The drawings on the upper right and lower left use a background of pastel to give a sense of darkness in the sky.

incorporating human diversity. The primary issue is when and at what point does consideration of human characteristics and human performance become part of the criteria defining the direction of design? The authors have chosen to state unequiv-ocally that these considerations must be included at the very beginning of design process. This means that the notion of context is inclusive and requires a thoughtful visualization of the human form with respect to gender, age, ability, race, and ethnicity as well as culture. The last of these, culture, means

addressing the issue of body covering and clothing appropriately as well as understanding and depict-ing appropriate settings for the figure and the cor-responding designed object or environment.

It was not so many years ago that gaining a realization of female characteristics was an issue and that women were not included as part of overall human factors. The last three decades have given rise to inclusiveness and eliminated that bias. The challenge of making full "universal" inclusiveness part of the design process is far from

Figure 5-49

(Joseph Koncelik)

This is another three-step drawing illustrating the sketching process of quick line drawing, application of marker, and refinement with additional marker lines and pen and pencil lines. In this instance, the drawing is on tracing paper—providing the opportunity to use both sides of the paper to reduce the intensity of specific markers such as those used to convey flesh tones. In drawings such as these, the first stage does not require completion. Note the addition of ski goggles occurring in the final stage of completion rather than developing them in the earliest stage of drawing.

The human figure—as context for design—can act as background providing a sense of ambiance for environment. Drawing the figure requires sensitivity to anatomy and the "draping" of clothing over the human form. Otherwise, clothing might either look like armor or convey the image of a robot. This figure conveys a sense of awkwardness on skis; the clothing might be appropriate, but there is a sense of trepidation. As the designer becomes more skilled at drawing the human figure, drawings move beyond indications of scale to convey humor, intensity, man/machine relationships, and other information important to the conceptual development.

complete and much work remains to ensure that aging adults, individuals with differing abilities, and the full range of ethnicities and races are included in the process of design.

With design becoming international, populations of every nation becoming multi-cultural, and our sensitivities toward individuals with disabilities and aging adults becoming heightened, inclusiveness is not optional. It is mandatory. New computer-assisted full-body scanning technologies have enhanced the science of anthropometry (body measurement) as well as two- and three-dimensional visualization. Just-in-time manufacturing and mass-customization of goods is the order of things in the twenty-first century. Design process must open up to embrace the depth, differences, and broadness of the human condition—or fail to find markets. Therefore, that first step into conceptual drawing carries a heavy burden of understanding and the responsibility to eschew prejudice and cynicism in the depiction of the human form.

The processes included in this chapter outline a possible methodology to increase the ability of the designer to incorporate "conventions" for drawing the human figure in the process of conceptual design. The intent of this incorporation is to develop design practice for advanced designers with accomplished conceptual drawing skills. Nevertheless, motivation to develop this form of conceptual inclusiveness is an important step for every designer. Eventually, it is likely that conceptual development, full-body scanning, and the application of anthropometry with concept development will merge and become a seamless operation. At the time of this writing, it is possible to look ahead and see that future, but that day has not yet arrived. Designers must develop sufficient skill to depict the human form in appropriate scaling to the designed object and environment.

This section of the chapter addresses four techniques where communicating ideas represented in the concept sketch are enhanced by including a

Figure 5-50a
Figure 5-50b
(David Tompkins)
The conceptual drawings,
Figures 5-50 a & b through 5-51 a & b,
by David Tompkins represent a range of
context relationships through which ideas
are presented in relationship to the user.
The drawings are at the highest level of
professionalism and press forward novel
product directions for a corporation with
multiple profit center operations. In each
case, color is minimal—emphasizing the
product. Also note the interaction of white
space to keep the drawings fresh.

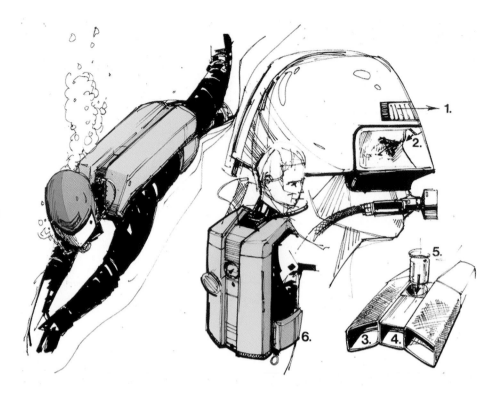

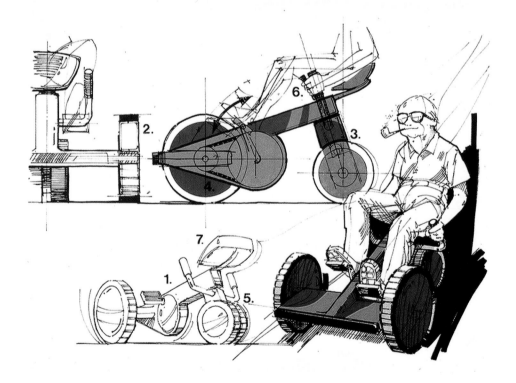

figure, contextual "elements" such as objects
within the environment, and an environment or
surrounding to enhance the impact, sense of
scale, and appropriateness of the conceptual idea:

1.   Drawing/constructing the human figure
through traditional proportions to easily communicate the product's size for the designer, to the
design team, and others who are involved in the

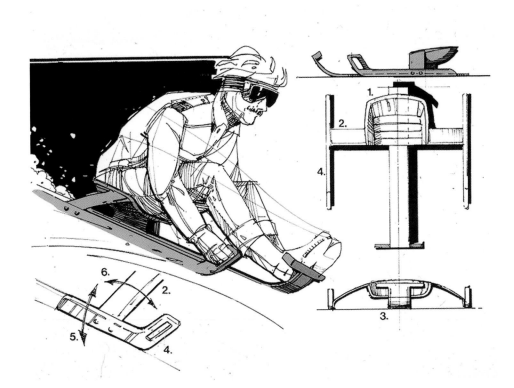

Figure 5-51a
Figure 5-51b
(David Tompkins)
The designer who created these product
images has a strong background in the
educational environment through which
"empathic drawing" became conceptual
drawing—Pratt Institute during the late
1950s and early 1960s. Drawing courses
were numerous, including drawing the
human figure—largely absent from
curricula in the contemporary design
program. Over time, Tompkins found
his own style that was applicable in both
the corporate and consulting design
environments.

decision-making process regarding product
development.

2. Drawing/constructing a "visual storyboard"—
a visualization of the process in use and the
sequence of operations involved in all aspects of

product development—including appropriate
human figure(s) and the product concept to
communicate broad issues of product use, storage, maintenance, and safe operation.

See segment 4, Human Figure in Context, for sequential development of both head forms and the human figure.

Figure 5-52
(Joseph Koncelik)
A "spot" drawing extracted from a presentation on uses of technology to enhance the educational experience.
Figure 5-52
(Michael Butcher)
A demonstration of the use of the human head form as the basis for development of a conceptual biking helmet.

3. Drawing/constructing the figure with appropriate physical characteristics to examine issues of fit, reach, and physical relationship to different people of differing anthropometry and body proportion.

4. Using the interior as an important context for visualization—aside from the design of interiors in and of themselves. As a context for product design, the use of interior spaces poses many problems in drawing, especially freehand drawing

without the aid of mechanical perspective, which is appropriate for the advanced student.

5. Designers meeting their responsibility to capture and draw the human body in a responsible way. While other forms of depiction—including cartooning—inform designers about posing and gesture, exaggerations of the human figure take away the emphasis from the technology, product, or environment that is the real focus of the conceptual design process.

Figure 5-53
(Kevin Reeder)
A concept for a play object is given additional playfulness by adding a figure, a male child, who looks ready for the fun implied by the riding toy. Note the use of a blue pencil underline to rough out the sketch before either pen or pencil line pulls out detail in the drawing.

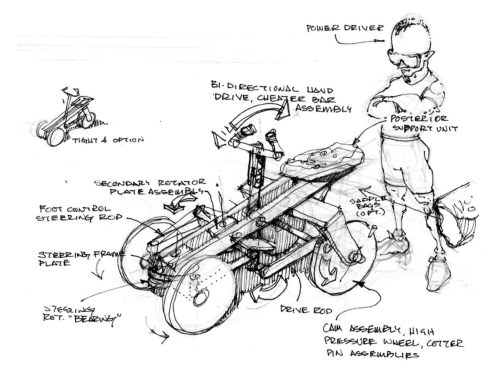

6

**Interior
Conceptual
Drawing**

Developing Interior Design Concepts

Drawing interiors in sketch form is a difficult undertaking when the designer/drafter begins with mechanical perspective. Even applying the long-lived and useful Lawson Charts (revised versions, 2005) that provide a series of grids to develop the perspective does little to speed up the process of conceptualizing interior design ideas. Interiors are both a design issue and a context for design. The product designer confronts the problem of interior design development to show where and under what conditions a product is in use or placed. Therefore, developing a methodology to visualize interiors rapidly is important to all designers—including the graphic designer who confronts the issues of exhibition design or the placement of signage in an environmental context.

An advantage of sketching an interior setting for a product design is the ability to develop multiple ideas about the product's appearance in one setting to assess fit. To do this, it is essential to take a *microenvironmental* approach to the drawing problem. This means that interior visualizations are placed in smaller settings that are more intimate. In such visualizations, the interior drawing has bounds, limiting the amount of the interior visualized, rather than requiring that the interior be drawn in total. In the design and drawing of a restaurant, for example, a single drawing depicting the entire setting would require many hours of work. The same problem would occur in the conceptualization of educational settings, commercial sales spaces, office landscaping in an open office setting, and many other large interior settings. It is advantageous to view the interior in "chunks." The designer should plan an approach to the drawing problem that permits sketching the setting in discreet parts for quicker representation.

The complexity of interior design visualization would seem to move the method of conceptualization in a different direction from that of product development or even graphic design. Interior designers must develop consistent themes using furniture, architectural hardware, wall and floor surfacing materials, and other artifacts and products—even plantings—to achieve their desired design result. It is appropriate and entirely natural that interior designers gravitate toward larger constructed drawings with plotted two- and three-point perspectives to provide complete visual information to convey design. Experience with interior design instruction shows that many—if not the majority of students—do just that from the beginning conceptual phase of design projects. This means that the effort put forth has the same drawbacks as with product development that begins with single rendered

Figure 6-1

(Kevin Reeder)

Sketching the interior is difficult for the novice unless the viewpoint permits overlap of objects in space. There would be an immediate tendency to turn to straight edges and other tools to sketch such environments. This chapter discusses such tools and adds helpful suggestions about tools and mixed medial drawing. The empathic approach helps develop control of line and this enhances the ability to freehand sketch interior space.

Figure 6-2
(Kevin Reeder)
An interior drawing illustrates the importance of overlap of objects to convey spatiality as well as avoiding the use of color to limit the drawing time. Quick sketching using line can be an appropriate way to communicate interior concepts, preventing the drawing from becoming visually overworked.

forms without exploring alternatives. Finished drawings have a psychological impact upon the viewer; frequently, the viewer cannot envision change or raises objections to the design. Finished drawings are exclusive by nature—not inclusive. Inclusiveness is one of the most valuable assets of quick sketching and allows for decision making with other parties, such as clients, as opposed to banking on one design that has not had input or exchange. It is impractical and costly to develop several complex drawings to explore a variety of concepts.

Interior designers who develop a personal conceptual drawing style have a distinct advantage over their contemporaries who do not. It is possible to generate quick spot sketches—samples of which will be developed and shown in this section of the text. With practice and careful treatment of subject matter to convey spatial arrangements of materials and products, the interior designer who uses conceptual drawing effectively engages the client in a dialogue about the design direction at the process's beginning. This will ensure ultimate acceptance and success of the design by achieving buy-in throughout the process of design.

Figure 6-3
(R. Preston Bruning)
A mixed media freehand sketch demonstrates the effective use of "negative" space, the white light coming from the passageway defining the shadows in the room.

Sketching interiors is similar to the process of sketching products. Designers should consider what information the drawing needs to communicate. In addition, to expedite the conceptual interior sketch, it is necessary to determine the appropriate visual information and drawing techniques to successfully communicate ideas. It is important to consider the functions taking place in the space and to understand the people who will be using it. This includes understanding individual and group uses of the space, how people will move through and around the room to develop adequate passage, and what sort of image or theme the space should present. For example, when designing a fine restaurant, designers should consider how customers enter, move to their table, sit/order/eat, use the restroom, provide payment for their meal, and leave. Interior designers consider how employees will service the customers, move in and out of the kitchen to the dining space—both to deliver food and remove and clean plates and utensils. The image of the restaurant that attracts the customers is an exploration in initial conceptual sketching so that customers' experiences are expanded through the overall spatial experience. Conceptual interior sketching should be the initial attempt to develop visual ideas in

relationship to human function and overall environmental theme.

Just as the product designer provides engineering drawings of the technology aspect of the product's development, the interior designer typically acquires architectural plans that provide accurate dimensional information to help generate interior design development. The drawing will depict the space (the overall collection of rooms that make up the selected environment) by visually removing the roof and ceiling. The walls, windows, bathrooms, doors, structural columns, or interior walls, et cetera, use a standard line vocabulary, as if they project from the floor without perspective effects of any kind. The purpose of the drawing is to present the room in scale so that all the design features, as described, are integrated and presented in a clear visual manner.

In addition to these considerations, electrical, plumbing, and heating/ventilation/air-conditioning drawings depict the space the same way. The walls of the room appear in elevation drawings—as two-dimensional rectangles—where the vertical structures in space, columns and beams, appear in scale without perspective effects. This flat (without perspective convergence) view helps communicate features of the space to those

Figure 6-4
(R. Preston Bruning)
This mixed media freehand sketch demonstrates the breadth covered by the term "interiors." For design professions, interiors are not limited to residential or commercial interior applications, the largest areas of design activity, but also include such diverse areas of design as vehicles, transportation systems, and commercial aircraft.

Figure 6-5
(R. Preston Bruning)
A freehand marker sketch shows the
application of interior design to vehicular
interiors. As automobiles change over
time, the impact of interior design is
a significant part of consumer appeal
and sales.

responsible for construction because the walls, windows, et cetera are in a consistent scaled relationship to each other in the drawing. This type of drawing communicates a dimensionally consistent view of the space that makes building the space possible.

Perspective drawings, on the other hand, communicate theme and qualitative aspects of the interior design but do not provide the necessary information for construction. Where interior space requiring redesign is in whole or part in an existing building, the floor plans may be part of the greater building package—or possibly nonexistent. If drawings do not exist, then the designer will take dimensions from the space and rooms and produce the drawings necessary to generate interior design before doing the interior conceptual drawing. Regardless of whether the designer is working with new or existing construction, the plan and elevation views are necessary tools for the interior designers who will generate conceptual directions in perspective drawings for the space to get client participation and approval. Construction or architectural drawings are useful communication tools for people who are familiar with and able to understand such visual information. Unfortunately, others who are crucial to the building and design process, such as developers, investors, potential users of the space, and those who will eventually manage the environment, frequently have difficulty figuring out construction drawings and visualizing a three-dimensional image of the space. Perspective drawings of the

space, on the other hand, present images of the space that open up the imagination for all participants in the design process.

From the plan view, designers can decide where to place the point of view for the perspective sketch. Choosing a specific view may be helpful to explore the view of customers as they enter. Seeing the space from this point of view may also help the design team explore the necessary textures, colors, and lighting needed to communicate the appropriate environmental ambience to others—such as customers in a commercial retail space. In developing a restaurant, a view of the overall dining area will help the design team show the client views of the conceptual restaurant, the intended flow of foot traffic, and the intended design theme of the space. Perspective sketches of the space can be quick line drawings for discussion and conceptualization; more developed line drawings with color will draw attention to specific focal points of interest. Perspective conceptual interior drawings begin with the goals of communicating to other project participants, development and exposure of issues relevant to full design problem-solving, and satisfaction of project schedules.

A one-point perspective can emerge from plan and elevation views showing an extended horizontal view of one wall and shorter, foreshortened views of other walls. A two-point perspective of the space will appear more dynamic than a one-point perspective and is preferred when accentuating an area of the space. If the space includes several tables and extended counters, placing the horizon below eye level will accentuate the walls and the larger space. Placing the horizon at eye level helps viewers relate to the space and achieve a sense of size or volume. Placing the horizon above eye level will present a larger, broader view of the space. Specifically placing the horizon at the top of a ladder or eye height on the second floor will make the view easier to read and understand. There are trade-offs, however. The lower the eye point, the less drawing time is involved in completing floor space and the quicker the resulting drawing. The higher the eye point, the more information appears regarding spatial relationships.

Rules of Thumb Regarding Interior Concept Sketches

Advocating a conceptual drawing approach in no way means to dismiss the complexity of interior design drawing and the multiple decisions interior designers make about objects, products, surfaces, treatments, lighting, and other aspects of their design responsibilities. There is no dismissing the necessity of generating finished drawings relatively early in the process of designing interiors. However, the question remains: When

does this happen? The answer should be that it occurs after initial conceptualization has taken place in a quick sketching mode. Conceptual drawing for interior designers requires attention to eight specific aspects of design drawing including the following:

1. Point of view
2. Perspective
3. Establishing "ground"
4. Overlap of objects
5. Vignette
6. Use of the human figure to establish scale
7. Judicious use of color
8. Use of text

Each aspect of generating interior conceptual drawing follows in the order of the previous list.

Point of View

As with the drawings generated by novice product designers, beginning interior designers will have even more of a tendency to move the eye point above the floor plane to visualize the relationship of furnishings and other accessories in space. For the interior designer using conceptual drawing, this poses even more problems than for the product designer. Great expanses of floor area must either remain untreated with color and

Figure 6-6
(R. Preston Bruning)
This Prismacolor pencil drawing is of a playground idea within the limiting dimensions of a rectilinear space. Such interior designs have become important in the food franchise business—offering attractive and entertaining activities for children.

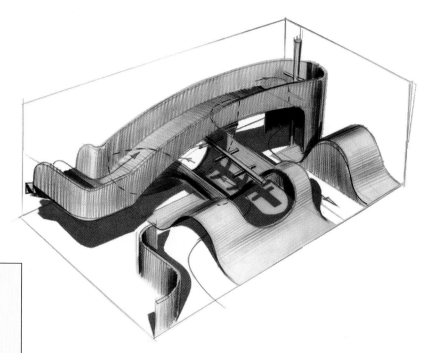

TIP - Use shadow to differentiate objects in close proximity. If one object is under another, let the top object cast a simple shadow onto the lower to help place it. ■

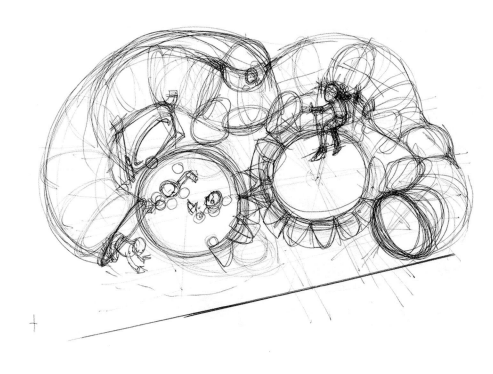

Figure 6-7a
Figure 6-7b
(Kevin Reeder)
Using the high eye point can be useful to describe design concepts better visualized from the plan view (from above) than from the elevation view (from the front). Such is the case with these two drawings of a playground. The top sketch is a rough pencil line drawing and the bottom sketch is an overlay with specific areas more fully described.

PLAY AREA

texture or "colored in" in a time-consuming process that affects drawing other objects placed on the floor. At the very onset of generating the interior sketch, *the eye point should lower to standing height.* This diminishes the amount of floor space that makes objects and furnishings overlap. Further, it provides a visual framework within which most objects appear quite realistically rather than in a diminished and foreshortened perspective. As shown in the step-by-step drawing following this discussion, the sketching

process begins with a lowered point of view using a three-plane relationship. The designer should draw connecting lines from corner to corner on the floor or ground plane and attempt drawing a freehand circle or ellipse on the ground plane. A vertical line from the center of the sketch will establish just where that eye point can or will exist. Without this first step realized, the interior sketch becomes laborious and time intensive.

Figure 6-8a
Figure 6-8b
(Noel Mayo)
These two marker sketches in single-point perspective show effective use of markers to capture textures such as plant materials, wood paneling, and materials for furniture coverings. Note the use of limited marker to depict carpeting without "deadening" the sketch by oversaturating the drawing with dark marker.

TIP - As a general rule, draw interiors from a standing eye point. Drawing interiors from a higher point of view means having the floor dominate the drawing. ■

Perspective

Interior designers favor single-point perspective drawing more than other design professionals—mainly because the setup is far easier with much

larger drawings of space possible on the same size and format of paper. Unfortunately, single-point perspectives can be distorted with little spatial room available to objects in the rear sections of

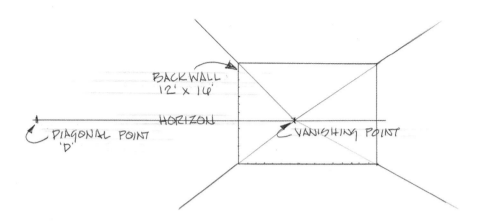

Figure 6-9

(Kevin Reeder)

Interior drawing is inherently complex regarding the amount of objects to be located in space as well as developing the indicators of spatial relationships. The first grid method uses a vanishing point and the back wall to project a grid into the space. A sequence of three drawings—including Figure 6-9, Figure 6-10, and Figure 6-11, shows the steps necessary to construct a single-point perspective with a proportional grid. These drawings and their notations remain in a sketch mode of visualization to emphasize the possibility of using such systems in the conceptual drawing process.

The first step in this process is: draw a diagonal point D (for diagonal) on the horizon, to the left or right of the vanishing point, about one and one-half times the width of the space.

the drawing. It is possible to use a modified one-point perspective similar to that shown in the chapter on perspective in this text. This entails shifting the eye point away from the center of the vanishing point at the middle of the drawing to either the left or the right. In essence, the drawing becomes a two-point perspective with only slight

diminishing of the horizontal lines at ceiling and floor plane to indicate a vanishing point far off the paper. Students are encouraged to try another method: freehand sketch the three-plane set up in two-point perspective—as shown in the step-by-step drawing—to allow for greater realism in the drawing. After the tree planes are established, a

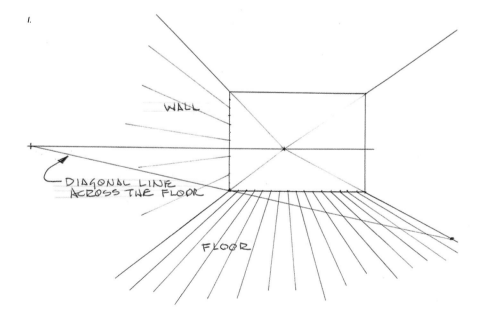

Figure 6-10

(Kevin Reeder)

The second step in this process is: draw a line from this point through to the nearest corner of the floor and across the space. The third step in this process is: draw an intersecting line with a series of vanishing lines from the back wall at the junction of the floor along that floor into the space.

Figure 6-11

(Kevin Reeder)

The final step in constructing a proportional grid system is: draw horizontal lines where the two lines intersect on the floor. The grid produces a proportioned pattern of squares on the floor to locate objects in space. For instance, if a table is eight feet from the back wall and three feet from the center of the room, it can be located accordingly. Conversely, a table can appear arbitrarily on the floor surface and then located on a plan view drawing because of its location on the grid surface.

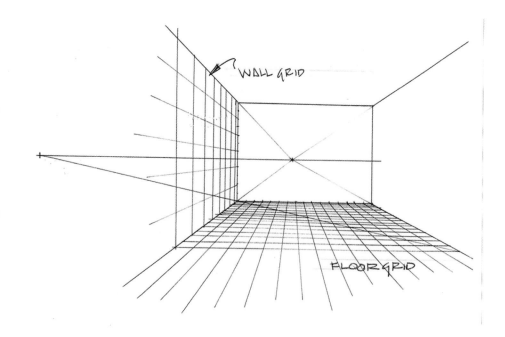

Figure 6-12

(Kevin Reeder)

Another method for determining proper proportioning is "the proportional square," using the broadest sidewall in the drawing for the same purpose as developing a floor grid system. The steps to achieve both proper proportioning as well as extensions of the single point perspective drawing of space appear in Figure 6-13 and Figure 6-14.

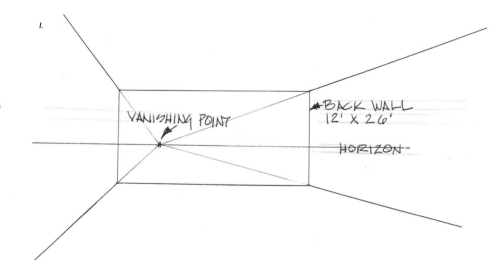

Figure 6-13

(Kevin Reeder)

1. Draw a square whose height projects from the back wall on the broadest sidewall. Given the foreshortening of the wall, project a square that appears to be proportionally correct. The height is an extension of the marked off measurement from the back wall. Therefore, the square will project along the wall at the same dimension. 2. Mark the center "C" of the vertical wall that is farthest from the back wall.

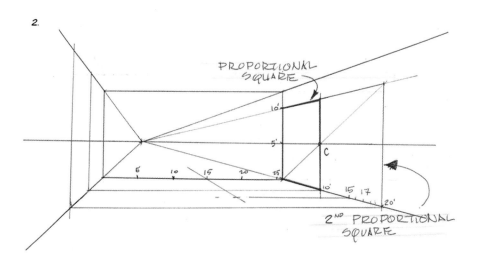

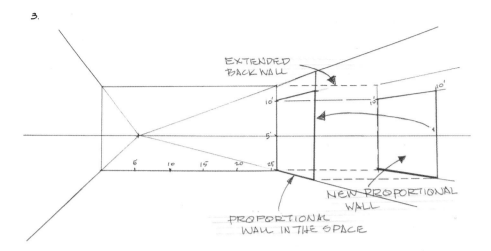

3.

EXTENDED
BACK WALL

NEW PROPORTIONAL
WALL

PROPORTIONAL
WALL IN THE SPACE

Figure 6-14

(Kevin Reeder)

3. Draw the next proportional square by connecting the line through "C" with the extended line that marks the top of the proportional square. After doing this, drop a vertical line to the floor. This creates another square of the same proportion on the wall into the space. 4. In the proportional square, draw dimensional marks on the floor/wall corner. For instance, if the proportional box is 10 feet square, points can be spaced proportionally along the floor to mark one-, two-, and three-foot increments. When the broader wall's convergence is insufficient to determine the proportional square, the back wall can be an extension and a new proportional wall. 5. From a point at the corner of the floor, the back wall, and the broader wall, draw a line that intersects the mark "C" on the vertical wall. The new extension provides a broader view of the space that will facilitate the construction of the proportional square. Floor dimensions are marked as before and projected into the room. As described earlier, objects can be located and constructed in the space from dimensional markings on the floor.

"belt line" should be drawn on the two wall plane surfaces that indicates the approximate height of surfaces. In dimensional terms, this belt line would be approximately 30 inches off the floor plane. Since all of these planes and lines are approximations, the designer must modify the spatial descriptors. For example, ceiling heights may have to be higher and walls extended.

Establishing Ground

Readers of this text will recall that one of the major difficulties in drawing objects in relationship to an environment (discussed in Chapter 2 on perspective) was the difficulty of placement on a floor or ground plane. As mentioned earlier in "point of view," defining the ground—now referred to as "floor plane"—is essential to get the chairs to stick to the floor. Interior designers use many mechanical perspectives that use a system of squared grids to establish the floor plane. This allows visual recognition of just where that surface is to make the gravitational connection between object and surface. In the quicker conceptual sketch, it is difficult and time-consuming to draw a full grid. Drawing diagonal lines from corner to corner of the floor plane will help establish surface for the more limited depiction of space. In addition, chairs, sofas, and tables all contact the floor plane at four contact points. These contact points can establish the position of a square on the floor plane that references four vertical lines that "box" the chair or other object. Simply put, interior conceptual drawing is from the floor plane up.

Overlap of Objects

When a high eye point is used, objects separate from one another in space. Using the lowered eye point, objects *overlap*. One object appears in front of another in a sequence of overlapping

Figure 6-15a
Figure 6-15b
(Kevin Reeder)
Using the proportional square method
covered earlier , a complex interior drawing
has been generated—first as a sketch on top
of the proportional system and then as an
overlay allowing "truing" of the perspective
and emphasis of the critical line work.
Having gained a sense of the overall
perspective, details can appear in place,
further increasing the visual identity of the
interior.

 See DVD
segment 5,
Interior Space.

relationships. This form of drawing has advantages. One advantage is that less of the object is visual when it is behind another—reducing drawing time. The designer should avoid awkward three-point perspectives. Most important, interior space develops through overlap of objects—not merely by distance between objects. Several of the drawings provided in this section support this idea of drawing in overlap.

Overlap occurs by the lowering the eye point and, as a result, objects are more readily seen as they truly are—devoid of awkward points of view.

The horizontal surfaces of desks and tables will have a minimal amount of surface area shown, but enough to indicate objects on that surface and the material and texture of that surface.

Vignette

Use of the concept of vignette has been discussed previously when objects, products—even vehicles—require a context of environment requiring less finish as the focal point of the drawing. In the use of vignette, the focus of attention (focal point) receives the highest amount of drawing

Figure 6-16a
Figure 6-16b

(Kevin Reeder)

One-point perspective interior drawings: interior spaces can be complicated to draw because there are several objects that need proper proportioning to communicate the intended design of the space that depends on an association of products, artifacts, and objects. Accurate proportioning of objects in space is readily achievable using a "measuring wall." In one-point perspectives, one wall of the space follows the measurement and proportioning on the plan and elevation views.

This entire wall becomes the measuring wall and becomes the "back wall." For instance, the floor and ceiling edges appear as horizontal lines with the wall corners described by vertical lines. The height and width of this wall is drawn in scale as the wall is parallel to the picture plane. (See Chapter 2.) The horizon line is placed as described earlier and one vanishing point (VP) is located on the horizon within the room.

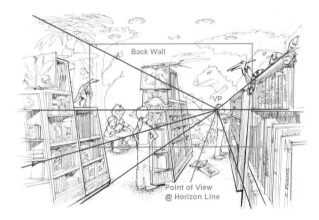

finish and less finish is applied to all other components of the drawing the farther they are away from the center. This concept is especially important for interior conceptual drawings. It is virtually impossible to contain the time frame of drawing interior concepts by finishing the entire drawing. The designer must pick the point of view, choose the relationship of objects, and quickly provide enough information to give an accurate impression of the intention of the design. It is far better to do several drawings of different areas of the space or different points of view than it is to attempt full interior drawing of the entire space in one drawing. The time consumed will be greater in the fully developed spatial drawing than with several impressionistic drawings of that space.

In vignettes, emphasizing the focus of attention is achieved by greater uses of color and shading, attention to the line work, and attention to surfaces such as floors and walls. This attention fades away from the center—in a manner similar to that shown in drawings to follow (refer to Figure 6-26 and Figure 6-27).

Figure 6-17a, Figure 6-17b
(Kevin Reeder)

One-point perspectives can become dynamic and complex. This drawing has multiple vanishing points—two of which appear in this drawing. Placing the vanishing point outside the room as constructed by the back wall means the viewer is not in the room and cannot see into the room. From the vanishing point, perspective lines move through the wall corners at the ceiling and floor lines of the back wall. At this stage, definition of the room space is in hand. In the use of a one-point perspective method for developing an interior space, the viewer is outside the space and looks inward at the space perpendicular to the back wall. To place an object in the space, such as a table, a vertical line appears on the back wall from the floor to the ceiling. Estimate or measure the height of the table on this line. The designer should sketch lines from the vanishing point through the vertical line at the floor as well as the height of the table. In this way, the height of the table projects into the space from the back wall. If the object is more complicated in form, then a side view of the object projects from the back wall into the space.

Human Figures as Scale and Context

All design students have difficulty drawing the human figure and the interior designer is no exception. Nevertheless, as discussed earlier in this specific chapter, use of the human figure—learning to draw the human figure—gives distinct advantages to designers. There are advantages for the conceptual drawing as well. The human figure establishes the human scale of spaces. Without human figures, interior spaces can seem empty or barren.

It is not necessary to become Peter Paul Rubens in the attempt to draw the human figure. As discussed earlier, there are methods that will help designers depict men and women—and children—convincingly and in a consistent manner with the drawing of space and objects. Frequently, designers will use cutout figures in design drawings. They are usually effective as long as perspective is not involved in the drawing. Flat constructions with figures behind tables or desks in conceptions of displays and exhibits can

Point of View

Figure 6-18
(Kevin Reeder)
As stated in this chapter's text, interior conceptual drawing begins with architectural drawings to accurately depict the boundaries of the space and gauge the shaping of the space. In this instance, the space is not a simple rectangle but a rhomboid with the right wall angling in.

The designer is likely to take advantage of this aspect of the space by juxtaposing the counters and display surfaces at angles within the space, as shown in this drawing. Angularity reflects in the design of banners and display advertising, providing part of the overall theme of the space. As this commercial space is quite small, the addition of surface level change as depicted with steps adds a sense of overall depth.

It is important to create an understanding of the point of view location—in this instance it is actually outside and to the lower-left corner of the space as defined by the architectural drawing to the left. Establishing a point of view means that all objects receive consistent placement in the space as seen from that point of view.

Careful attention has been given to the space details that convey its function as a retail commercial space for selling cosmetics. The designer is skillful enough to depict the details of shampoo bottles, lotion containers, and other products so that the purpose of the space is clear.

This drawing is the second in a sequence that begins with constructing the space in blue-line pencil as shown in Figure 6-17a and Figure 6-17b and ends with the drawings shown in Figure 6-19a and Figure 6-19b. The drawing on this has additional refinement done as an overlay on the first.

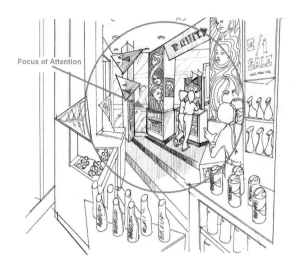

Figure 6-19a, Figure 6-19b

(Kevin Reeder)

This final drawing in the sequence of three further defines the space through its level of finish. Later in the text, vignette is discussed. This method of drawing—especially appropriate to interior conceptual drawing—allows the designer to convey as much information as necessary without having to give the drawing a level of finish that might take too much time away from developing other conceptual drawings. In this drawing, the area within the circle defining the "focus of attention" receives shading and pencil line definition of form. From the focus outward, the level of finish diminishes, but the essence of the idea has sufficient visual attention.

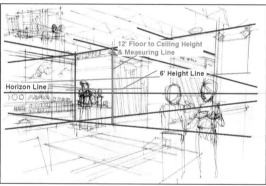

Figure 6-20a, Figure 6-20b

(Kevin Reeder)

Two-point perspective interior drawings: In a two-point perspective drawing of a space, it is important to remember that the viewer's point of view is not perpendicular to the back walls and that there is not a back wall constructed of horizontal floor and ceiling lines. Instead, the construction lines of adjoining walls converge at two vanishing points on the horizon. It is important to set the vanishing points farther apart to have the corresponding corner appear to be correct. Otherwise, the perspective will be too severe, conveying an impression of scale that is not accurate. In the case where the vanishing points are too close, the corner between the walls, their convergence will appear to be less than 90 degrees. Referring to the plan view and locating the viewer is a simple way to select the appropriate view and approximate the convergence of the corresponding walls. A measuring line or edge is useful in a two-point construction just as a measuring wall is useful in a one-point construction. The measuring line works best when a full-length, floor-to-ceiling line is shown in the sketch—similar to the freehand construction lines drawn in the quick thumbnails in this chapter.

Proportional dimensions follow along the line and project into the space from the vanishing points. When an object is not parallel to the adjoining walls, a new vanishing point and vanishing lines project through the measuring line.

In keeping with the functional analysis that determines use of space, this drawing has been given those attributes such as exchanges over product and bins of lumber that indicate a commercial hardware store. In the foreground, there is an indication of a table saw and graphic displays point to the area where hand tools are available. Even the roof supports, steel triangular reinforced beams, provide visual indicators to represent the type of commercial space.

Figure 6-21a, Figure 6-21b

(Kevin Reeder)

In retail spaces (as depicted in Figure 6-20a and Figure 6-20b as well as these drawings) the visual excitement caused by objects that are not parallel to the architectural walls can appear in the two-point perspective. Using the plan view, with the measuring line drawn as a point (in the top view), projection lines can be drawn from an object to the vanishing line to a rear wall. This construction repeats in the perspective and the nonparallel perspective construction of an object can be located in the space using different vanishing points placed on the same horizon line. It is important to note that the sketch uses only one vanishing line. The consistency will help the drawing look correct and help the viewers understand the concept.

Projecting an object into the space is similar to the process discussed with one-point perspective.

Constructing a proportional grid on one of the walls is a simple way to determine the depth of the space. To do this, project a line along the wall at a known height based on the measuring line. Visually determine a square on the wall and project it by the far corner-to-midline projection method. This will produce the next proportional square. In this manner, if a six-foot square projects along a wall, proportional divisions are possible allowing the further projection of an eight-foot dimension along that wall. This point projects into the space from the other vanishing point and the table or chair appear in place with accuracy.

Also note that, once again, interest in the drawing has been created in a specific area of the drawing as opposed to developing the entire surface of the drawing equally.

Figure 6-22

(Kevin Reeder)

This particular interior line drawing assumes a relatively high eye point off the floor. The choice of this point of view includes the visualization of the top of the structure of the unit. Note also the use of a grid to determine the floor plane to establish the placement of not only the unit of display but also the figures.

Figure 6-23
(Kevin Reeder)
In this variation of a previous drawing, the eye point remains higher off the floor to capture the essence of the micro-environmental concept. Also note that the floor on which this unit is sitting remains untreated—largely because it is not relevant to the "floor" of the unit being described.

Figure 6-24
(Kevin Reeder)
This drawing places the eye point at standing eye height. The viewpoint looking in at this space is on the same level as the eye plane of the two individuals at right-center. Of the greatest importance, the sense of space develops through the "overlap" of objects and people cast against one another and the floor plane. There is a visual progression in this space from the exercise machine in the foreground overlapping another such machine and others—leading the eye to the back window wall.

The lowered eye point allows for the development of a floor surface. However, this surface remains without color over the entire visual area of the floor. In so doing, the designer has depicted the floor, but has not "overwhelmed" the drawing with too much color. This concept represents the points made in this chapter about vignette and judicious use of color. Limiting the use of color—marker color in particular—keeps the drawing fresh and the background is prevented from visually pressing forward of the objects in the drawing.

TIP - Do not "over-color" interior conceptual drawings; it will flatten the sense of space. ■

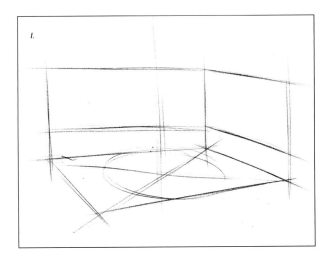

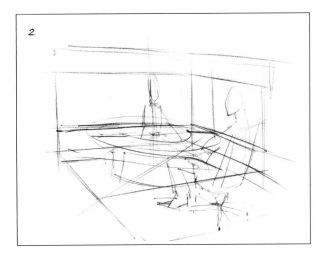

Figure 6-25a
Figure 6-25b
Figure 6-25c
Figure 6-25d
(Joseph Koncelik)

This sketch was developed quickly in freehand using many of the principles offered in this text from the beginning chapters through to the use of mixed media.

The first sketch scan (1) illustrates a method for developing the point of view and perspective at just above eye level. This point of view minimizes the amount of time-consuming top-down floor space drawing. The freehand circle and cross-referencing corner-to-corner lines help establish the floor plane. A "belt line" appears at a level that will help establish surface heights and the proportion of wall to window.

In the second image of the sketch development (2), a quick sketch illustrates a relationship between human figures—helping establish scale and context. Also note that alterations occur to wall height to indicate a "valance" line for draperies and lighting.

The third image (3) shows the development of color to indicate floor plane, desk front surface, and the color indicators for the garments clothing the figures.

The fourth image (4) provides most of the indicators that will show the entire conceptual drawing and one of the ideas for part of the spatial development.

Sketches of this kind should be quick and are useful as communication tools to assist design teams in coordinating ideas in complex interior-development projects. The drawings are fast sketches—taking minutes to do such concepts—and therefore not precious. In the initial exploration of interior design ideas, complicated constructions of perspective with a broad-based view of the entire interior space are costly and less than useful.

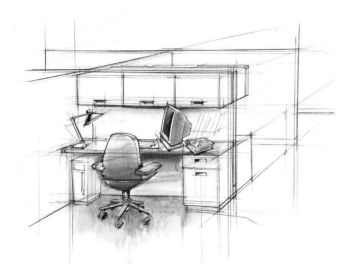

Figure 6-26
(Kevin Reeder)
The most common form of vignette is the drawing focusing attention on a specific location and allowing the remaining detail to fade away. This concentrates attention on a specific aspect of the design and leaves other aspects of the design to additional drawings.

Figure 6-27
(Kevin Reeder)
Another treatment of the concept of vignette is the use of media to focus attention on a specific location of the drawing. This requires additional skill with media that might prove difficult for the novice.

work well. Where there are more complex interior perspectives, pasting in figures can be difficult and inappropriate. They will seem to float in the space, disconnected from their surroundings. It is far better to develop a figurative technique that is consistent with drawing style, but stylized

so it isn't labor intensive. A fine line is frequently crossed regarding this form of figure drawing—the result is cartooning. Many forms of cartoon figure rendering have become popular among designers, but they are not always appropriate to every form of product or interior drawing.

Figure 6-28
(Joseph Koncelik)
This initial image of a step-by-step drawing utilizes the process that has been repeated many times—beginning with simple line drawing in Verithin pencil (as with this image) outlining the concept in a quick visualization. One important aspect of this drawing is that the eye point is on center—literally in the crosshairs—of the "belt line" of the table surface and the vertical junction of the two walls at the rear of the drawing. This is a low eye point, but one that enables the designer to develop the drawing quickly without the time-consuming delay caused by drawing floor and table surfaces.

2.

Figure 6-29
(Joseph Koncelik)
The figure is a context for scale and infers functionality to the drawing of an office space, so it receives the initial marker treatment—always drawing the marker in accordance with the direction of the body form and clothing.

3.

Figure 6-30
(Joseph Koncelik)
Keeping in mind that the figure/desk relationship is central to communicating concept, the products and architectural hardware receive attention—including indications of shadow. However, note that marker use is not a "fill-in" to line work. White space remains—first to provide liveliness in the drawing and to avoid a flattening of space and to allow for "bleed" of the marker color that would otherwise overpower the line work.

Judicious Use of Color

In the interior concept drawing, less color is better than more color. Since most conceptual drawing discussed so far in this text uses markers or pastels—or both—the designer must beware of the rawness of these colors and the difficulty in color mixing. Mixing marker colors is virtually impossible, with the exception of some overlays of gray on color to indicate changes in shade. The use of color in the interior sketch is part and

Figure 6-31

(Joseph Koncelik)

This drawing receives an appropriate level of finish—as a quick conceptual sketch—not as a finished interior drawing. As the drawing progressed, some details appeared at the last stages. Note the inclusion of a telephone on the desk surface as well as a "tack-board" seemingly used to display page layouts for study or presentation.

Also note that an abstracted tree form is present behind the figure and chair to indicate that there is a window wall to the rear. This was done without modeling the exterior.

It is essential to keep drawings of this kind at a level of finish that does not make them precious—or expensive to produce. This drawing—without the repeated scanning of stages—took minutes to produce. Initially, all the lines were produced freehand, but then "tightened up" using a cardboard straight edge to provide a cleaner set of lines to describe surfaces and structures such as table legs. This technique is discussed in a following section and is appropriate for all forms of drawing, including product and interior sketches.

Initial discussions in this text about drawing process have noted that time is a critical factor in producing these images. The designer must be able to discard a drawing, literally crumple it up and throw it away without feeling a significant amount of time has been wasted.

Figure 6-32

(Kevin Reeder)

This drawing is a concept for a glazed elevator permitting a view to the external world. Judicious use of color is well represented in this sketch. The boundaries of floor and wall are defined (the wood railing defines the two exterior walls of glass). The focus of attention is obviously the surroundings and not the interior of the elevator cab.

Figure 6-33a,
Figure 6-33b,
Figure 6-33c
(Joseph Koncelik)

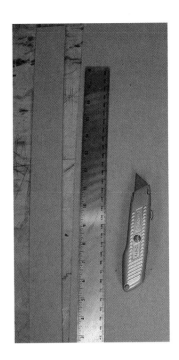

The beginning of this text emphasized that the novice student/designer should not become dependent on the use of tools such as straight edges, circle guide and ellipse guide templates, and other mechanical drawing aids at the onset of learning conceptual drawing skills. Using such tools at the beginning of the learning process distracts attention from the need to draw freehand with confidence. As skill increases, the use of tools is appropriate. Placing an ellipse guide at the end of a tubular shape without having learned how to draw the circle in perspective typically results in awkward selections of ellipses that are not "true" to the drawing's perspective. The practiced designer will freehand sketch all parts of a drawing and use the tools to "true up" the line work. This process advocated in this text—and is especially appropriate for interior conceptual sketching.

In the preceding photographic images, scrap cardboard is used to fashion a straight edge for use in sketching. The line work produced can be seen in the sketch to the right (part of the step-by-step drawing to follow). Using the cardboard straight edge has several advantages. First and foremost, it can be used with markers without the marker color bleeding beneath the straight edge. The cardboard absorbs the additional marker ink, saving the drawing. In addition, the cardboard edge is light and—depending on how much cardboard is desirable for the edge—smaller than a triangle and easy to use in the sketching mode. After use, it can be discarded without the problems of cleaning edges using solvents that eventually destroy the edges of plastic triangles and other tools.

The drawing at below, right, shows the cut-out cardboard edge being used to "true up" freehand sketching lines in a step-by-step drawing shown in this chapter.

parcel of the development of vignette. Color is strongest at the focus of attention and less color is used away from the focal point. Color can also be modified using pencil and ink lines—reducing its intensity.

Interior designers must invest in colors away from the more basic blues, reds, and greens. Marker colors have become relatively sophisticated with a selection of earth tones and muted colors that are appropriate for interior conceptual

drawing. Regardless, intense colors should be used only sparingly and not over large surfaces. As with most design drawing, the object is what the designer wants to convey to the client or to the instructor. In many cases, the choice of color was an arbitrary act that could be changed with another drawing overlay. Designs should not be rejected simply because the designer chose a crimson marker for the rug on the floor.

Figure 6-34a
Figure 6-34b
Figure 6-34c
(Joseph Koncelik)

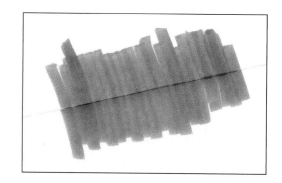

The images at right illustrate two fast techniques that will help any designer—especially the interior designer—with edges. The top two images illustrate a simple method for controlling the edges of areas where marker is used where it should not bleed over a specific line.

A sheet of scrap paper with a true straight edge is placed against the line or just above the line. The marker is drawn from the scrap paper up to and through the area where the tone or area of color is to be placed. Strokes of marker are drawn in this manner repeatedly until the area has the desired amount of marker. In the middle image, the scrap paper is pulled away, revealing an edge that is controlled rather than bleeding over line work.

In the bottom image, a cardboard straight edge is used to draw marker lines below the area of marker just described. Ordinarily, using a plastic triangle to make such lines results in a build-up of marker underneath the triangle and the lines will "fray" when the triangle is pulled away. Cardboard will absorb the excess marker. Looking closely at the edge of the cardboard marker, color can be seen where it has been absorbed into the cardboard edge. However, each of the three lines was drawn without any fraying or bleeding.

Obviously, it is necessary to be sensible about how much one cardboard straight edge can be used in this manner. The cardboard will become saturated with marker and actually lose its edge—even disintegrate. Therefore, it is wise to cut several cardboard straight edges and use them until they are no longer serviceable—a judgment call! In addition, each piece cut for the use of guiding lines has two useable edges

Figure 6-35
(Joseph Koncelik)
The initial line work of a more complex interior sketch shows how "overlap" is used to indicate the depth of the space—using objects placed in the foreground of other objects to produce spatial depth.

Figure 6-36
(Joseph Koncelik)
Two figures are placed in juxtaposition on a sectional couch, inferring a relationship that is an additional visual indicator of the function of the space.

Figure 6-37
(Joseph Koncelik)
In this step-by-step sketch, the process of using markers has been altered over the previous example in that objects are given color before the figures. This can be a useful variation when the complexity of the interior increases beyond the development of figures as context.

Figure 6-38
(Joseph Koncelik)
The function of the space becomes apparent as a back wall is given detail, indicating the inclusion of a media wall—implying that the male figure is listening while the female figure is reading.

Figure 6-39a, Figure 6-39b
(Joseph Koncelik)
In stages 5 and 6, the level of finish is "decided." It is always a subjective issue to determine how finished a sketch should become. As a rule of thumb, pulling back from the image on the page and not being able to decide what to add indicates that it's time to stop. There are only slight differences between the two sketch images above, including line work and shading.

  This sequence was produced on tracing paper allowing for the use of marker on two sides of the page. This reduces the intensity of the marker color and is useful in producing a color "mixing" when one marker is used on both sides of the page in an overlay.

Use of Text

Unlike the product designer, the interior designer does not have the option of hand-lettered text surrounding an object that has been drawn in isolation from the rest of a spatial environment. Yet text is useful as "notation" in the development of architectural spaces and the relationship to a building program. It is likely that the interior designer will find it useful to describe an area at the base of a drawing as the row in which text will be placed in a uniform organized manner. Again, developing a decent hand-lettering style—similar to architectural hand lettering—is extremely useful to the interior designer. This is especially true because many opportunities for interior designers come through architectural

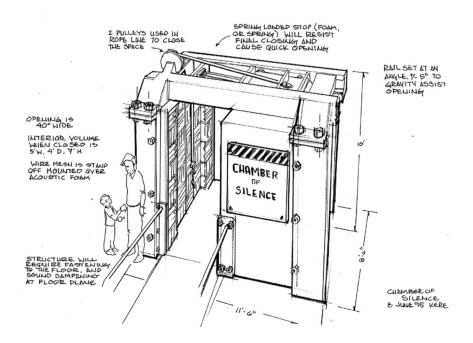

Text on drawing:

2 PULLEYS USED IN ROPE LINE TO CLOSE THE SPACE

SPRING LOADED STOP (FOAM, OR SPRING) WILL RESIST FINAL CLOSING AND CAUSE QUICK OPENING

RAIL SET AT AN ANGLE, ≈ 5° TO GRAVITY ASSIST OPENING

OPENING IS 40" WIDE

INTERIOR VOLUME WHEN CLOSED IS 5'W, 4'D, 7'H

WIRE MESH IS STAND OFF MOUNTED OVER ACOUSTIC FOAM

CHAMBER OF SILENCE

STRUCTURE WILL REQUIRE FASTENING TO THE FLOOR, AND SOUND DAMPENING AT FLOOR PLANE

10'

8'-6"

11'-6"

CHAMBER OF SILENCE 8 JUNE 95 KERE

Figure 6-40

(Kevin Reeder)

Well-conceived line drawings use the human figure to convey scale as well as a relationship to the exhibition within an open space. The notations on the drawing explain what cannot be stated visually. Text is an important part of interior drawing as well as in architecture—sometimes referred to as drawing notation. In product design, the text is used as indicators of function, use of materials, and processes of manufacturing. In interior design, the notations are also functional but also may indicate anticipated use, traffic flow, types or associations of appliances and products, or surface treatments to floors walls, and ceilings—if not complex descriptions of lighting. Frequently, the interior drawing—even the sketch—is sufficiently complex so that the text content must be "designed" into the drawing in specific locations so as not to interfere with the imaging of the space.

design offices. The more consistency there is between the style of presentation between disciplines, the better the chances for employment and successful design.

Another aspect of the argument that design professions must have interchangeable skills—especially conceptual drawing skills—is that there is free-ranging employment of design skills throughout design professions despite the educational background of the designer. Graduates from product or industrial design programs find their way into interior design or graphic design and the same "professional drift" is present for the other specializations. Since the ability to draw well is the critical component of entry-level design employment, conceptual drawing skill is the common language of all design professions.

Conclusions about Interior Conceptual Drawing

The central point of this chapter is that interior conceptual drawing is not only a useful aspect of design process, it is a viable means of communication to design process participants. Interior designers have a natural tendency to gravitate to mechanical methods for generating spatial concepts. As with any other field of design, mechanical methods are usually time-consuming, expensive, and risky. The risk lies in the gamble that clients or others involved in decision-making will reject the single concept presented in finished form, thus returning the designer or design team to the drawing board to repeat the entire process. In addition, finished drawings typically intimidate clients. There is an

A CORRUGATED BUSINESS

USING CORRUGATED BOARD + PLASTIC SNAP RIVETS, A 'BUSINESS' PLAY ENVIRONMENT COULD BE CONSTRUCTED. IT MAY INCLUDE A DRIVE THROUGH WINDOW/CASHIER COUNTER WITH A CASH REGISTER, INFORMATION BOARDS AND SERVICE PAD.

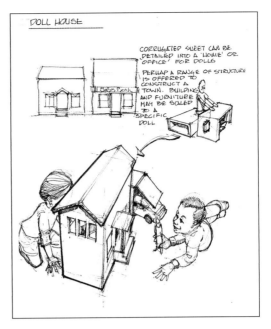

DOLL HOUSE

CORRUGATED SHEET CAN BE DETAILED INTO A 'HOME' OR OFFICE' FOR DOLLS

PERHAP A RANGE OF STRUCTURE IS OFFERED TO CONSTRUCT A TOWN. BUILDING AND FURNITURE MAY BE SCALED TO A SPECIFIC DOLL

Figure 6-41a
Figure 6-41b
Figure 6-41c
Figure 6-41d
(Kevin Reeder)
The interior is also context as well as the objective of design. The drawings at left illustrate the development of objects in space and also the use of the appropriate figure to demonstrate use as either a play object or a place to store personal items with a sense of play. Text accompanying the image explains aspects of the concept that either cannot be visualized or require further elaboration.

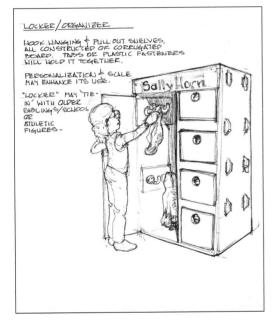

LOCKER/ORGANIZER

HOOK HANGING + PULL OUT SHELVES, ALL CONSTRUCTED OF CORRUGATED BOARD. TABS OR PLASTIC FASTENERS WILL HOLD IT TOGETHER.

PERSONALIZATION + SCALE MAY ENHANCE ITS USE.

"LOCKER" MAY 'TIE-IN' WITH OLDER SIBLINGS/SCHOOL OR ATHLETIC FIGURES -

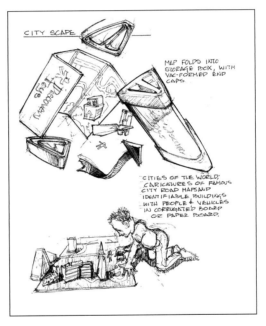

CITY SCAPE

MAP FOLDS INTO STORAGE BOX, WITH VAC-FORMED END CAPS.

CITIES OF THE WORLD; CARICATURES OF FAMOUS CITY ROAD MAPS AND IDENTIFIABLE BUILDINGS WITH PEOPLE + VEHICLES IN CORRUGATED BOARD OR PAPER BOARD.

emotional barrier presented by finished drawings at the beginning stages of design that prevents interaction and engagement with the design process. Many design services clients believe that a finished drawing means the process is so complete that any suggestion of change is fruitless or unwanted. Even if the design is acceptable overall, finished drawings at the beginning stages of design diminish interaction and full acceptance of the design direction.

Conceptual interiors, as presented in this chapter, spring from the architectural drawings that describe the structure of an environment. Such architectural drawings and details are initially to guide construction. Plan views in particular are useful starting points to describe spaces. With regard to perspective, both one- and two-point perspectives are useful in interior conceptual drawing. One-point perspectives allow for a relatively easy method to gauge proportions of objects from a flat two-dimensional rear wall. Diagrammed drawings in this chapter illustrate the development of relatively quick one-point perspectives that use one and two vanishing points derived from the same horizon line. Two-point perspectives present other possibilities,

Figure 6-42
(Noel Mayo)
The complexity of an interior may require accuracy in the initial conceptual drawings. This drawing and the one below of the interiors associated with a financial institution required such accuracy.

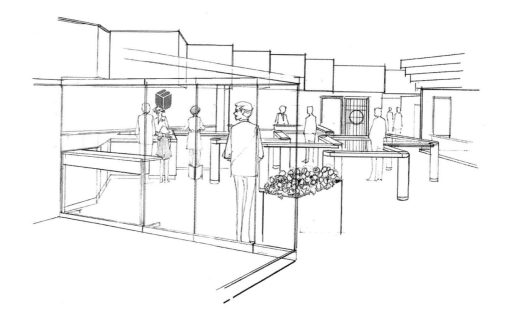

Figure 6-43
(Noel Mayo)
These drawings were shaped over Lawson Charts, published perspective grid systems that permit a layout without the time-consuming issues associated with constructing a perspective manually.

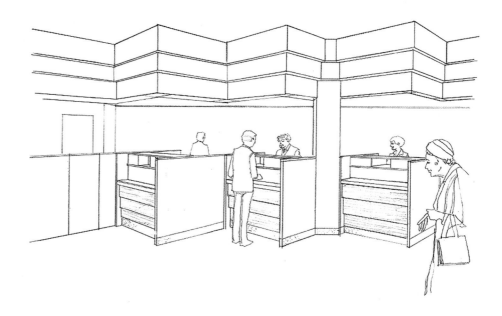

but require extending vanishing points beyond the drawing surface in most cases—otherwise, the perspectives become either too severe or distorted. To gain an intuitive understanding of creating freehand perspectives, it's a good idea to review Chapter 2 on perspective.

Another important aspect of establishing the interior conceptual drawing is placement of the eye point in space. There is a tendency to place the eye point too high off the floor plane in many instances—when space is indicated by the overlap of objects. Nevertheless, as shown in

drawings in this chapter, there are instances when the eye point should be on the "second story," so to speak, to describe a concept adequately. The drawing of the playground shown in this chapter is one conceptual drawing where a high eye point is necessary. The view into space is a more complicated issue than establishing the view of a product. Many of the fundamentals remain the same, but interior drawing can have points of view or eye points that are inside the space, external to the space, perpendicular to the rear wall in a one-point perspective,

TIP - Detail in an interior should be more highly refined at the focal point of the drawing. ▪

Figure 6-44a-
Figure 6-44b
(Noel Mayo)
Here again, the designer meets the demands of accuracy by constructing an interior over Lawson Charts. The upper drawing shows the reception area in front of a walled office and the lower drawing has the wall removed to show the interior.

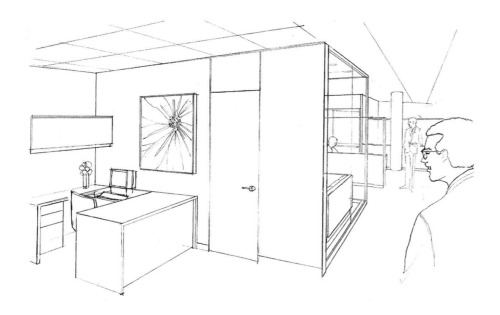

or juxtaposed to an association of two walls, as in two-point perspective.

It is essential to grasp the concept that freehand drawing of interior spaces is possible and useful. The process of developing freehand drawings requires attention to the following eight important rules of thumb:

1. Point of view appropriate to the interior design

2. Perspective—especially the efficacy of one-point perspective

3. Establishing "ground" to place objects

4. Overlap of objects to create a sense of space

Figure 6-45

(Noel Mayo)

As with previous drawings in this chapter, this drawing uses extensive "overlap" of objects and people in space—as well as perspective—to define the space. The plantings and other textures are abstract, yet very convincing.

Figure 6-46

(Michael Butcher)

A progression of steps in the development of an interior perspective as developed in the DVD, Segment 5, Interior Space.

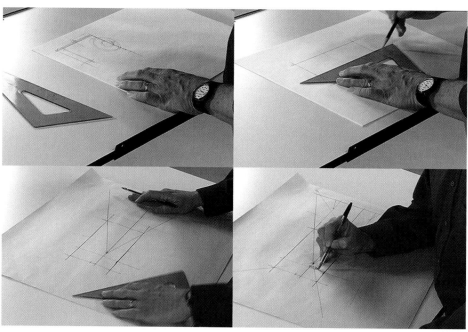

Figure 6-47
(Michael Butcher, Kevin Reeder)
This image shows further steps in
the progression of an interior
perspective conceptual drawing. A
final image of the sketch has an
appropriate level of finish.

See DVD
Segment 5,
Interior Space,
for complete inte-
rior perspective
demonstration.

5. Vignette—allowing background detail to fade away to emphasize the focal area

6. Use of the human figure to establish scale

7. Judicious use of color—especially in marker sketching

8. Appropriate use of text to explain and enhance the design

Finally, the interior designer who develops conceptual drawing skills has a definite edge over his or her peers and competitors. Essentially, the conceptual interior drawing is a form of communication that is used to engage design process participants. It is a useful expenditure of time to produce such drawings and certainly a useful pursuit for any designer who wishes to develop those skills that will ensure success.

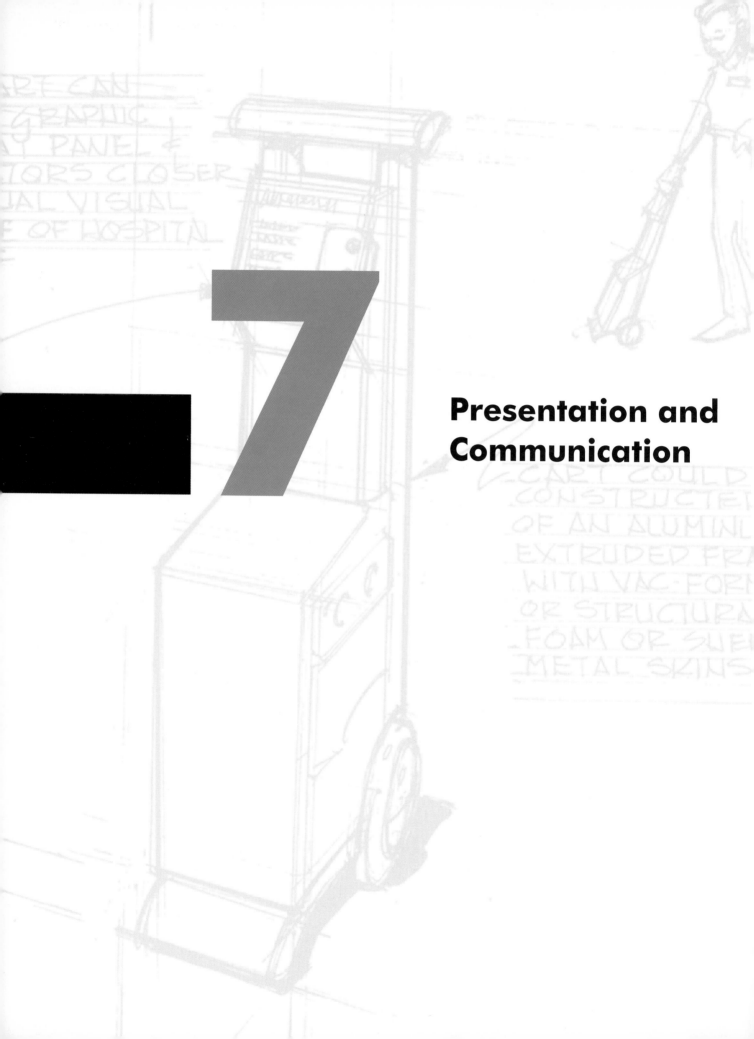

7

Presentation and Communication

Selecting Tools for the Drawing Process

Tools to produce conceptual drawings have evolved over time. Conté crayons, pastel pencils and chalks, even watercolors have been used to produce design visualizations. For the past three decades, the general term that describes both the type of drawing and the tools is *mixed media*. Mixed media drawing is the use of multiple drawing instruments to achieve effective communication. The range of tools used for generating these types of visualizations can be as limited as two drawing instruments or as broad as several different instruments used in a specific sequence to create effective communications through drawing.

Among artists, there is a sense of purity in the use of drawing instruments even though there are many examples of mixed media that created stunning images. Design visualization is not art, and the purity of use of drawing tools is not important compared to the need to communicate ideas to others. Any means to produce drawings is acceptable, especially where using multiple forms of media saves time and expedites the number of alternatives that might be available.

It is important to establish that the simplest form of conceptualizing ideas is through a single tool such as a particular pencil or use of pen

lines. Most of Preston Bruning's line drawings shown in this text are executed with a ballpoint pen. This form of drawing requires great confidence because none of the lines can be removed. Generally speaking, lines drawn on the paper surface should not be removed—even if those lines are placed there using a pencil. Erasure is time-consuming and does not allow instructors to fully examine the thinking process. As stated earlier, erasure is itself a drawing technique, used to model the surface of an object, not to correct line work or improperly drawn objects and environments. Beyond the quick sketching mode of drawing, designers frequently refine rough sketches by using overlays of vellum or tracing paper. This is the quickest way to eliminate line work that is not relevant to communication.

Students of conceptual drawing are advised to experiment with a number of drawing tools. Graphite pencils are, generally, not suitable for line work and line drawing. Graphite smudges as the drawing hand moves over the paper surface. Unless smudging is intentional and the draftsperson can keep their hand off the paper surface, graphite drawings are not acceptable. Preferred pencils are the *Eagle* or *Berol Verithin Black* pencil and the *Eagle Prismacolor Black* pencil. These pencils produce a deep black line that has fewer tendencies to smudge. They can be used with

Figure 7-1
(Joseph Koncelik)
This drawing represents some of the typical drawing media designers use in mixed media drawing. From left to right: Verithin pencil, Prismacolor pencil, non-photo blue pencil, Berol design markers (2), a fine-line ballpoint pen, a fine-line Sharpie, and a broad-tipped Sharpie. Preference may dictate other choices. Nevertheless, each of the tools is used in a sequence to provide quick and clear conceptual drawings.

other media more effectively than graphite (to be discussed further on). The Verithin pencil is extremely useful for general line work that describes the object being visualized. The Prismacolor black pencil is more useful as a finishing tool for laying in deep black lines that emphasize an object's shape and detail.

It is important to note that there are no "art rules," as many designers humorously state when they discuss rigid ideas about how designs should be visualized. Art rules are meant to be funny. A typical example would be, "Never leave your Crayola Crayons on the radiator." (Actually, that is not such a bad art rule.) Such art rules also call attention to the false assumption that someone can dictate the process of artistic image making or, for that matter, design visualization.

It is more appropriate to think of the information here not as rules per se, but as *conventions*. Conventions are practices that have evolved over time through repeated use and that produce desired results. The convention for using the two pencils mentioned is to use the Verithin pencil first and the Prismacolor pencil second. There are several designers who sketch using only one of these pencils. It is wise for students to observe

and utilize conventional ways of drawing before they become too inventive. Regardless of how uniform are the practices among a class of students, every student will exhibit uniqueness in their work. Uniqueness as an aspect of creativity does not need to be a conscious effort to achieve a personal style. Personal style is unavoidable and will emerge and become refined over time.

Another pencil that has become part of the basic form of mixed media drawing is the *Eagle Verithin Non-Photo Blue pencil*. This pencil is used frequently to describe objects, people, and environments in rough sketch form because it produces a light blue line. Such drawings are further refined by over-drawing with either pens or other black pencils. The term "non-photo blue" is misleading. It infers that the lines cannot be reproduced photographically. There are examples provided in this text that show blue lines exposed as well as the over-drawing in examples of conceptual drawing provided by Kevin Reeder. However, all of the drawings have been converted to black and white, so the "blue" lines have also been converted to black. Examples of this technique can be found in the CD-ROM that accompanies this text.

Figure 7-2

(R. Preston Bruning)
In this small sketch of a hovercraft concept, Bruning demonstrates his mastery of mixed media. The white of the craft and the buildings in the background is the paper showing through the drawing. The drawing makes extensive use of markers, Prismacolor pencil, and pastels.

It is also important to state that when students are developing drawings that take advantage of the complexities of mixed media, they must have mastered the fundamentals discussed earlier. Achieving line quality, sense of perspective, and other aspects of visualization must be well developed before a student proceeds with more complex forms of drawing for communication. Nevertheless, virtually all design students must progress to the point where the efficient use of mixed media drawing is attempted and mastered.

Discussing pens and all permanent ink media is difficult because there are so many different types that in turn produce differing line weights, effects, and colors. The evolution of the magic marker from a tool used in industry to mark metals on the production line into a tool called a *Design Marker* is a phenomenon that dramatically changed conceptual drawing and overall design visualization. Most of the advanced visualizations shown in this text with tone, shadow, and backgrounds are mixed media marker drawings.

One of the best texts on the subject of "marker rendering" is Ronald B. Kemnitzer's *Rendering with Markers* (1983). Kemnitzer discusses and demonstrates process—how to create such drawings step by step. His book is also filled with drawing examples from some of the most talented designers in the field. One cautionary note: Kemnitzer's book is meant for advanced students, those who have progressed beyond fundamentals. Students frequently become enamored with the intense colors of markers and the use of backgrounds to "pop" drawings off the page. Both of these aspects of marker rendering and several others can become counter-productive when attempted by the novice. In addition, as noted in previous discussions, rendering is not conceptual in nature; it is illustrative. It can be an essential part of a presentation, but it is the final form of design visualization that is time-consuming and expensive.

Pens can be divided into two groups. The first group is those hard-tipped roller ball pens called ballpoints. Variations in this group include pens with soft rollers that create lines similar to felt-tipped pens, which are the second group. Felt-tipped pens comprise a spectrum of drawing instruments and include versions ranging from those that make very fine lines to those that make broad lines of ½ inch or even broader. This text will concentrate on those pens that are useful in the initial stages of conceptual drawing and design visualization. Students will find a wide variety of these tools, ranging from *Pilot Fineliners* to fine-tipped and bold-tipped *Sharpies*. The refillable

Figure 7-3
(R. Preston Bruning)
This freehand mixed media drawing on vellum uses both sides of the paper to change the intensity of markers.

felt-tipped pen has disappeared from use and most of the current tools are disposable—not a very good commentary on the ecological aspect of pen development and use. Nevertheless, speed and efficiency are important in conceptual drawing and many of these tools fit the requirements.

Finally, it is important to discuss the use of gray scale and color markers because they are so frequently used as line-drawing instruments as well as for surface rendering. There are several brands, but the felt-tipped marker with the greatest range of colors and shades of gray is the double-ended *Berol Prismacolor Art Marker*. Berol has manufactured cool and warm gray markers, basic colors, and sophisticated mixes of color. This double-ended version of the marker has one felt tip that is a relatively medium-weight line and has another broad felt-tip generally used for surface rendering and backgrounds. The Prismacolor marker is an extremely flexible tool that is effective in generating quick sketches as well as more complicated and time-consuming renderings.

Owing to the emphasis on freehand drawing in this text, there will be no discussion of guides, templates, sweeps, and other devices meant to assist in the development of straight and curved surfaces. The exception is two guides, the cardboard ruler and the scrap-paper mask. Felt-tipped inking tools tend to bleed under plastic triangles and ruling guides. If it is necessary to true up a line—even to delineate a straight perspective line from point to point—students are advised to cut out a cardboard straight edge as a cheap throwaway guide. When used with most felt-tipped pens, there will be little-to-no bleeding when the surface of the cardboard is clean. As it becomes saturated, bleeding can become a problem. Eliminate that difficulty by cutting several guides from waste cardboard. It is also possible to cut a sweep-line guide as well, but that is beyond the realm of conceptual drawing generation. If it is necessary to produce a very straight edge to an area of marker that provides either shading or color, a sheet of scrap paper with a straight edge can be placed at the edge of the area to be marked and the marker drawn from the paper to the drawing surface.

In developing a mixed media drawing that is an appropriate extension of a refined conceptual drawing, the conventional sequence of use of tools is likely to be:

1. Development of an under-drawing using either a Verithin or non-photo blue pencil

2. Placement of surface shading and/or color using a felt-tipped marker

3. Development of the edges and surfaces of the object or environment using pencils or felt-tipped pens

4. Shading or further surface treatment using the Prismacolor pencil

Figure 7-4
(R. Preston Bruning)
Line quality is the essential ingredient in all conceptual drawing. As in this dynamic juxtaposition of aircraft, deft handling of line is critical to the character and clarity of the drawing.

Figure 7-5
(Aaron Bethlenfalvy)
This conceptual drawing of a
carbon fiber bicycle frame for
Pacific Cycle is enhanced by
computer graphics.

To keep a reasonable time frame for drawing, it is essential that any developed conceptual drawing *not* use complicated mechanical perspectives or templates and guides. When students begin drawings using mechanical layout techniques, their investment in the drawing becomes greater than their investment in communicating the design.

An argument frequently used in the classroom is that the professional designer at the "entry" level will have his or her time billed to a client at a minimum of $30.00 per hour. A three-hour drawing is going to be billed at $90.00 or more. In the initial stages of design, it's necessary for the designer and client to communicate about the numerous potential directions a product or environment might take. It is far better to generate drawings that consume less time and explore a greater number of ideas. Thus, design students must learn how to generate a number of design ideas quickly—with clarity, detail, and a well-developed sense of the aesthetic.

This abbreviated discussion of tools can be expanded by referring to the text by Kemnitzer or several other books on drawing and rendering available at art supply stores and craft stores. One problem for students is knowing the limitations of the tools. Pencils need to be continually sharpened to produce consistent drawings. Pens need to be fresh—and that requires a fairly substantial investment of money. The most preferred pens—both hard-tipped and felt-tipped—are expensive

and have a limited lifespan. Experimentation with tools will result in an accumulation of numerous tools over time and that is to be expected. Students are advised that the cost of a design program may increase from 30 to 50% because of the purchase of materials and supplies.

It is also important to discuss the media of papers or the drawing surface. Since students will be doing large numbers of drawings both in class and on their own, using an inexpensive surface is highly recommended. Newsprint is easily the best choice for the early stages of learning conceptual drawing. There are varying textures of newsprint and the better choice is a smooth surface paper. Buying newsprint in pads is costly. Students should attempt to find sources where 18 by 24-inch newsprint can be procured in reams of 500 sheets—all loose. There are two significant advantages of using this paper: 1) it will be cheaper and far more disposable; 2) the sheets of paper are already loose and need not be torn from a pad, thus preserving the edges when a drawing is a "keeper." There are drawbacks to newsprint, however. First, markers bleed into the surface—unless they are used as instructed in this text. Second, the paper has a color, a given background that is both good and bad—but deters its use in presentations. Third, newsprint marker drawings have a lifespan—while there may be no initial bleeding from markers, the paper will absorb marker ink slowly over time and the drawing will become "fuzzy."

Figure 7-6
(Joseph Koncelik)
A freehand mixed media drawing on opaque white paper illustrates a way to depict the sea using marker.

It is recommended that tracings not be done to perfect or correct drawings in the initial learning stages of acquiring drawing skill. Students should retain drawings that include the keepers and the rejects. This helps inform instructors about the struggles an individual may be having. In the first generation of conceptual drawings, there is no precious idea or revelation that cannot be drawn again from scratch. Just as erasures are rejected in this process, redrawing through overlays adds time to the initial process and is counterproductive.

The most expensive paper used in conceptual drawing and design visualization is what is now termed vellum—a bright white translucent paper with excellent surface texture accepting mixed media. Historically, vellum was a form of animal skin used to reproduce ancient texts. During the industrial age, velum became a paper with high

Figure 7-7
(R. Preston Bruning)
This line drawing montage of images was created to illustrate Bruning's love of model airplane building.

rag (cloth) content. Today, vellum may contain many different substances. It is not economical to use vellum the way one uses newsprint. However, the skilled designer uses vellum when his or her abilities are at a level commensurate with generating multiple images at a reasonably refined level of communication. These papers can also be used for tracing or over-drawing to reproduce images and show variations in design.

Automotive designers—perhaps the most skilled designers at conceptual drawing—use a form of vellum that can accept media on both sides without bleeding through. Marker on one side has a slightly different effect than on the "front" side of the page. This allows creation of subtle backgrounds that accentuate the drawing. Pres Bruning's drawings frequently use this technique and several examples—all freehand drawing—accompany this text.

Conventions for Hand Lettering

Drawing notation is as important in conceptual sketching as it is in more elaborate drawing visualizations of designed objects and spaces. If a picture is proverbially worth at least one thousand words, it is important to set boundaries for interpreting the visualized information in a design context. An object's shape, texture, and surface treatment may not convey important thoughts such as method of production, fastening, power requirements, et cetera. The designer chooses between what information must be visual and what information must be verbal. For the sake of the drawing's quality, it is important to develop a legible, aesthetically consistent and pleasing lettering style. Few designers, if any, can write in cursive on the surface of their drawings and have their writing aesthetically (if not legibly) complement the drawing.

Emulating Leonardo Da Vinci, who wrote in backward script left-handed, would not be prudent. Emulating the "architectural" hand-lettering style is highly recommended because this lettering form is an established standard in all design fields. In addition, it is not cheating to place rule lines on the drawing page to position text and ensure that the text is not sloped out of relationship to the drawing. Examples of architectural hand-lettering style are shown on student drawings in this section and in other locations in the text. Developing this style of lettering is also important because such lettering is a professional expectation both from the standpoint of employers in the design fields and also for the sake of clarity to clients who review designers' work.

Developing a lettering style that's adequate for presentation purposes takes practice. In the contemporary design education studio, few students have had any training in cursive writing or calligraphy. Two rules of thumb should be observed regarding the developing a hand-lettering style:

1. Observe the work of others who have mastered hand lettering in the "architectural" style so you can understand its appearance and determine the required clarity of lettering.

2. Practice. As with the initial stages of developing drawing skills, practice is essential to develop hand-lettering skills.

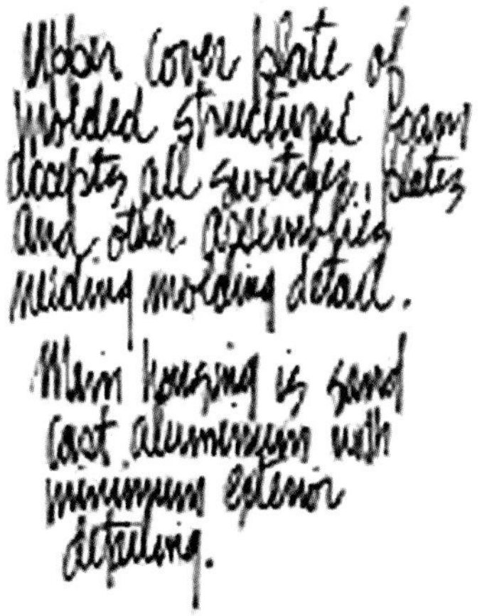

Figure 7-8a
Figure 7-8b
(Tim Gasperak and David Tompkins)
On the left is a derivative of the "architectural" hand-lettering style that is acceptable for the majority of design professionals. On the right is a more personalized cursive style that is sufficiently legible and has enough aesthetic merit to be used in conceptual imaging.

Presentation of Conceptual Work: Case Studies

Throughout this book, it has been repeated that conceptual drawings are essentially a tool to communicate ideas to others. This is a major theme and as stated, it is the fundamental division between drawing for its own sake and drawing to achieve a design goal. To achieve the most desirable level of communicating ideas to others, presentation cannot be neglected. The word "presentation" is significant for designers. Whatever materials are generated for a presentation, they are always prepared with the highest regard for quality, organization, sequence of idea development, and clarity. Design instructors are frequently confronted with presentations of conceptual materials that blatantly disregard these criteria—at least in the initial stages of learning. All presentations should essentially follow a specific organization and sequence, including:

1. Conceptual drawings demonstrate the range of possibilities open for further investigation. Designers do not reject ideas that have been generated in the conceptual process before others have an opportunity to review them. All ideas should be "on the table" when the design process commences.

2. The order of presentation is not arbitrary or without direction. Designers decide the logic of that order to communicate not only range but also their assessment of the most fruitful direction(s) to pursue.

3. Aesthetics is never abandoned. A lack of quality or concern for the appearance of a presentation usually results in negative commentary—even unspoken subjective reactions—which affects the choices of directions in the design process. A lack of attention to the look and feel of a presentation may result in a stage of the conceptual process that increases costs and reduces time necessary for other steps in the design process.

4. Designers must decide how to communicate ideas represented within the limitations implied by conceptual drawing. Most of the information must be visual, but visualizations are often enhanced through the effective use of text (as seen in numerous drawings in previous chapters). In addition, presentations are frequently accompanied by the designer's oral discussions. These discussions must reflect the designer's confidence in his or her own conceptual abilities and the resulting work on display.

5. Conceptual drawing presentations should promote open discussion and should result in all parties being on the same path to a design problem's eventual solution. Affectations should be avoided—including strong color use that masks an idea and misdirects attention to nonessential aspects of the design.

6. If the conceptual presentation is properly developed and organized, the designer should experience closure regarding which direction is best to develop the conceptual work. If clients and others move in directions contrary to the most desirable path, the designer must decide whether the focus has changed, a direction is unknown, or whether some ideas were not adequately communicated.

Some sequences of drawings shown in prior chapters might have been seen as presentations. However, this section of the book provides visualizations of ideas that follow the premise that conceptual drawing presentations require that the artist explore the broadest range of possibilities.

Figure 7-9
(Kevin Reeder)
This is the first in an extended series of conceptual drawings for developing complex electronic medical equipment technology. This sequence is all line drawings—easily transmitted by scanned computer imaging or by facsimile. They are also easy to copy using a Xerox machine.

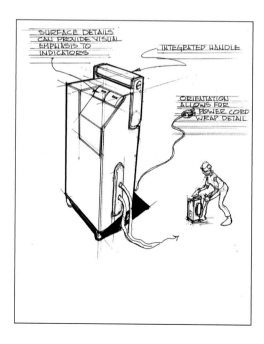

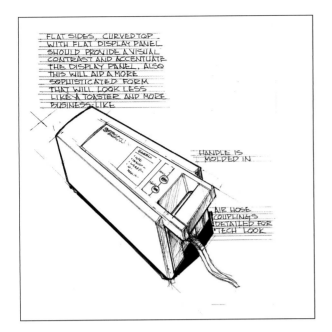

FLAT SIDES, CURVED TOP WITH FLAT DISPLAY PANEL SHOULD PROVIDE A VISUAL CONTRAST AND ACCENTUATE THE DISPLAY PANEL. ALSO THIS WILL AID A MORE SOPHISTICATED FORM THAT WILL LOOK LESS LIKE A TOASTER AND MORE BUSINESS-LIKE

HANDLE IS MOLDED IN

AIR HOSE COUPLINGS DETAILED FOR 'TECH' LOOK

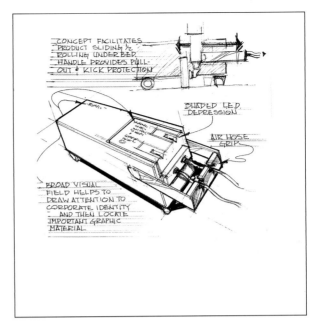

CONCEPT FACILITATES PRODUCT SLIDING ½ ROLLING UNDER BED HANDLE PROVIDES PULL-OUT & KICK PROTECTION

SHADED L.E.D. DEPRESSION

AIR HOSE GRIP

BROAD VISUAL FIELD HELPS TO DRAW ATTENTION TO CORPORATE IDENTITY AND THEN LOCATE IMPORTANT GRAPHIC MATERIAL

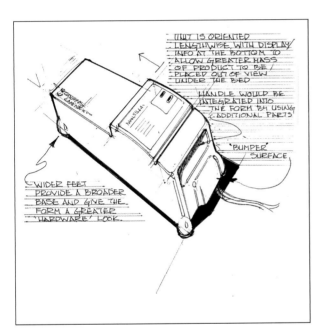

UNIT IS ORIENTED LENGTHWISE, WITH DISPLAY INFO AT THE BOTTOM TO ALLOW GREATER MASS OF PRODUCT TO BE PLACED OUT OF VIEW UNDER THE BED

HANDLE WOULD BE INTEGRATED INTO THE FORM BY USING ADDITIONAL PARTS

'BUMPER' SURFACE

WIDER FEET PROVIDE A BROADER BASE AND GIVE THE FORM A GREATER 'HARDWARE' LOOK.

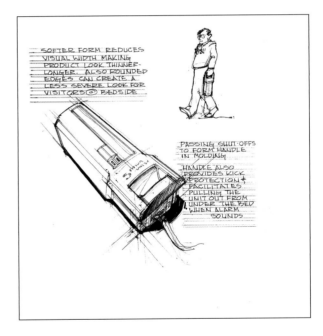

SOFTER FORM REDUCES VISUAL WIDTH MAKING PRODUCT LOOK THINNER-LONGER. ALSO ROUNDED EDGES CAN CREATE A LESS SEVERE LOOK FOR VISITORS @ BEDSIDE

PASSING SHUT-OFFS TO FORM HANDLE IN MOLDING

HANDLE ALSO PROVIDES KICK PROTECTION & FACILITATES PULLING THE UNIT OUT FROM UNDER THE BED WHEN ALARM SOUNDS

Figure 7-10a
Figure 7-10b
Figure 7-10c
Figure 7-10d
(Kevin Reeder)
These four drawings in the extended sequence illustrate ideas about form and function, portability, and accessibility.

See DVD demonstration on product drawing.

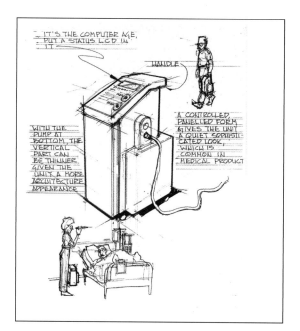

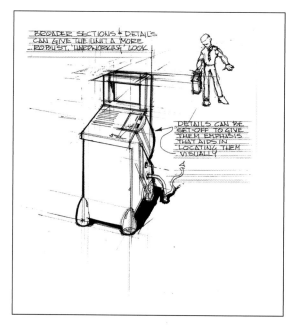

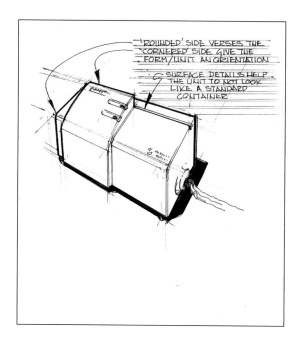

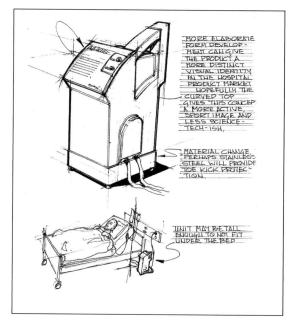

Figure 7-11a
Figure 7-11b
Figure 7-11c
Figure 7-11d
(Kevin Reeder)

These drawings represent a continuation of the sequence, further developing the full range of possible design solutions and uses. This sequence makes the point that conceptual drawing requires full exploration of as many possible solutions to a problem—at the initial state of development—as are possible by the designer or by the team.

TIP - When sketching a keypad, draw the closest five switch caps in the set and let a simple outline describe the rest. ■

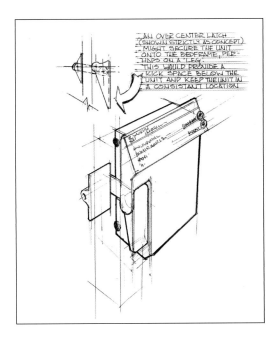

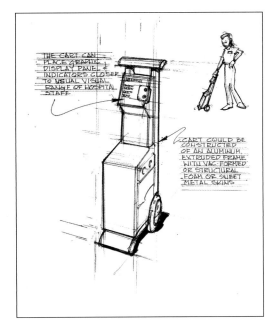

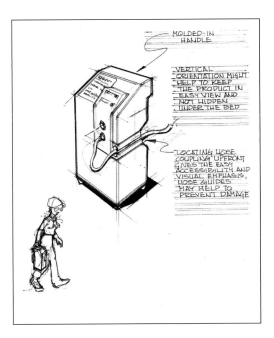

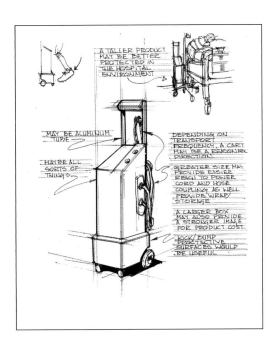

Figure 7-12a
Figure 7-12b
Figure 7-12c
Figure 7-12d
(Kevin Reeder)

These drawings represent another continuation of the sequence, further developing a range of possible solutions to transportability and portability. Most of the development is focused on the technology packaging as well as the location of controls and display and critical connection/disconnection of power cords and critical wires, cabling, and leads. Subordinate drawings illustrating use, position, and portability enhance the conceptualization and develop a sense of scale.

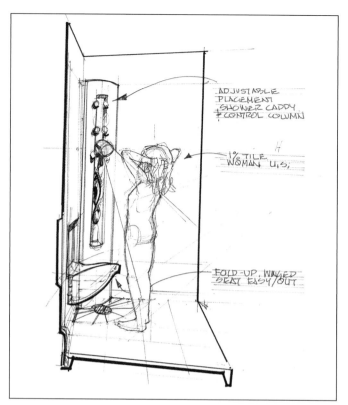

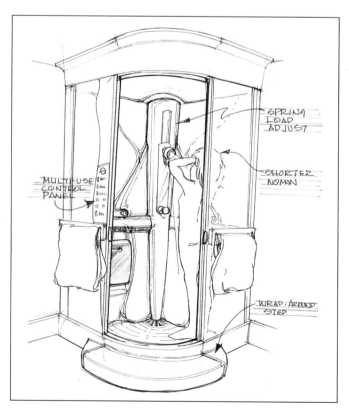

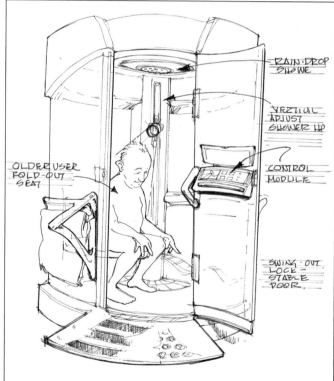

Figure 7-13a, Figure 7-13b, Figure 7-13c, Figure 7-13d
(Kevin Reeder)
This sequence of initial variations on a shower stall is an "after-build" installation, requiring a rise from the base flooring to install technology driving the showering equipment and other amenities of the product. The rise requires variation in steps and ramps to accommodate different users—from the youngest child capable of showering without assistance to the older adult who will require grab bars and seating.

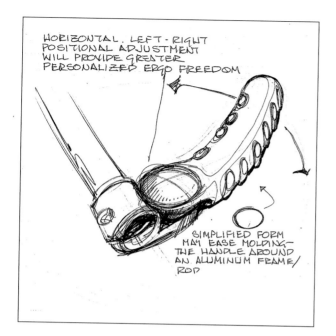

HORIZONTAL LEFT-RIGHT POSITIONAL ADJUSTMENT WILL PROVIDE GREATER PERSONALIZED ERGO FREEDOM

SIMPLIFIED FORM MAY EASE MOLDING— THE HANDLE AROUND AN ALUMINUM FRAME/ ROD

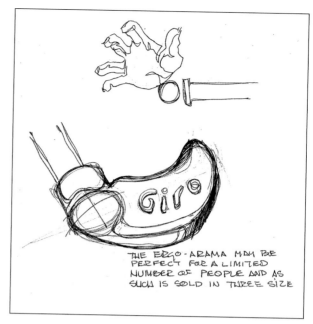

THE ERGO-ARAMA MAY BE PERFECT FOR A LIMITED NUMBER OF PEOPLE AND AS SUCH IS SOLD IN THREE SIZE

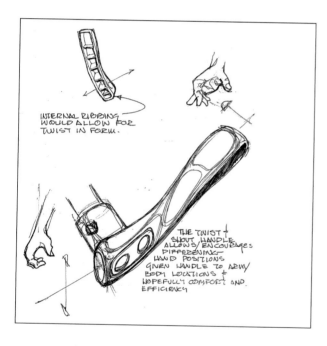

INTERNAL RIBBING WOULD ALLOW FOR TWIST IN FORM.

THE TWIST + SHORT HANDLE ALLOWS/ENCOURAGES DIFFERENT HAND POSITIONS GIVEN HANDLE TO ARMY BODY LOCATIONS & HOPEFULLY COMFORT AND EFFICIENCY

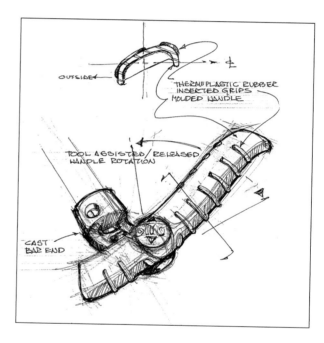

OUTSIDE

THERMOPLASTIC RUBBER INSERTED GRIPS MOLDED HANDLE

TOOL ASSISTED/RELEASED HANDLE ROTATION

CAST BAR END

Figure 7-14a
Figure 7-14b
Figure 7-14c
Figure 7-14d
(Kevin Reeder)
This is a short sequence of conceptual drawings similar to the
more extensive previous sequence. However, these drawings focus
on the development of an articulated handle requiring the
designer to go beyond form to explore how the articulation will
work in relationship to materials and connection hardware.

Figure 7-15

(Joseph Koncelik)

These "thumbnail" drawings use pen line on white copy paper. These drawings are part of a presentation on bathing and toileting products used by older adults.

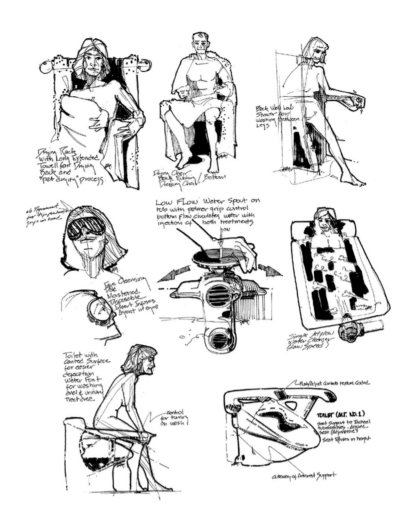

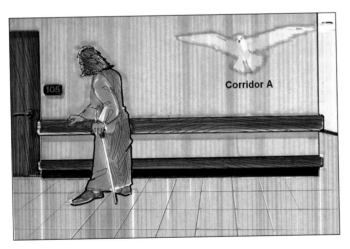

Figure 7-16a

Figure 7-16b

(Joseph Koncelik)

Two freehand mixed media drawings illustrate developing a conceptual visualization of a long-term care facility. In the drawing on the left, graphic images and text signify the place within a corridor setting. Handrails and lower bumper rails accommodate users with differing levels of ambulatory ability. The drawing at right provides information about using a divider to split a double room space—but also indicates the necessity of socialization.

Figure 7-17a
Figure 7-17b
(Joseph Koncelik)
These are initial conceptual
drawings in a presentation using
mixed media, including: Verithin
pencils, Berol markers, and fine-
line and broad-tipped marker
pens. The sequence illustrates the
possible development of a long-
term care bed using bolsters to
house the mechanism of an
motorized adjustable bed
mechanism. Controls are
duplicated on either side to
enable use by individuals who
might be paralyzed on one side
of their body.

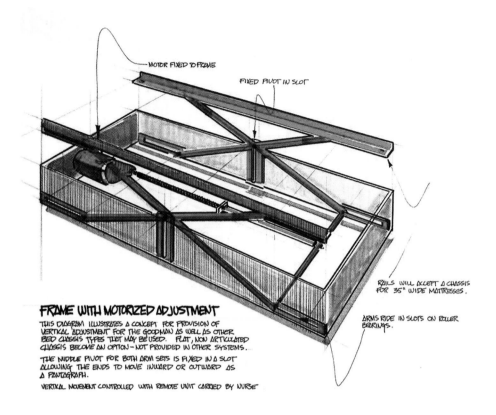

MOTOR FIXED TO FRAME

FIXED PIVOT IN SLOT

RAILS WILL ACCEPT A CHASSIS
FOR 35" WIDE MATTRESSES.

ARMS RIDE IN SLOTS ON ROLLER
BEARINGS.

FRAME WITH MOTORIZED ADJUSTMENT

THIS DIAGRAM ILLUSTRATES A CONCEPT FOR PROVISION OF
VERTICAL ADJUSTMENT FOR THE GOODMAN AS WELL AS OTHER
BED CHASSIS TYPES THAT MAY BE USED.   FLAT, NON ARTICULATED
CHASSIS BECOME AN OPTION - NOT PROVIDED IN OTHER SYSTEMS.

THE MIDDLE PIVOT FOR BOTH ARM SETS IS FIXED IN A SLOT
ALLOWING THE ENDS TO MOVE INWARD OR OUTWARD AS
A PANTOGRAPH.

VERTICAL MOVEMENT CONTROLLED WITH REMOTE UNIT CARRIED BY NURSE

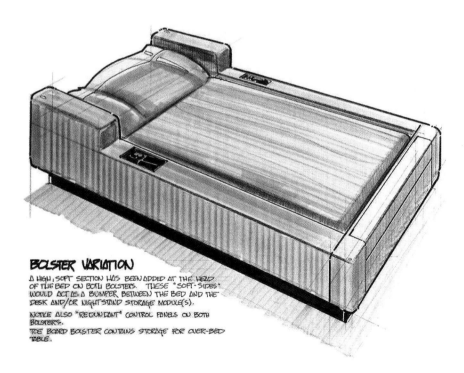

BOLSTER VARIATION

A HIGH, SOFT SECTION HAS BEEN ADDED AT THE HEAD
OF THE BED ON BOTH BOLSTERS.   THESE "SOFT-SIDES"
WOULD ACT AS A BUMPER BETWEEN THE BED AND THE
DESK AND/OR NIGHTSTAND STORAGE MODULE(S).

NOTICE ALSO "REDUNDANT" CONTROL PANELS ON BOTH
BOLSTERS.
TOE BOARD BOLSTER CONTAINS STORAGE FOR OVER-BED
TABLE.

Figure 7-18a
Figure 7-18b
(Joseph Koncelik)
The bed must provide amenities such
as an over-bed table (variations shown
at right). The drawing of a human
figure further enhances the context of
use and scale.

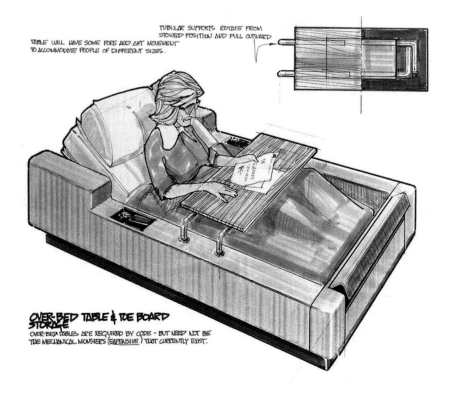

Figure 7-19a
Figure 7-19b
(Kevin Reeder)
The side panel illustration is graphic treatment for a traveling exhibition on the Columbus Zoo in Columbus, Ohio. Reeder's capacity to handle human figures consistently with the level of drawing used to depict the vehicle is in evidence.

Figure 7-20a
Figure 7-20b
Figure 7-20c
(Kevin Reeder)
Three portable phone sketches in this composition are represented overlays from one base drawing, illustrating variations in surface treatment. Note the manner in which the recess for the speaker is handled—giving the visual impression of edge radii and plastic material.

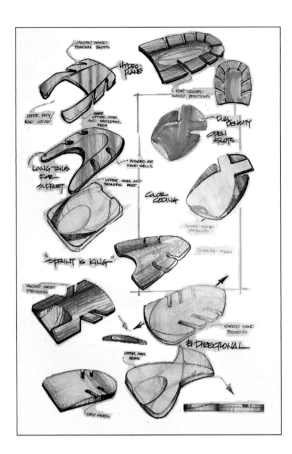

Figure 7-21
(Paul Reeder)
This composite of drawings is a novel way to present conceptual drawing information on design variations for swimming practice kickboards. This is a collection of drawings assembled in a collage (paste-up) that provides potential solutions to the problem.

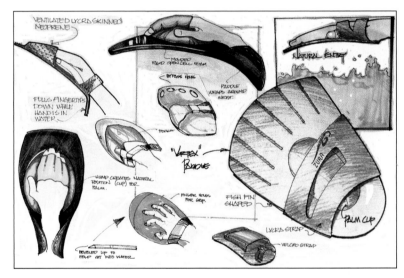

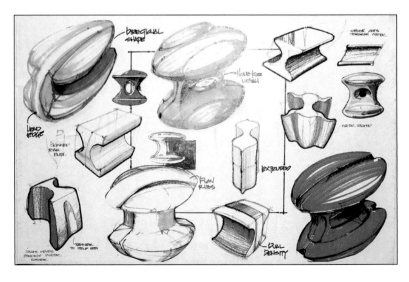

Figure 7-22a
Figure 7-22b
(Paul Reeder)
Additional variations are shown on practice equipment for swimming training including flippers, hand-paddles, devices to keep legs together, and other ideas.

Figure 7-23a
Figure 7-23b
(R. Preston Bruning)
These drawings represent two mixed-media drawings on vellum tracing paper. They are two conceptual vehicles drawn in their operating environment. Both drawings are freehand and are complete with regard to background—using both sides of the tracing paper to obtain the desired visual effects.

Figure 7-24a
Figure 7-24b
(R. Preston Bruning)
These concepts are mixed-media drawing on vellum tracing paper and show Bruning's deft handling of form in transition, geometric form development, reflections, and surfaces. The media include Prismacolor pencils, marker, pastels, and fine-line pens. Of significance is Bruning's ability to capture the essence of imaginary landscapes—the result of careful observation over time.

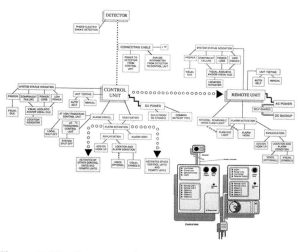

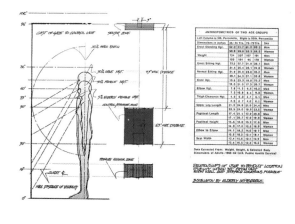

Figure 7-25a, Figure 7-25b

(Joseph Koncelik)

Presentation of initial concepts may include issues related to project development through research. This presentation begins with the development of systems information (left) and anthropometry (right) critical to the development of a residential fire-detection system.

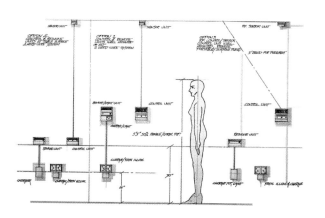

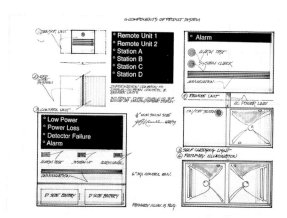

Figure 7-26a, Figure 7-26b

(Joseph Koncelik)

Understanding the potential of the system and the characteristics of various users is illustrated to provide information about the locations of devices as well as the array of information that must be displayed by the units. In addition, lack of electrical current requires battery-charged illumination.

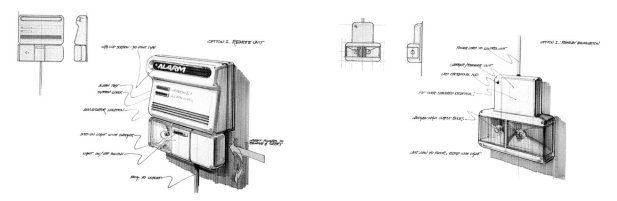

Figure 7-27a, Figure 7-27b

(Joseph Koncelik)

Beyond the presentation of research information and establishment of the criteria for design, there is the development of specific products—their look and feel. This sequence of drawings provides variations on the theme of wall-mounted devices, including ideas about materials, assembly, power packages, control, and display.

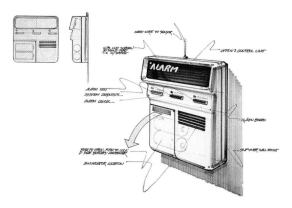

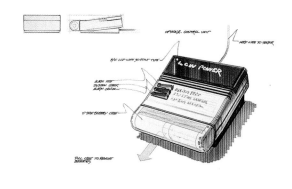

Figure 7-28a, Figure 7-28b
(Joseph Koncelik)
Variations of power pack placements as well as adaptation to
surface are important concepts to explore. These drawings have
been executed in mixed media (pencils, pens, and markers) using
freehand techniques and line work is made true by using cardboard
straight edges.

TIP - When drawing a vent pattern, include a
darker shadow line to show that the vent is
an opening. ■

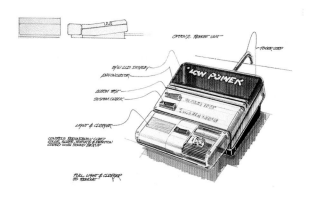

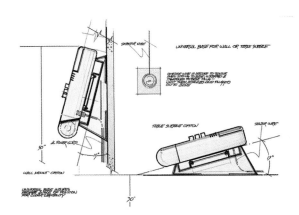

Figure 7-29a, Figure 7-29b
(Joseph Koncelik)
These additional detailed conceptual drawings show the potential for developing a reversible base allowing for wall-mounted and
tabletop use.

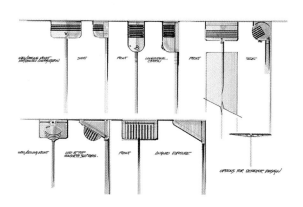

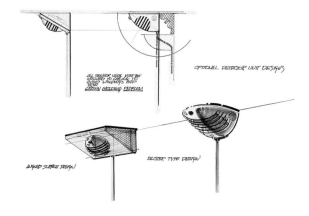

Figure 7-30a
Figure 7-30b
(Joseph Koncelik)
Multiple concepts for the sensor end of the smoke detector are shown in this set of initial drawings where the sensor was placed at the
junction of the wall and ceiling. Later drawings show a change in this conception since the "boundary layer" of air at the ceiling prevents
smoke from reaching the ceiling height. The sensor is best placed six inches below the ceiling height.

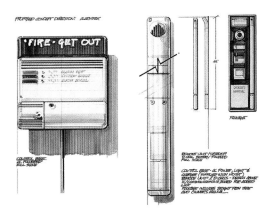

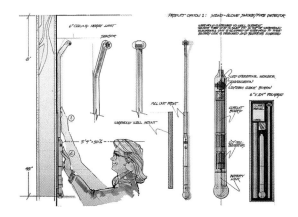

Figure 7-31a
Figure 7-31b
(Joseph Koncelik)
As conceptual development progressed, the idea about power source and total array of products changed. From the initial conceptual development of a hard-wired system, the product envisioned became a battery-powered device without the use of consoles for control and display.

Figure 7-32a
Figure 7-32b
(Joseph Koncelik)
The initial concept development was a very small part—in terms of time consumption—of the entire project. The intent from the beginning of the project was to develop an operational prototype. The photographs at right illustrate that culmination of the project.

The idea was to produce a fire-warning system that could be used and maintained without the usual overhead problems from using current technology. All of the anthropometric data reviewed at the beginning of the project were essential in devising a product that could be operated by adults of various heights and sizes—yet prevent access by children too young to understand this technology's uses. The product parts were eventually drawn in ProEngineer

and those data were used to generate stereo lithographic prototype cases and extension rods. Battery access was from the bottom of the lower casing. The warning signal is audible for adults with moderate hearing loss—meaning that the frequency of sound selected is in a lower register. This required more power from the batteries than the standard technology.

This project's conceptual process ran parallel to technology development—and several changes occurred along the way. A hardwired system gradually gave way to battery power. Accessory units were abandoned, and, most important, the original concept of a linked system with a central control unit was also abandoned. However, it was far less expensive to explore these options in conceptual drawings than to push ahead with full design development including prototypes that would eventually prove to be useless.

Additional problems for such novel technology and design arose because most fire alarm unit manufacturers have a vested interest in the technologies they produce. The costs to bring completely different technology and product forms into the market proved too expensive.

Again, explorations through visualization prior to engaging in full-bore engineering development saved time, energy, and resources. This validates the conceptual design process of which conceptual drawing is the most important aspect.

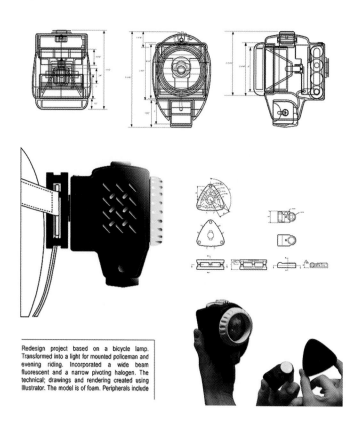

Redesign project based on a bicycle lamp. Transformed into a light for mounted policeman and evening riding. Incorporated a wide beam fluorescent and a narrow pivoting halogen. The technical; drawings and rendering created using Illustrator. The model is of foam. Peripherals include

Figure 7-33

(Suzanne Boyden)

This composite of engineering drawings, illustrator drawing, and dense foam model mockup is the first in a sequence of web site pages representing a portfolio. As such, great care was taken to present the work well graphically for the highest amount of visual impact.

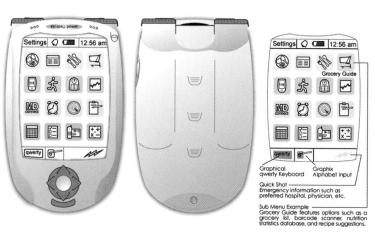

Nutrition
Tools assist with tracking eating habits, invigorating meal plans through a recipe database, opening up dining possibilities beyond the home through a restaurant nutrition planner, and a similar grocery shopping feature.

Maintenance
The maintenance tools focus on daily guidance with an e-mail system for medical help, programmable alarms, and a logbook for life goals and plans to accomplish those goals.

Monitoring
This feature set includes an integrated glucose meter, an exercise log that calculates the effects on insulin and glucose levels, documentation areas for other statistics, and visual charts for statistics over a specified period of time.

Utilities
These tools are standard on most existing hand-held computers and contain a calendar that tracks diabetic actions as well as others, a daily to do list, a comprehensive address book, and a basic calculator.

Figure 7-34a
Figure 7-34b

(Suzanne Boyden)

The second in the sequence of Web-based portfolio images, this is a graduate thesis project requiring the development of a three-dimensional product as well as the graphical interface related to health care use.

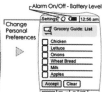

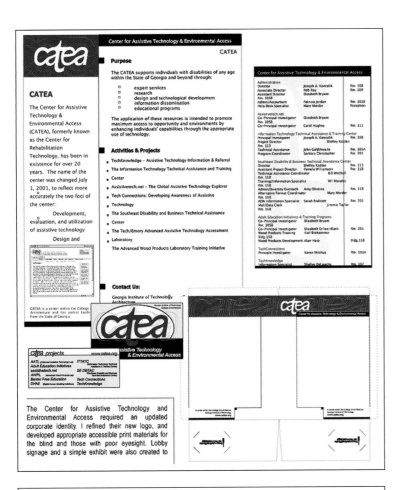

Figure 7-35
(Suzanne Boyden)
In reality, the design fields have no boundaries. Individuals educated as product and interior designers find themselves contributing to the graphic development of organizations as well as to their product design. Figures 7-35 and 7-36 represent work on a research center's identity as well as organization of information for the center's web site.

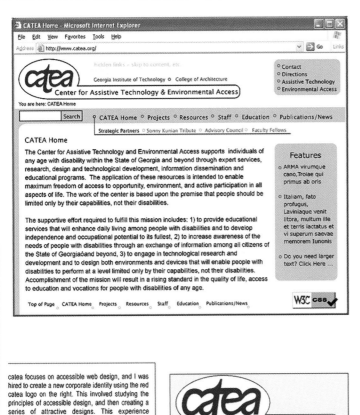

Figure 7-36
(Suzanne Boyden)
This is another in the sequence of Web-based portfolio pages. At left is the organization of materials beyond the "home" page. In addition, the center for which this web site was designed required that the materials on the web be accessible. The "W3C/CSS" designation in the lower right of the upper-boxed text indicates compliance with World Wide Web accessibility standards.

Figure 7-37
(Suzanne Boyden)
This page is the last in a sequence of six images representing Boyden's portfolio. The graphics and glove design were both results of a class project from which individual students drew their own project directions.

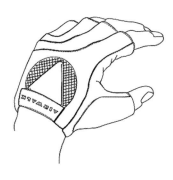

This group project focused on extending the corporate identity of a company into a sporting goods product. The glove's name, 'Aegis,' follows the group's use of an A for the first letter of each product. The graphic on the front of the package illustrates the mountain gloves with a simple biking

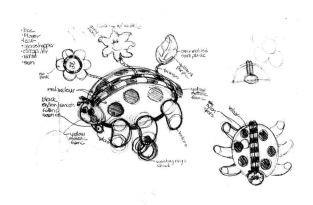

Figure 7-38a
Figure 7-38b
(Anne Letherby)
These initial drawings and refined conceptual drawings for the Sassy Company were intended to explore the company's next generation of product directions. This stroller toy is designed for an infant, and is placed on a stroller's front bar. The ladybug's body is made of soft velour. The middle legs are rings of varied colors and textures. The back of the ladybug opens to reveal a domed mirrored surface and three small ribbon-tethered toys. The flower contains a rattle and the sun is sewn with reflective material that crinkles when touched. The leaf is a soft plastic meant for teething.

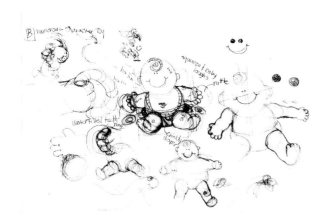

Figure 7-39a
Figure 7-39b
(Anne Letherby)
These two images represent an initial drawing and refined conceptual drawing of a plush stuffed baby doll for the Sassy Company. The doll is sewn of terrycloth and laughs when squeezed. The body parts are labeled so the baby can start making word associations. One of the doll's hands holds a water-filled "teether," while the other holds colorful textured rings.

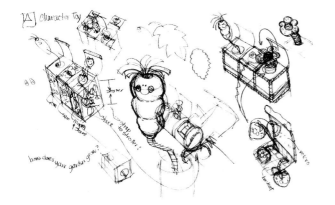

Figure 7-40a
Figure 7-40b
(Anne Letherby)
These two drawings represent another infant toy for Sassy: a stroller toy with a garden theme. It is sewn of colorful cotton material and attaches to the front of the stroller bar with short Velcro straps. Three material flaps open to show toys hidden inside. The image of the toy inside is shown on the outside of the flap. The first section of the garden holds a terrycloth stuffed carrot. The carrot is "planted" inside a hole and can be pulled out by the ribbon tuft on the top. The next section of garden contains a flower on a spring that pops up when the flap is opened. The third section houses a basketful of ribbon-tethered strawberries.

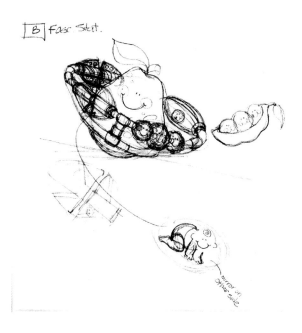

Figure 7-41a
Figure 7-41b
(Anne Letherby)
Additional explorations of infant toy concepts incorporate bright colors and interesting surface designs to visually intrigue and occupy the child. Called the "Fascination Station," Letherby's design is a reworking of an earlier toy with a new theme, look, and revamped activities. The product is meant for attachment to a highchair tray. The new version has a textured bottom that produces sounds as the toy wobbles around on the surface of the tray. Four different activities are placed around the perimeter.

B Fascination Station   Concept by Anne Letherby for Sassy, Inc.

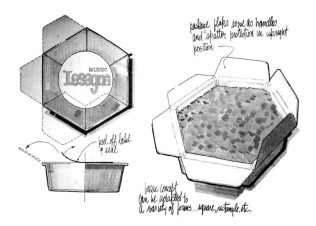

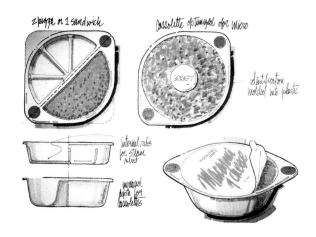

Figure 7-42a
Figure 7-42b
(David Tompkins)
Designers may be called on to serve a myriad of client needs—including the development of convenience food packaging. In such conceptual development, the graphic resolutions are integral with the product development—in this case, the provision of molded plastic containers with seals. Notice that the foodstuffs are abstract, but sufficiently representational to convey the contents.

Figure 7-43a
Figure 7-43b
(David Tompkins)
These two drawings are initial concepts for Gilbarco, the manufacturer of gasoline "vending" machines for several of the largest oil companies. These drawings have been done as modifications to a "blue-line" print. A basic perspective outline is developed that can be reproduced in quantity and then "over-drawn" using mixed media—in this instance markers and pen line—to convey the form and also the relationship to use.

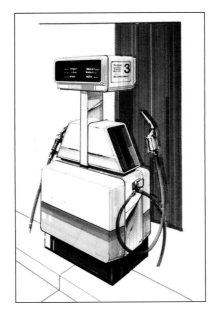
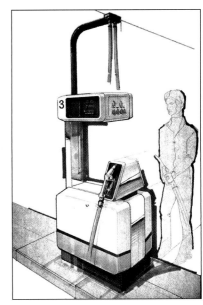

Figure 7-44
(David Tompkins)
This perspective construction is essential for developing multiple drawings that contain complex visual information. The over-drawings are shown in Figures 7-45, 7-46, and 7-47 Constructing the perspective rather than intuitively sketching freehand perspective guidelines was necessary in this phase of conceptualization because consistent details were required from drawing to drawing. In addition, a number of components for the "Shopsmith" product were and are interchangeable—and that visualization was required for consistency.

Note, however, that even with the development of a mechanical two-point perspective, there are elements of the under-drawing or "underlay" that are developed without construction—such as the large ellipsoid form that is the guide for the saw blade as well as the center shaft location for the lathe fixture.

The final conceptual drawings are large, in the format of 18" by 24" with the visualized parts on the page composing the full machine base and fixtures as well as enlargements of specific parts.

The media include markers, pens, and, of course, Prismacolor blue and brown lines for guides on the underlay.

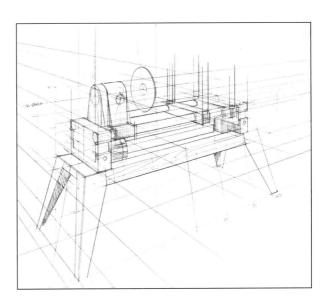

TIP - It is okay to use ellipse guides and straight edges while you sketch—especially to "true-up" a drawing. ▦

Use of Storyboarding in Presentation

Conceptual drawing can be used to go beyond specific images of form and space to include exploring the problem conditions, the environment, and sequences of use. The product designer is typically charged with developing form as well as control and display for specific technologies. The appropriateness of the form and its functional characteristics will also be determined by the environment of use, times of use, characteristics of specific users, and also the relationship of one technology to other technologies. These are only a few of the considerations that should be examined as part of a conceptual exploration.

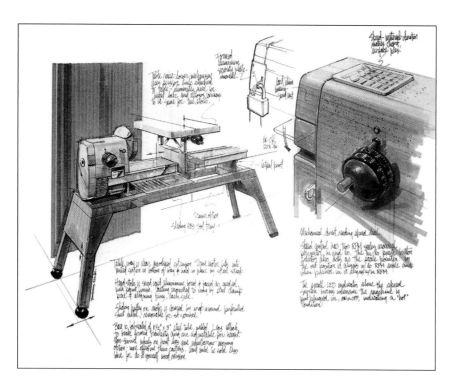

TIP - Be sure to construct graphics on a cylinder to the curve of the object and to the shortening curve of the cylinder. ▪

Figure 7-45

(David Tompkins)

The next set of drawings is relatively more complex than typical conceptual drawings. The Shopsmith product is an interesting multiple-tool workstation that has several functions: lathe operations, drilling, shaping, and cutting. The role of the industrial designer, in this team-based project, was to bring specific applied human factors in conceptual development of control and display. Over time, the Shopsmith product has been successful and has evolved to meet or exceed consumer demand as well as ever-changing technologies.

The conceptual drawings for this product were larger and more complex than for other products. The drawings had to be large enough to capture details, but remain smaller than the actual product. The mechanical perspective shown previously was the underlay drawing used to position various views of the full product and exploded views of components.

The drawings provide critical human-factor information, including: positioning of controls and display with an emphasis on safe operations; selection of controls; and positioning of components—including locking mechanisms—that prevent accidents with machine use.

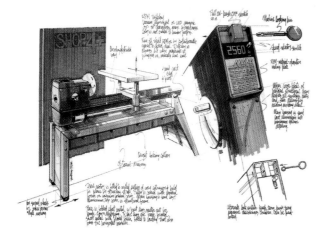

TIP - Draw through the object so that you sketch it as if it is transparent. This will allow you to draw the object and features on the back that may be seen from the selected point of view. ▪

Figure 7-46

(David Tompkins)

In terms of novice design students approaching conceptual drawing for the first time, the Shopsmith drawings exemplify the breadth and depth of the conceptual drawing. Conceptual drawings are not simply vague conceptions of a generalized idea without detail. Rather, as these drawing illustrate, conceptual drawing provides specific information about details. As drawing capacity is developed, it is possible to convey ideas about materials and production methods. Functional attributes such as moving parts, locking mechanisms, and membrane-switch control pads can be drawn and shown as options.

Earlier text covered the use of backgrounds. In this conceptual drawing, the background is deftly used as a graphic panel.

The process by which these drawings were executed begins with an underlay drawing—likely done using a Prismacolor Verithin pencil. High-quality vellum tracing paper would be the final surface medium— one that accepts marker readily. The general form of the object would be drawn with gray markers. Backgrounds such as the blue rectilinear form would be placed in back of the gray marker forms and then the drawing "tightened up" using pen and pencil lines.

Regardless of the large amount of information provided on each drawing, there is ample white space and careful attention to the overall composition of both drawing and text.

Figure 7-47
(David Tompkins)
Each drawing shows variations in
design. Each of the three drawings
shown has different ideas for the base of
the machine. That base is the support
structure for a variety of components
that can be mounted alone or with other
tools for various machining operations.

Clearly, the higher the level of
visualization in two dimensions, the
better the communication of ideas to
others. The Shopsmith drawings are
examples of the importance of
communication through visualization.
Decisions for the Shopsmith's design are
the result of communication between the
designer and other members of the
product development team.

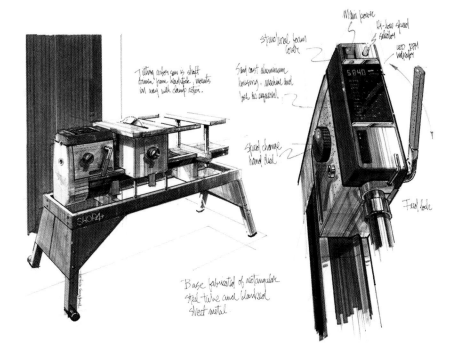

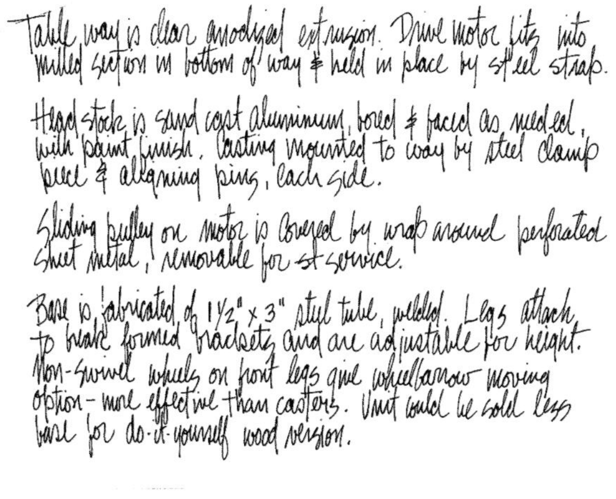

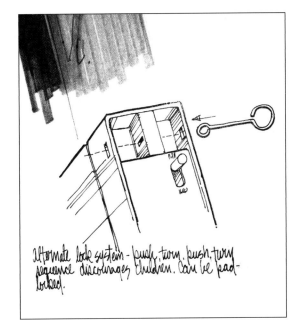

Figure 7-48a
Figure 7-48b
(David Tompkins)
Tompkins exhibits a unique style in the use of text. His writing is a form of vertically oriented script. This is unusual because
few individuals have a cursive style of writing that would be sufficiently clear—or complementary to conceptual drawing—as
to be useful.

This style of writing text is difficult to emulate, but effective for the talented individual who created these drawings.

Figure 7-49a
Figure 7-49b
(Noel Mayo)
Designer Noel Mayo was given the challenge of conveying accuracy from the very beginning of the design process for the development of interior concepts that ranged from interior architecture at entrances to the more personal spaces of individual offices. His designs were developed over Lawson charts, allowing rapid development of conceptual information with complete fidelity to the spaces for which the designs were intended.

Storyboarding can be similar to task analysis in that it permits visualization of the order in which a device or and environment (especially a work environment) is used. This converts the "deductive" process of visual thinking to a form of analysis that permits a broader and deeper understanding of the design problem. In addition, using storyboarding will help communicate project-development issues to others with immediacy and readily understood methods.

The motion picture industry relies heavily on storyboards to describe the visual sequences of the cinematic filming process (Shay and Duncan, 1991, Fraioli, 2000 and Tumminello, 2003, Begleiter, 2001). Storyboarding describes visually how the motion picture flows from beginning to end, how the characters interact, and where transitions and/or gaps exist in the storyline. Beyond its use in the film and advertising industries, storyboarding has applications in the design process,

Figure 7-50a
Figure 7-50b
(Noel Mayo)
Interior design and specification encompasses challenges that include the product development of millwork as well as the suppliers' specification of furnishings—rather than using furnishings created by the interior designer. Therefore, the fidelity that begins with dimensional accuracy extends to providing the appearance and dimensional accuracy of the specified furnishings.

as discussed by Landay and Myers, and also in the development of business strategies on a web source by Murphy and Salinas. In addition to books and articles on this subject, Brian Bailey's Web-based publication discusses storyboarding's wide application in the development of computer interactivity. In the design of products, storyboards also can be used as an analysis, conceptualization, and communication tool. A storyboard visually describes how users will interact with the product from start to finish and also can depict individual steps in that process that need further examination and possible change. This detailed examination leads to innovative product solutions that can successfully address a greater share of the users' needs and expectations.

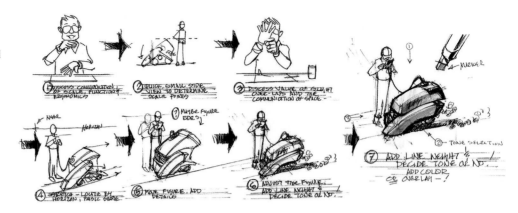

Visual Storyboards can be generated in several ways. Movie storyboards are often hand-drawn for speed and visualization of the story and action. For industrial designers, both photographic and hand-drawn methods may be used. Hand-drawn methods are most appropriate when it is necessary to quickly examine the process of use and conceptualization is the intent. It is important to note that hand-drawn storyboards are not limited by the designer's skill and, as such, stick figures communicate images as well as a full-color rendering. Regardless of the media, the storyboard allows the designer to examine the sequences of use, a form of task analysis.

Visual storyboards can help designers analyze the process of using a product and can encourage an expanded development of additional new product concepts. For instance, the operational process (sometimes drawn as a link diagram) for a common electrical kitchen product may include the following operational steps:

1. Remove the product from storage.
2. Plug the power cord into the outlet.
3. Turn the product on.
4. Complete the task.
5. Turn the product off.
6. Remove the power cord from the outlet.
7. Clean the product.
8. Replace the product in storage.

In the process of designing this product, Step number 4, "Complete the task," may be given priority. By storyboarding the overall process, designers can visualize and develop solutions for steps in the process that are not prioritized and perhaps are not addressed by competitive products. In this manner, the new product can surpass the user's expectations by offering more than "complete the task" to the consumer. As a conceptualization exercise, the design team can use visualization to examine how the priority of the design objectives may change through product use. For instance, in Step 1 of the process described earlier, storing the power cord is a significant issue, while in Step 4, cord storage is not as significant.

Employing visual storyboarding to achieve innovation is demonstrated in this chapter through the drawings of Kevin Reeder. In

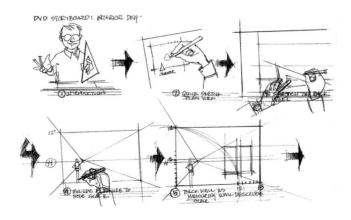

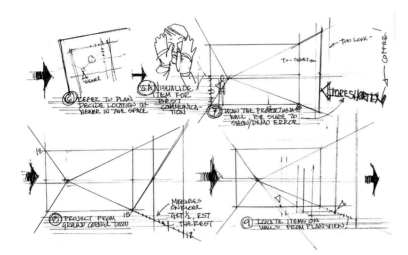

Figure 7-53a
Figure 7-53b
(Kevin Reeder)
These selections are the first in a series of
storyboards that guided the development of the
DVD video sessions for Kevin Reeder. The drawing
below is the first overlay on a single-point
perspective construction.

Reeder's drawings, the designer addresses the stable market of lunchboxes where change and innovation have been traditionally limited to product graphics or surface material treatments. In this example, storyboards were used to examine the process of commuting to an office with a lunchbox and briefcase. By addressing the issue this way, several product solutions were generated that potentially address new market segments for the production and sale of adult lunchboxes. An experienced designer might search his or her mind and identify opportunities for alternative products without using a storyboard. However, even in that situation, the images created by using this technique are valuable communication tools to other people involved in the design process—including clients who may better understand the importance of specific product ideas as a result of visualizing the process of use.

A product development team often includes people representing different disciplines: industrial design; design and marketing research; product development engineering; electrical engineering; marketing and sales; business and finance; and manufacturing and engineering. User advocates are frequently brought into the product-development process through so-called "focus groups." All these individuals have different input to the developmental process and contribute to the new product's success. Their points of view, though initially different, will move toward

Figure 7-54a
Figure 7-54b
(Kevin Reeder)
This demonstrates further refinement and development of the initial single-point perspective sketch, as Reeder explains in the DVD.

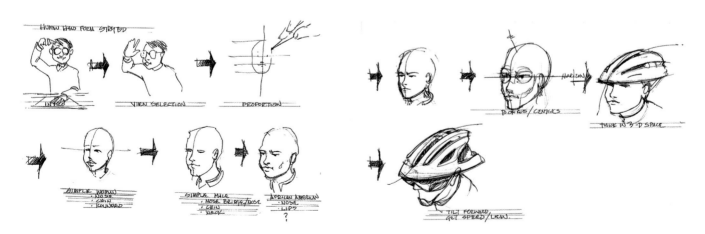

Figure 7-55a
Figure 7-55b
(Kevin Reeder)
These selections represent a segment in the DVD on developing products for the human head, in this case a helmet. Reeder guides his own discussion of the development of the sketch that begins with drawing the head and surrounding it with a form meant for protection.

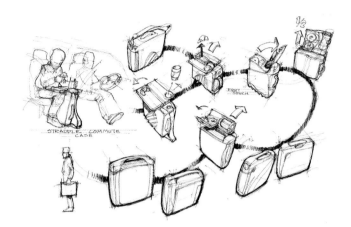

Figure 7-56
(Kevin Reeder)
Conceptualizing requires an analytical approach as well as one that combines different ideas. Reeder conveys the use of a "storyboard" form of conceptual drawing that permits the designer to investigate various aspects of the design task that otherwise might not be seen as part of the problem or the solution.

Figure 7-57a
Figure 7-57b
(Kevin Reeder)
The sense of storyboarding completely explores a sequence of activities that will provide the designer insights into conditions and criteria for product development—and explore situations and activities where multiple products are operated within environments. This sequence of "boards" explores female and male operators as they use a lift truck from a delivery's beginning to using it at the destination. It starts when packages are taken from the delivery van.

Figure 7-58a
Figure 7-58b
(Kevin Reeder)
These drawings continue the
sequence of operations related to
lift-truck design and operation. The
delivery person moves the lift truck
off and over the rear end of the van
and then must assemble the
packages for specific destinations.
From a human factor standpoint,
lifting is a key aspect of the task.
The package placement must also
expedite the process to avoid undue
back stress. One critical safety issue
is that the delivery person must exit
the truck by jumping to the ground.
This might make designers consider
a fold-out stepping surface that
would reduce the possibility of falls.

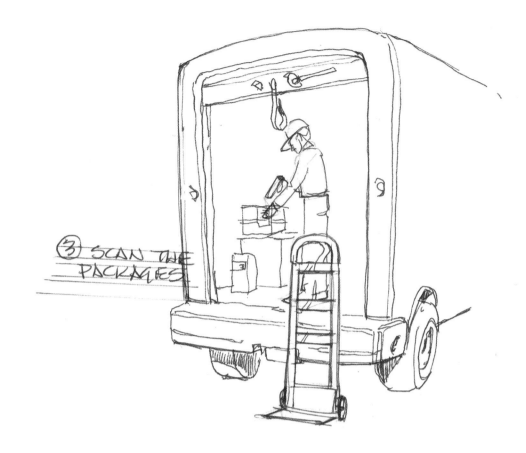

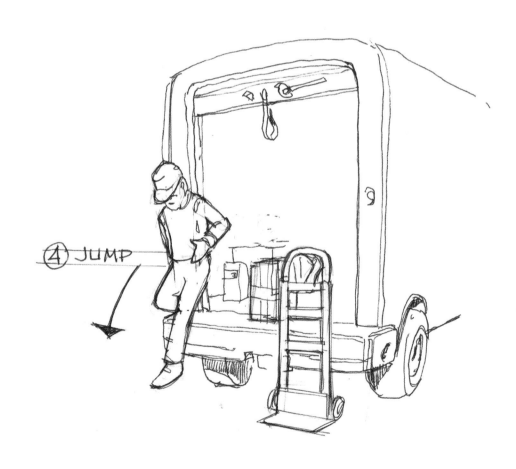

Figure 7-59a
Figure 7-59b
(Kevin Reeder)
Loading the hand truck should raise the consideration of reach to the packages and then placement of the packages on the lift truck—requiring bending and stress on the back. In the image on the left, the visualization should provoke discussion—if not consideration—of developing design solutions in response to the physical stress issues arising from this aspect of the task.

Figure 7-60a
Figure 7-60b
(Kevin Reeder)
Lift trucks expedite movement of
objects over distances and also up
stairs. One critical consideration
that must be addressed regards the
disparity between male and female
users. When the lift truck moves, its
angle changes with the height of the
user. The smaller the user, the
further out the wheels will be from
the body—and more of the load's
weight will be carried by the arms.
Theoretically, the best condition of
use is when the truck's angle of tilt
is just beyond the load's center of
gravity, requiring less arm strength
to move the loaded truck over
surfaces.

greater harmony through understanding a product design in the context of use. Various professions utilize different languages, and the
storyboard picture becomes worth the proverbial
thousand words—and more. The storyboard can
then be a useful tool for keeping individuals with
a variety of viewpoints focused on common

objectives and in closer agreement about the
product design.

**Conclusions about Conceptual
Drawing and Design Visualization**
Everyone benefits from watching others draw.
Seeing how another designer or artist seems to

Figure 7-61a
Figure 7-61b
(Kevin Reeder)
Moving the loaded lift truck over surfaces requires constant maneuvering with the arms and positioning of the legs. Different surfaces will either provide vibration into the truck and/or jostle the load.

effortlessly accomplish their work is an important way to build drawing skill. Drawing instructors provide essential information for students, but the context is formal if not formidable. As this text has brought out, drawing instructors should demonstrate drawing and muster the confidence to show students their ability. An instructor must demonstrate drawing—or bring in others to do so—for a drawing class to be successful. One-on-one demonstration and working back and forth between the instructor and the student is also extremely beneficial.

The student of drawing is way ahead of students in previous generations because electronic media such as the videotape can be a marvelous tutor. Numerous videos and books on drawing are available. The modern technological world is replete with visual images and there is much to learn from the work of others. No lack of material inhibits those who want to know more about drawing. What may be missing is the tutorial. A relaxed personalized drawing session is an important form of tutorial removed from the pressure and dictates of the classroom. In the middle of the twentieth century, Pratt Institute's fabled undergraduate program in industrial design benefited from having supremely talented students who taught one another how to draw. The method of "empathic" drawing was carried on from student to student by upperclassmen teaching students in the beginning classes—informally—in apartments all over Brooklyn near the Pratt Institute campus, without the pressure of the course. This method became so

Figure 7-62a
Figure 7-62b
(Kevin Reeder)
Movement on and off elevators requires crossing a gap between the floor and the interior surface of the elevator floor. The larger the wheels on the lift truck, the easier this maneuver will be. Many lift trucks have a foot bar across the rear of the device to allow the user to push forward with the foot to move through this type of surface area. When positioning the lift truck in the elevator, others who may be using the elevator at the same time must also be considered.

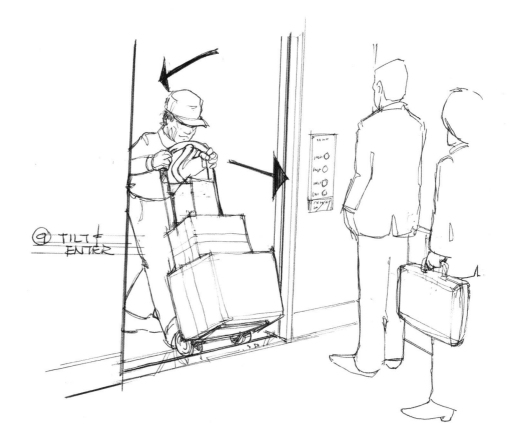

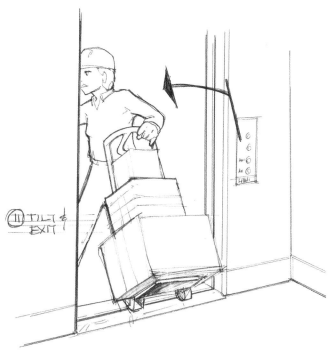

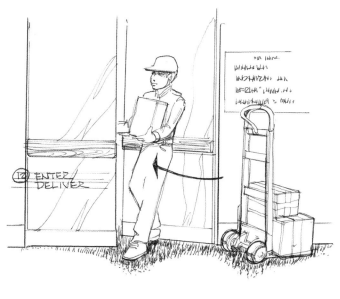

Figure 7-63a, Figure 7-63b
(Kevin Reeder)
Exiting an elevator means moving the lift truck by pulling rather than
pushing. Using a pulling motion makes it easier to move the wheels out of
the gap between floor surfaces. Nevertheless, arm strength is required and is
continually tested during these activities.

Figure 7-64a, Figure 7-64b
(Kevin Reeder)
Loading and unloading and manually lifting and carrying packages from the truck are the delivery person's job. Considerations that arise
include, but are not limited to, using support belts to prevent back injuries and protective footwear to reduce foot injuries from dropped
packages. OSHA requirements dictate the total weight of any given package, but size and proportion add to the problem, and awkwardness
can lead to lifting difficulties. These are considerations for the largest male and smallest female delivery persons.

standardized from the mid-1950s through the 1960s that instructors generally gave up teaching drawing in design classes and expected students to be able to produce conceptual drawings without much formal instruction.

History is an important teacher because it informs about the future. This text has empha-

sized the importance of mastering manual drawing skills because they are fast, efficient, timesaving, and economical. The more subjective side of conceptual drawing and design visualization is definitely more rewarding. The ability to draw well and to approach drawing with confidence translates into a designer believing that he or she

Figure 7-65

(Kevin Reeder)

The sequence of twelve drawings that begins with Figure 7-65 and ends with Figure 7-67, depicts the stages of behavior and use of amenities in showering. The storyboard technique provides clues to the range of product applications and the issues involved in using a curved wall-corner shower stall.

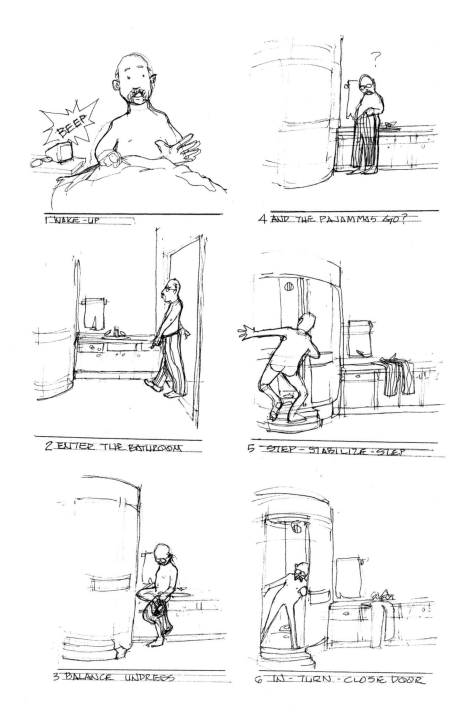

can always rely upon their creative "juices" in virtually any problem-solving situation. Hopefully, this text—a discussion of teaching and learning conceptual drawing and design visualization—has been fruitful for the reader and that their capacity for drawing and communicating will advance.

This chapter reinforces one of the most important points of the text: conceptual drawing is a tool to communicate ideas to others. Conceptual drawing is primarily a means of working through ideas on paper. However, the design process is not a soliloquy with the communication following a circular route from one side of the brain to the other.

To develop this form of visual communication, there are specific practice measures beyond knowing the fundamentals that are essential if

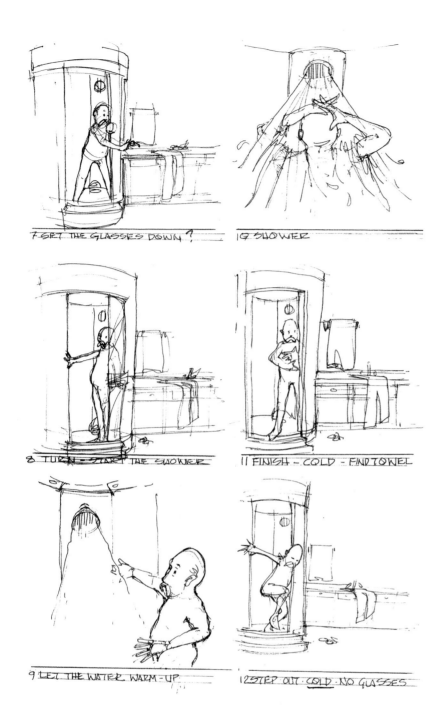

Figure 7-66
(Kevin Reeder)
The sequence of operations in using the
shower stall is shown here. Also identified
are serious safety issues that may arise from
the user exiting the shower with wet
slippery feet.

the skills of conceptual drawing are to be fully
understood, assimilated, and utilized effectively.
The following list summarizes the major points
of this chapter.

1. When communicating to others through conceptual drawing, allow the visual image to state
everything possible that is visual. Allow text in an
appropriate lettering style to communicate—and

supplement—everything that only verbal information can cover.

2. There is a sequence in the use of mixed
media instruments that is a workable convention,
starting with rough pencil drawings, moving to
the use of markers, and finalizing the drawing
with bold- and fine-line pens. While all uses of
tools can be varied in sequence, the order of
mixed media tools presented works well enough.

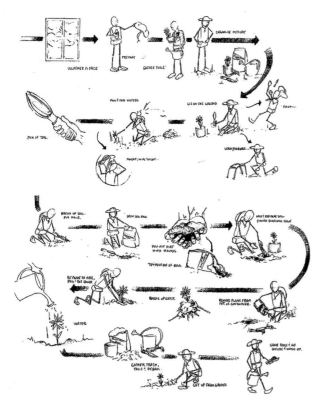

Figure 7-67
(Megan Roe)
This sequence of conceptual storyboard drawings examines the flow of operations involved in gardening. Through this analytical thought process, ideas about product development are revealed.

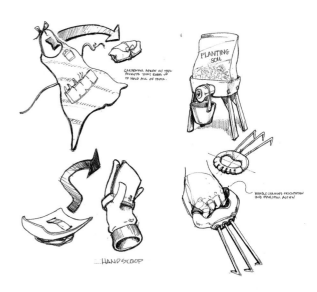

Figure 7-68
(Megan Roe)
These drawings represent outcomes from examining operations that were the subject of the storyboard In Figure 7-67.

3. The authors of this text emphasize that individual practice—outside the classroom—is the most appropriate way for the individual student to assimilate conceptual drawing skills. There are warm-up exercises that have been referred to as "running the scales." Students are advised to set aside time for drawing and focus on developing skills through freehand drawings of "favorite things" from memory. Inventive interpretation is also highly recommended.

4. Conceptual drawing has applications as design methodology. The use of image making in sequences called "storyboarding" has been a useful tool for many in the examination of a design problem, task analysis, exploration of human/computer interactivity, and even in the creation of business strategies.

5. Time management and focusing on the task at hand is part of the discipline of drawing. Students are advised to avoid distracting environments and the myth of "multi-tasking" by watching television or surfing the Internet while drawing.

Figure 7-69
(Kevin Reeder)
As a reminder of the fundamentals, conceptual drawing begins with the line work generated without erasures and refined through overlays. The steps in the sequence have been consistent throughout the examples uses in the text—even when enhanced using computer graphics software.

Figure 7-70
(Michael Butcher)
Reeder demonstrates the uses of storyboarding in identifying problems that arise in the use of products—a way to uncover potential design solutions.

See DVD Segment 6, Presentation and Communication, demonstrating uses of storyboarding in the development of products.

6. Seeking critical review of work is essential to growth and development. The classroom is a major component of critical review. However, seeking one-on-one reviews of work during an instructor's open office hours is a way to get a more focused individualized review of work.

7. Students should neither fear nor avoid review from others. There are rules to the game that both instructors and students should play by so that everyone benefits. The student then progresses and develops conceptual drawing skills to the highest level possible. Students who make excellent progress, produce presentation-quality drawing, and return favorable evaluations of teaching represent the instructor positively.

Forming good work habits—similar to the development of good study habits—is an enabling and empowering process. Rather than conceiving of the act of drawing as completely free-form in its practice, the student of design must be willing to accept a discipline and to work at it (practice) very hard. As has been illustrated in this chapter, developing good drawing ability is possible regardless of the starting point for any student. Some may progress to levels that are very high, while others may not. Nevertheless, every student in a design program should have adequate communication skills through conceptual drawing before their first interview for entry-level employment.

Figure 7-71
(Michael Butcher)
Segment 6, Presentation and Communication, of the DVD provides instruction on the uses of conceptual drawing in presentations with an emphasis on visual communication of ideas to others.

See DVD Segment 6, Presentation and Communication, demonstration on presentation using conceptual drawing.

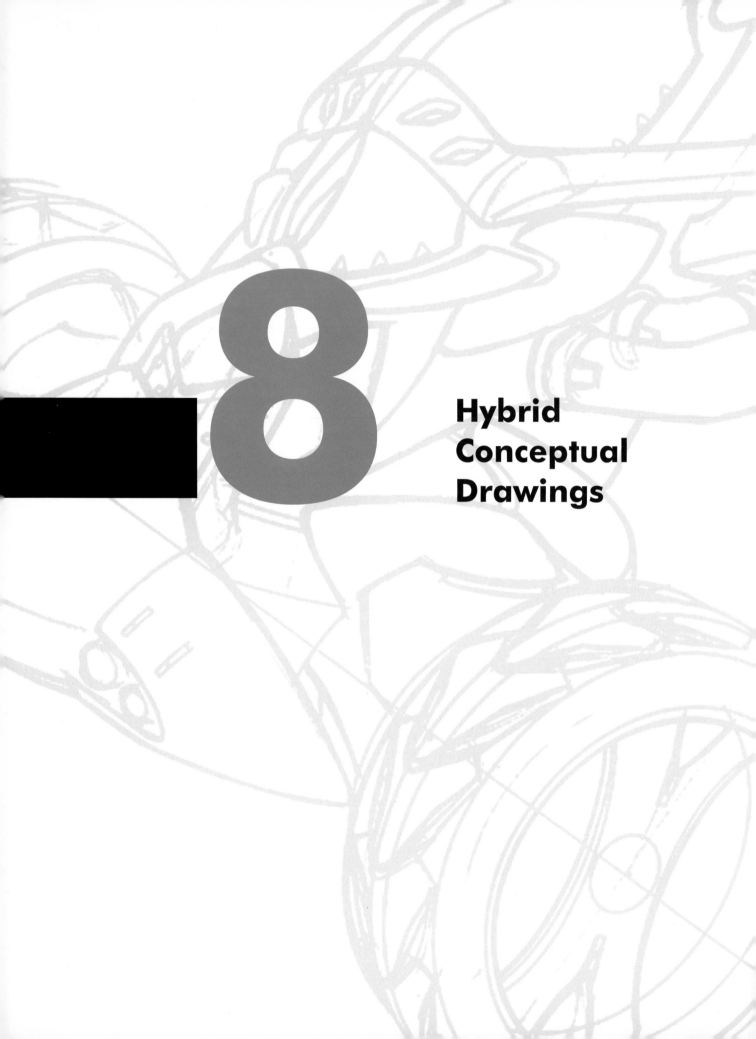

8

**Hybrid
Conceptual
Drawings**

Hybrids: The Fusion of Traditional Drawing with Digital Media

In the last three decades from 1970 through to the new century, CAD rendering programs and software such as Adobe Illustrator and Vellum have become widely used to generate visualizations of products—especially when definitive information was necessary for conversion to production. As stated previously, the initial process for developing three-dimensional views of objects is time-consuming on the computer and worthwhile only when it is necessary to create a database for repeated usage, production, and archiving. The computer is shrinking the time necessary for developing form when that form must relate to specific materials and manufacturing. From the quick sketch stage, designers move rapidly to solid modeling programs such as ProEngineer and AutoCAD, creating dimensionally accurate designs—*after* a series of decisions has been made about the direction of design. These three-dimensional computer visualizations are automatically translated into data used to generate stereolithography models and CNC-milled dies and molds. Computing has greatly reduced the time necessary to translate an idea into a manufactured product.

Another trend that surfaced relatively recently is known widely as "hybrid" conceptual drawing. This process allows for the speed of manually developed line drawings that are scanned and further "enhanced" using one or more software programs. In its simplest form, hybrid conceptual drawing uses tightly drawn images in line, which are scanned and then enhanced using Paint programs (commonly found in the operating software of most PCs and Macintosh computers. Adobe Photoshop and Adobe Illustrator are also frequently used in combination with Paint programs to enhance images. Hybridization does not stop there. Since all images in a computer are digitized, background photographic materials or architectural features such as the environment or setting for the designed object are easily applied and effective. In essence, the hybrid conceptual drawing process uses the best of two worlds, free-hand drawing and computer software enhancements, to produce effective visual communications.

It is worth noting that the concept of hybridization is far more broadly applied than just to conceptual drawing. The Internet has several web sites that have hybrid images—including fine arts abstractions as well as architectural applications. Architectural education and interior design

Figure 8-1a
Figure 8-1b
(Joseph Koncelik)
One of the easiest forms of "hybrid" computer-enhanced drawing is scanning in simple line drawings and then using a paint program to insert tone and color. A step up from this level would be to further enhance the drawing using Adobe Photoshop to "airbrush" in additional tones or to change the balance of the drawing by adjusting contrast and lightness as well as using other Photoshop tools.

programs have utilized the techniques of hybrid image making for a number of years. The concept has also broadened to include developing full educational programs. A paper presented at the *National Conference on Liberal Arts and the Education of Artists* by Sally L. Levine and Warren K. Wake (2000), entitled extols the virtues of hybridized education in the visual arts. As the authors of the paper state:

> "Hybrid teaching combines the best aspects of traditional education with the promising possibilities provided by new media to create a robust educational experience."

The authors envision a twenty-first century model of education in the visual arts utilizing aspects of traditional studio education combined with online education. In fact, institutions of higher education offering online courses—areas of study not necessarily intended for the on-campus traditional student—found that as much

as 60 percent of students accessing online courses reside on campus. In effect, students are designing their own hybridized education made up of the available components on campus and online—from any source across the globe.

It seems that hybridized design education as well as the development of hybridized image making are similar to forces of nature and possess an inevitability that is unstoppable. It also seems important if not critical for students learning the manual skills of drawing as well as becoming expert in the uses of computing and computer graphics to look for opportunities to combine both, to be inventive in the use of hybridization because efficiencies and cost benefits result.

"Hybrid" Computer-Enhanced Product Drawing

Recently, since the 1980s, a methodology called "reverse engineering" changed the process of designing. Three-dimensional models are

---

TIP - Make sure lines connect or intersect with all other lines to prevent "bleed" of colors applied through the software. ■

Figure 8-2a
Figure 8-2b
(Joseph Koncelik)
Color can be used to enhance the drawing's meaning, as in this case where a simple line drawing is converted in Paint to bring out the relationship between the sink, the water, and hand washing.

scanned—in the same way human figures are scanned for body measurement—and the shape of that model is manipulated using computer software to generate three-dimensional images. These images can become the basis for variations in form, making the computer-generated image a conceptual model.

The computer has not replaced the hand-drawn sketch, at least not yet. Manual quick sketching is done even faster than it was in the early 2000s out of necessity, but it is still done. It is inappropriate to characterize the difference between manually generated drawings and computer-generated imaging as a "rift." Rather than separate these two important aspects of generating design into distinct camps, the two forms of visualization can be melded into "hybrid" conceptual drawings. In its most simplified form, manually produced sketching is scanned into computer memory and then "enhanced" with the various tools and software available to the designer. This allows for the quick line sketch to become a more fully detailed object. It also permits the designer to make numerous variations of the design—especially to color—that can help clients decide all aspects of a finished product.

Conceptual drawing, as used by product designers, is not a major component of the graphic design process, so graphic designers have gravitated toward computer-generated imaging much faster than their counterparts in industrial and interior design. This is not to say graphic designers do not draw. Graphic design is a process that requires finished visualizations—especially including finished text—more quickly than in those professions where a two-dimensional drawing is only a precursor to a three-dimensional resolution of form and space.

This chapter intends to provide the student of conceptual drawing and design visualization a visual library. What follows is a series of portfolios that illustrate the diversity of approaches to visualization, from simple line drawings to fully

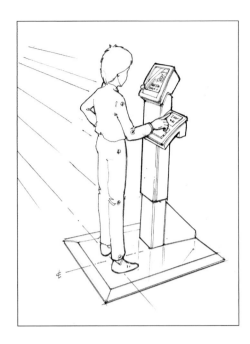

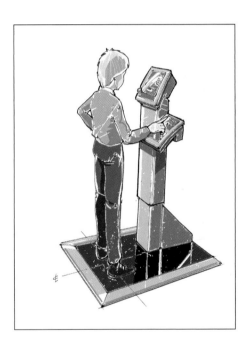

Figure 8-3a
Figure 8-3b
(Kevin Reeder hybridized by Joseph Koncelik)
As images become three-dimensional, color manipulation allows for development of shade and shadow.

Figure 8-4a
Figure 8-4b
(Kevin Reeder hybridized by
Joseph Koncelik)
There are significant advantages in
hybridizing interior drawings
through use of Photoshop tools
such as using "rendering" functions
to establish lighting effects and
running a "high pass" filter to
develop color gradation.

developed high-resolution computer-enhanced
drawings. Since rendering applies a formal and
mechanical approach to creating a single image,
these portfolios will not be regarded as collections of renderings. For the most part, the overwhelming number of drawings are freehand
perspectives that were enhanced using several
variations of computer software. Captions for
drawings and sets of drawings will provide information about how these visualizations were
generated.

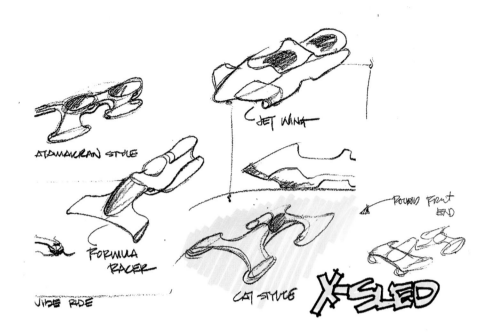

ATOMAKRAN STYLE

JET WING

FORMULA RACER

JIVE RIDE

ROUND FRONT END

CAT STYLE

X-SLED

Figure 8-5a
Figure 8-5b
(Paul Reeder)
The thumbnail sketches in Figure 8-5a and the first
rapid sketch of a molded plastic sled in Figures 8-5b,
8-6, 8-7 and 8-8a, developed by Paul Reeder begin a
sequence of drawings that progressively become more
refined and end with a hybrid computer-enhanced
version as a final concept.

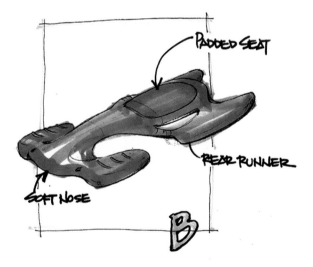

PADDED SEAT

REAR RUNNER

SOFT NOSE

B

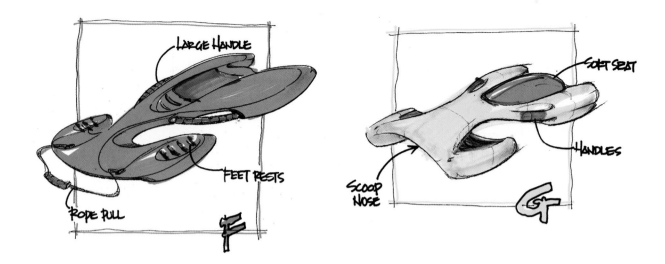

Figure 8-6a
Figure 8-6b
(Paul Reeder)
One aspect of this conceptual design process is that the designer is acquainted in depth with the uses of molded plastic in various forms such as blow molding and injection molding. This allows for the development of conceptual forms that have the potential for manufacture.

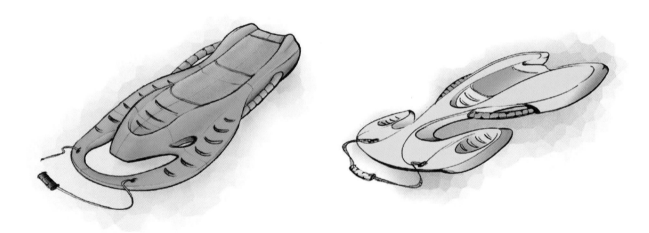

Figure 8-7a, Figure 8-7b
(Paul Reeder)
Additional variations are shown on the molded sled concept drawing using mixed media techniques.

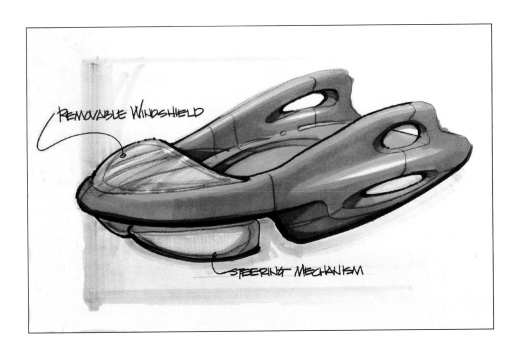

Figure 8-8a
Figure 8-8b
(Paul Reeder)
The drawing in Figure 8-8a is a
mixed media drawing using
markers and pens. The image is
Figure 8-8b is a computer-enhanced
drawing using Adobe Illustrator to
generate a sense of the material in
which the sled will be produced.

Figure 8-9a
Figure 8-9b
(Paul Reeder)
These two hybrid conceptual drawings are products potentially related to the sled concept. The goggles and the snowboard have been enhanced using Adobe Illustrator.

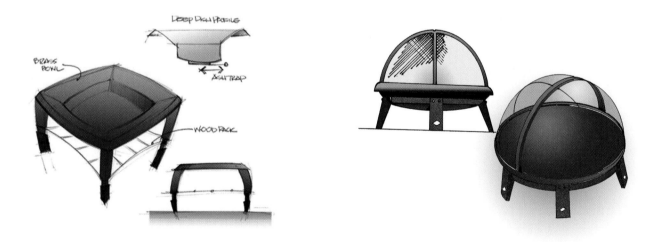

Figure 8-10a
Figure 8-10b
(Paul Reeder)
Line drawings of exterior patio fireplaces were initially drawn using pen line and then scanned and enhanced using Adobe Illustrator to achieve the gradient effect on both drawings.

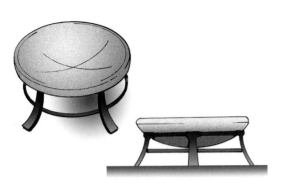

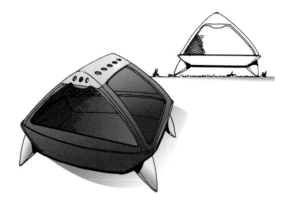

Figure 8-11a, Figure 8-11b
(Paul Reeder)
Additional line drawings of exterior fireplaces are shown, again initially drawn using pen line and then scanned and enhanced using Adobe Illustrator to achieve the gradient effect on both drawings.

Figure 8-12
(Paul Reeder)
One of the tasks many product designers frequently face is developing "point-of-purchase" displays. The drawing shows three differing products from the same manufacturer on a mobile display unit. The drawing has been executed in the same combination of media and computer enhancements as the previous drawings.

Figure 8-13a
Figure 8-13b
(Paul Reeder)
Shown are conceptual drawings of molded storage containers. The drawings were generated using line media and then scanned. The scanned images were enhanced using Adobe Illustrator, giving the units the gradients of color that provide a sense of the form's convex curves.

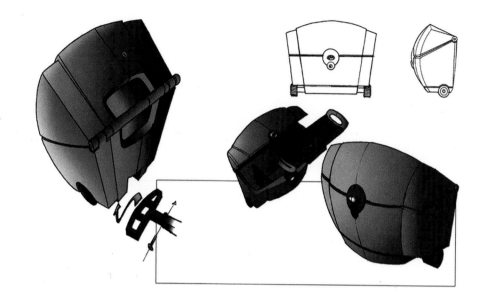

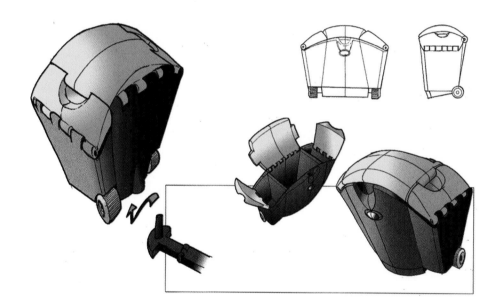

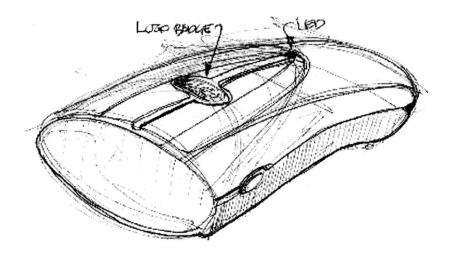

Figure 8-14a
Figure 8-14b
(Paul Reeder)
These two drawings illustrate the process of first committing the idea for an illumination device to line on paper and then scanning the image for further enhancement using computer software such as Adobe Illustrator. In this case, the object is highly refined with indications of surface reflectivity and a background to "set off" the product.

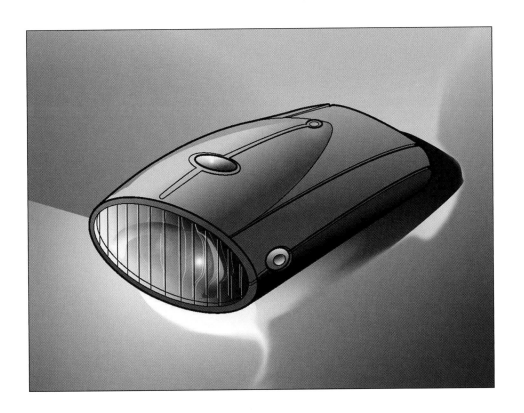

Figure 8-15a, Figure 8-15b, Figure 8-15c, Figure 8-15d, Figure 8-15e, Figure 8-15f
(Aaron Bethlenfalvy)
Six hybrid drawings in a series show variations that can be made in color, background, and even the treatment of wheels on these bike designs. The hybrid drawings were generated for the studios of George Barris, noted custom car designer for individuals and Hollywood movies. The original sketches were enhanced using paint programs for the bicycles and with regard to background and graphics.

Figure 8-16a
Figure 8-16b
(Aaron Bethlenfalvy)
Pedal-powered bicycle designs require a great deal of creativity to innovate continuously using tubular frame members. In the two images of scooters, the Schwinn Company contemplates expanding into motorized two-wheeled vehicles—and the resulting hybrid conceptual drawings show the range of material treatments available to the designer.

Figure 8-17a
Figure 8-17b
(Aaron Bethlenfalvy)
Pacific Cycle is an umbrella company with several brands. The advantage of having so many brands is the possibility of expanding lines because of the available means of production and technologies found in the various divisions. These two hybrid conceptuals demonstrate moving the company into toy design based on experience generated in other enterprises.

Figure 8-18a
Figure 8-18b
(Rob Englert)
Hybrid conceptual drawings provide a means to enhance careful line work using software tools that permit form and surface development akin to full rendering—without the requisite time consumption. Englert has used combinations of software programs and a "draw-on" monitor enabling the development of his conceptual child carry pod and sunglasses. He has obtained the look of the materials and still maintains the freshness of the drawing by keeping the descriptive line work on the exterior of the sunglasses. Note the careful use of photographic images of mother and child to provide scale and develop context.

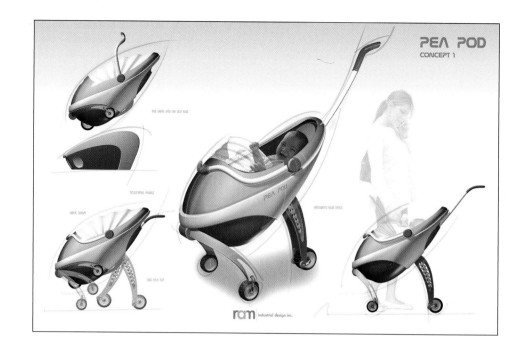

Figure 8-19a
Figure 8-19b
(Brian Lawrence)
A careful line drawing is scanned and used as the basis for generating this graphic image, enhanced with multiple graphic software programs. Note the use of the image as both background and foreground subject matter.

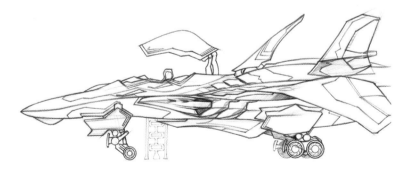

Figure 8-20a
Figure 8-20b
(Brian Lawrence)
These two drawings represent starting a composite image beginning with generating this jet fighter—first in line and then enhanced using the computer.

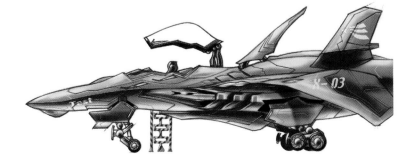

Figure 8-21a
Figure 8-21b
(Brian Lawrence)
The final stages of the composite are shown. Part of the image is the result of drawing, scanning, and enhancing using the computer. Another aspect of this image is the addition of color photography as a background. The sky is appropriately selected as a match to the modified single-point perspective indicated by the yellow stripes on the tarmac.

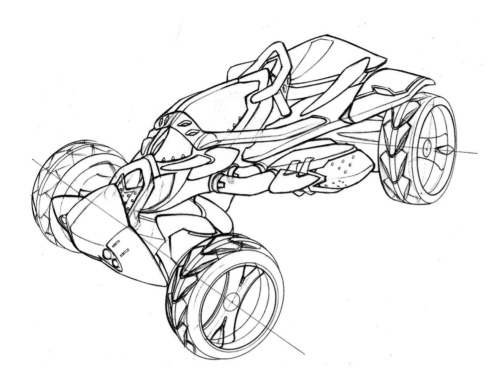

Figure 8-22a
Figure 8-22b
(Brian Lawrence)
Once again, a careful line drawing is used as the basis for generating a full-color image. In this sequence depicting the three stages of the drawing development, scanned line work is given an application of flat color as seen in the image in Figure 8-22b.

Figure 8-23
(Brian Lawrence)
The final stage of the sequence shows the application of enhancements that carry off the image's three-dimensionality. The flat colors of the previous stage are given surface treatments that provide a sense of the materials that would be used in such a vehicle.

Regardless of the technology that allowed the generation of such an image, the fundamentals are the same as discussed in Chapters 2, 3, and 4. The original line drawing must be seen in terms of its position in perspective and the observer's point of view. Complex form generation requires knowledge of how shapes interrelate and transform. Finally, the surface treatment must begin with a consistent direction for illumination and reflectivity.

Graphic software technology is available on desktop computers and is accessible to virtually everyone. The difference between competence and mediocrity in the use of this technology is the skill of the user—not the power of the machine. As demonstrated by both Rob Englert and Brian Lawrence in the sequence of images shown, their skill at drawing is the difference between their work and others without conceptual drawing skills.

"Hybrid" Interior Design Drawing

Interior drawing is far more difficult than object and product drawing because it captures many objects in relationship. Again, certain conventions for sketching an interior in a freehand style are given so that quick drawings and depictions of objects and space do not become tedious and burdensome tasks.

It is also interesting to see where the computer fits into the total methodology of design—depending, of course, upon the type of design being done. Graphic designers shifted to the computer faster than did any other design field. Architects and interior designers followed—

owing to the need for extensive specification and the reliance on plan views in designing.

Industrial designers have been slow to move to computing until the 1980s—with much rapid progress in the 1990s as so much powerful graphics software became available for desk-top computers. Developing three-dimensional views of objects is time-consuming on the computer and only worthwhile when the data created can be used repeatedly as a visual reference. Quick sketching is done even faster today than it was in the 1970s—prior to the advent of the computer—but it is still done. The computer seems to be shrinking the time necessary in the development

Figure 8-24a
Figure 8-24b
(Joseph Koncelik)
Hybrid conceptual drawings match manually drawn and scanned line drawings with use of computer graphics software. While they do *not* accomplish 3D effects available using CAD program rendering functions, they do provide the quickness and variability that is an important asset in conceptual development. These two interior images utilize a manually generated line drawing that has been modified and enhanced in Paint and Photoshop to develop color, paste-up photographic materials, and shading. Beyond line, color, and shading, the Photoshop applications allow changes in the look and feel of the final image. Two widely varying images are shown here that are both monochromatic and full-color with Photoshop "artistic" enhancements.

Figure 8-25a, Figure 8-25b

(Joseph Koncelik)

The following images in Figures 8-25 through 8-30 present a sequence of 12 images showing the step-by-step development of a residential interior concept sketch. Drawing 1 is the manually generated line drawing that is set up with a two-point perspective from a standing height point of view. The drawing was generated using a photo-blue pencil and then overdrawing—without erasures—using fine-line and bold-tip marker pens. Once scanned, the second step (drawing 2) uses selected materials scanned from photographic "clip files" of background exteriors applied by cutting and pasting into the window wells of the room. Drawing 2 shows how the material was transferred into the Paint program. A section of the couch that defines the lower edge of the paste materials was transferred over the paste material and used as a template to "cut" the material to fit the window position.

Figure 8-26a, Figure 8-26b

(Joseph Koncelik)

Drawing 3 shows all the exterior pasted materials placed in the window wells of the room. Owing to the continuity of the material used, there is a consistency in the exterior "scene" beyond the windows. In drawing 4, the same procedure has been used to clip and paste materials from a Persian rug to fit the floor.

Using photographic materials as backgrounds and other applications in a collage with drawing is not new. Drawings shown earlier in this text generated by R. Preston Bruning show applications of this type with actual paste-up of photographic background materials. It is important to recognize the similarity of perspective comparing the line drawing with the source from which the materials are taken. With practice, such applications using the computer are faster and quite effective.

Figure 8-27a, Figure 8-27b

(Joseph Koncelik)

Drawing 5 represents the finished interior sketch as it appears in the Paint program. Colors have been applied using "fill, line, and brush" functions. In addition, window treatments have been "drawn" in place in the Paint program, demonstrating the variability of drawing options when hybrid imaging is used.

At this juncture, the conceptual drawing is finished. However, using the computer provides options in the treatments of the drawing that are worth exploring. Drawing 6 is a manipulation of the light and contrast as well as the color in the "adjustments" function of the Photoshop graphics program. This function can be especially useful in varying the intensity of marker colors that can tend to be too bright. There is a noticeable "yellowing" of the drawing in number 6, compared with drawing number 5.

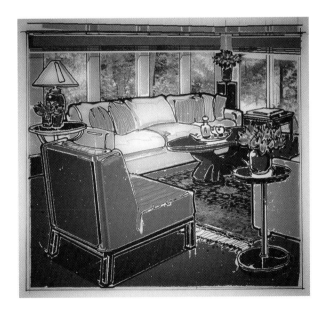

Figure 8-28a, Figure 8-28b

(Joseph Koncelik)

Drawing number 7 represents the beginning of an exploration process using Photoshop's "filter" function. Further manipulation of the contrast, brightness, and color saturation has been explored. However, drawing number 8 uses a focused "glow" lighting effect that can be effective when a designer wants to focus attention on a specific portion of the drawing.

These filtering functions—that can be used in combination—can produce interesting and useful effects. Many of the effects do not obscure the drawing's message and its communication of design ideas. It is important to be objective and selective in the use of these tools.

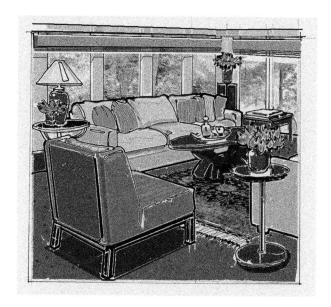

Figure 8-29a
Figure 8-29b
(Joseph Koncelik)

Drawing number 9 illustrates that the effects generated using Photoshop can obscure the visual information to be conveyed in a conceptual drawing. However, using these techniques can have an impact in the overall presentation as well as on the generation of reports for clients and others.

Drawing number 10 is less "graphic" in its overall visualization and retains most of the critical visual information that must be conveyed.

Figure 8-30a
Figure 8-30b
(Joseph Koncelik)

Drawings 11 and 12 are further variations using the filtering and mode functions in Photoshop. Looking back at drawings 6 through 12, color manipulation is clearly a critical factor in using hybrid techniques. The lounge chair in the foreground is the best example of the alterations. The color red has been significantly altered from deeper shades of crimson to lighter variations in muted orange.

There is a "learning curve" in the development of hybrid skills and knowledge. Each designer will find those specific techniques that allow the best expression of ideas. The drawings in this sequence use some of the most basic computer graphics applications. Many other programs are available for the designer and can expedite the drawing process.

Figure 8-31
(Noel Mayo)
The following is a four-drawing
progression from initial
"thumbnail" of an interior to a
marker sketch and a hybridized
interior of the space.

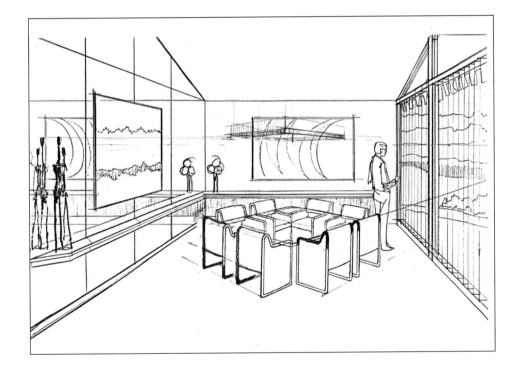

Figure 8-32
(Noel Mayo)
The initial sketch is refined using
overlays and the perspective has
been established using Lawson
Charts—a faster way to establish a
true perspective without difficult,
time-consuming construction.

of form when that form must relate to specific materials and manufacturing. From the quick sketch, designers move rapidly into the solid modeling programs such as ProEngineer or the rendering tools of AutoCad to create dimensionally accurate designs that are automatically translated into data used to generate stereolithography models and numerical-computer milled dies and molds. The computer has not replaced the hand-drawn sketch—at least not yet. It has greatly reduced the time necessary to translate an idea into a manufactured product. Nevertheless, there is something to be said for the satisfaction of doing visual work by producing a drawing by hand. Drawing is a deeply satisfying activity in and of itself.

Figure 8-33
(Noel Mayo)
The following is the continuation of a four-drawing progression from initial "thumbnail" of an interior to a marker sketch and a hybridized interior of the space.

Figure 8-34
(Noel Mayo hybridized by Joseph Koncelik)
The refined line drawing on the previous page has been used to develop a color conceptual drawing that attempts to treat the space similarly to the marker drawing, including mirrored surfaces and fabric-covered conference chairs.

Figure 8-35a, Figure 8-35b, Figure 8-35c
(Noel Mayo)
Photographs of the actual finished interior show the close resemblance to early sketches by Mayo. Generally speaking, experienced interior designers have a deep working knowledge of the architectural hardware, furnishings, and surface treatments that permit close approximation of the interior design in the earliest conceptual drawings.

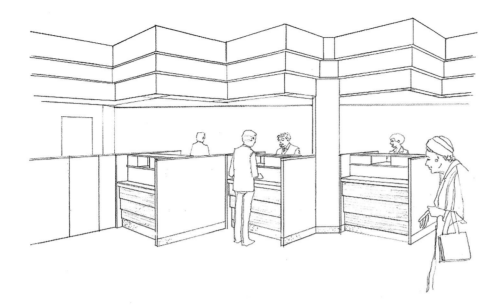

Figure 8-36a
Figure 8-36b
(Noel Mayo hybridized
by Joseph Koncelik)
Another sequence of hybridized
conceptual drawings begins with a
refined line drawing and progresses
to a version that has carefully
balanced color combinations.
Marker drawing would not provide
the level of balance between colors
that are available in programs such
as Paint and Photoshop.

Conclusions about Hybrid Conceptual Drawings

Hybrid conceptual drawing can be defined as the use of traditional freehand sketching—or even mechanically generated manual drawing—combined with computer software enhancements to create effective, efficient communication of visual ideas. Hybridized image making is broadly utilized in the design professions with the most developed forms of the practice found in both architectural design and visual communications or graphic design. Interior designers have followed close behind in the generation of hybrid visualizations owing to the advantages of quick "image-grabbing" to establish interior environments and settings. Product design has lagged to some degree

Figure 8-37
(Noel Mayo, hybrid conversion by
Joseph Koncelik)
Lighting effects available in
Photoshop allow the space to be
further softened in appearance.

Figure 8-38a
Figure 8-38b
(Noel Mayo)
Two photographs of the finished bank interiors—quite
different from the hybridized versions—that again
demonstrate how close the initial conceptual drawings are
to the final interiors. Note the use of both direct and
indirect lighting in this space.

owing to the requirement that conceptual drawing requires that multiple potential product solutions be generated. The freehand line drawing sketch still proves to be the most efficient, fastest method for generating such images.

Nevertheless, as this chapter has demonstrated, the hybridization process is taking hold in the industrial design and product development arena and there are numerous variations in the approach to developing such images. One important point remains, however. Developing freehand sketching skills is essential before using computing to generate images. Developing the hand and eye coordination necessary to produce excellent images is critical.

It remains to be seen just how hybridization of the image-making process as well as the full development of hybrid education in general will develop. This is truly a twenty-first century evolution of education and the image-making process. Students will be just as instrumental in this development as their instructors. The accessibility of online courses to all has not been fully realized as an educational direction either institutionally or by the faculty who generate the curriculum. In the fullness of time, hybridization from the broadest educational perspective down to the generation of visual images will become the accepted educational models.

 See DVD Segment 7, Digital Integration, for a complete demonstration of hybrid conceptual drawing.

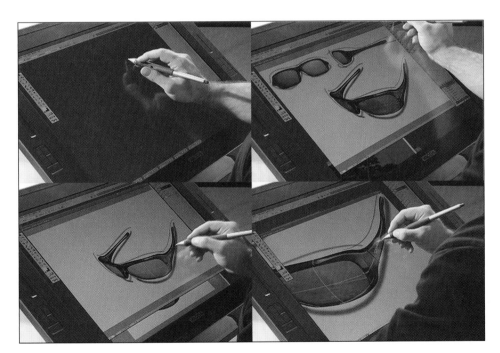

Figure 8-39
(Michael Butcher)
Rob Englert is a master of developing images directly on a Wacom computer screen using Photoshop as well as other software to produce images that are initially hybridized or completely visualized in software. Segment 7, Digital Integration, of the DVD provides a sequential demonstration of how these images are created.

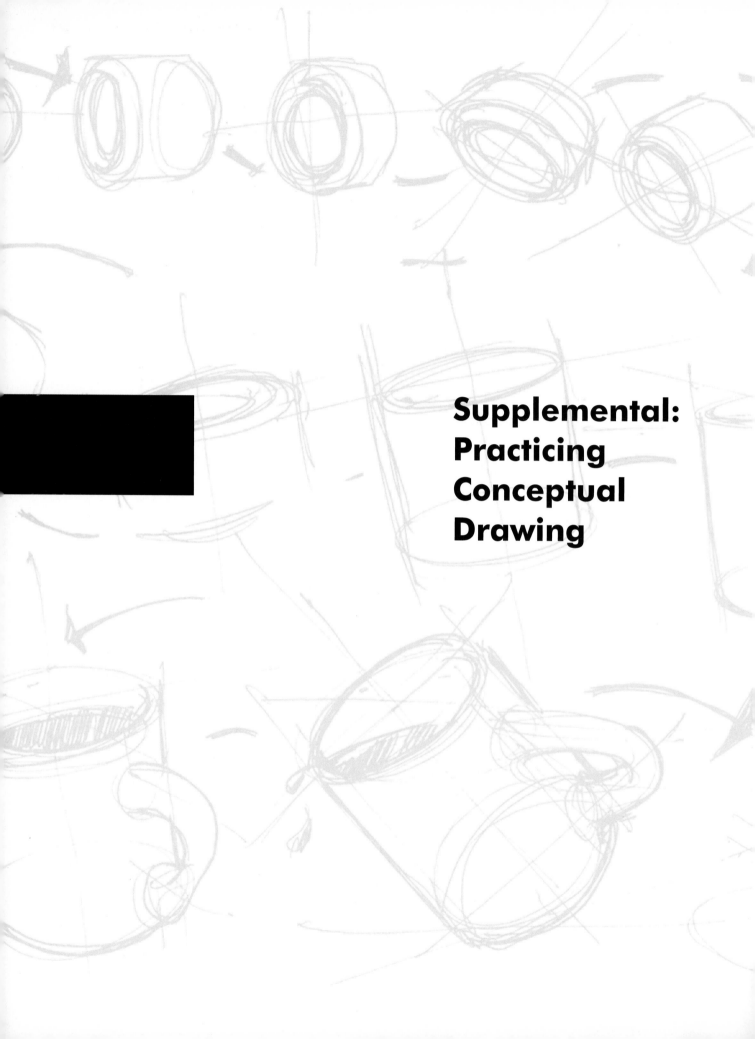

**Supplemental:
Practicing
Conceptual
Drawing**

Faculty members debate about the best way to orchestrate the "doing" of drawing by students of design. Some argue that keeping students in long class sessions with all work done in the instructor's presence is the best way to ensure the skill development improves. This idea is hard to implement as total credit hours diminish and content expands in design curricula. One important saying about college education is that responsibility for education rests with the student. Removing individual self-guided learning prevents individuals from meeting that responsibility. Personal commitment is essential to developing conceptual drawing skills. If students can perform only under the watchful eye of an instructor, they have limited personal commitment and students and instructors both will find that skills evaporate with the completion of each successive class.

Figure SUPP-1a
Figure SUPP-1b
(Kevin Reeder)
Ideas originate from the collection of combined memories resulting from combining different subjects. Creativity is the ability to fashion ideas from the most dissimilar sources—making sense out of combinations of things that do not necessarily relate. Hence, the swan becomes the door handle and the play on the form of a cylinder becomes the coffee mug.

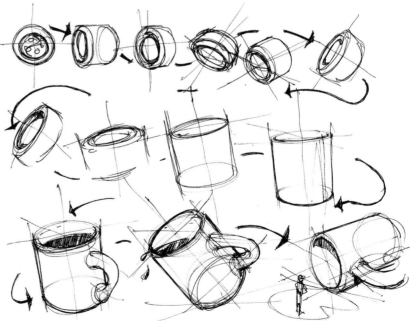

In the shortening of classroom time, in-class practice and the total time available for all subjects is lessening. It is understandable that having students perform under the watchful eye of the instructor ensures that all assigned work is completed. On the other hand, younger students are adept at short-term memorization of information and instruction, but information and capability are frequently lost shortly after class time ends. Skills development must become integral with the discipline of following through individually—without supervision. The student must use his or her own time to build on the instruction provided in class. Otherwise, instruction cannot be committed to long-term memory and develop into the capability that will automatically come to mind when needed.

Students should follow five practice guidelines. These guidelines include, but are not limited to, the following:

1. Run the scales.
2. Draw objects and places from memory.
3. Manage time properly.
4. Focus on the task at hand.
5. Seek out critical review.

Each of these aspects of practice is explained in detail in the following sections.

Running the Scales—Musicians develop the dexterity to play difficult pieces by performing the calisthenics of hand-to-instrument sound production and control. The great pianist Arthur Rubinstein once said, "Skip one day of practice and I know it, two days and the critics know it, three days and the public knows it." It is the same with developing excellence in drawing. Even the best designers and drafters know that continuous practice ensures the sharpness of their skills. Practice fundamental drawing exercises should include, but not be limited to, drawing circles in one motion or developing ellipses as the three-dimensional view of circles in perspective. The beginning design student should practice daily for at least one hour. Students should set goals for completing a number of drawings on a weekly, quarterly, or semester basis. As time goes on and skill develops, the practice sessions can be fewer—but the need for them never really disappears.

It is possible to lose skill, to become "rusty." It is also important to retain the dexterity and

Figure SUPP-2
(Kevin Reeder)
Moving from the doodle to ideas about form, the thumbnail is a useful means to explore idea "nuggets." This first series of sketches is part of a progression that only stops when the designer wants to move on to more detailed drawing.

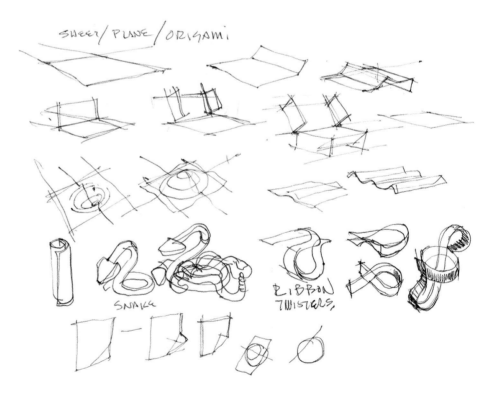

Figure SUPP-3a
Figure SUPP-3b
(Kevin Reeder)
From the first series to the second, the drawing effort produces more recognizable forms—leading to the third in the series that begins a progression Reeder calls the "box with wheels."

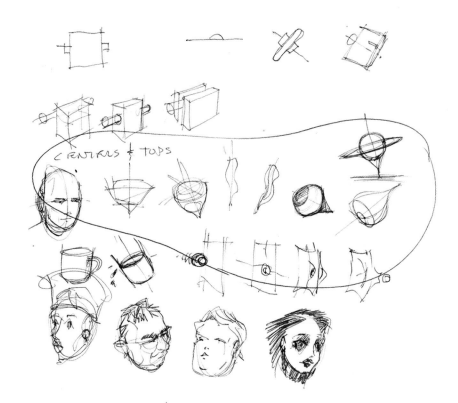

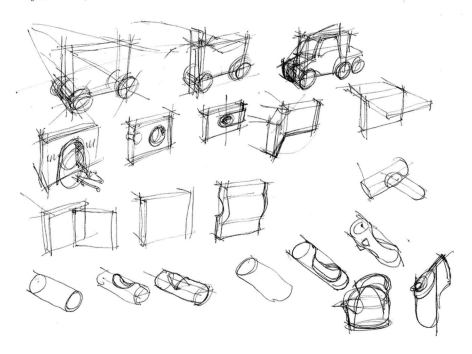

hand-eye coordination required for drawing. Long periods of absence from drawing can mean loss of facility. Placida Domingo, the great operatic tenor, works continuously, even in his advanced years, and has said, "If I rest, I rust." His example is important for anyone hoping to

achieve a high level of excellence in any skill. Students will perform under the watchful eye of an instructor in the classroom. Will those same students of design perform or sustain practice on their own? The requirement for individual unsupervised practice is necessary or the discipline of

Figure SUPP-4a
Figure SUPP-4b
(Kevin Reeder)
The personal exchange using the media has resulted in an idea that seems worth pursuing in greater depth. The "box with wheels" is the jumping-off point to explore several design ideas.

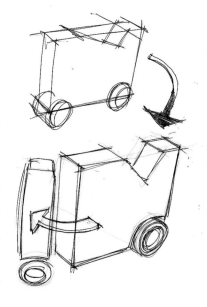

drawing will not become an integral part of the artist's personal ability to excel in design.

Drawing skill seems to lessen between courses— or wanes more heavily during long breaks over summer months. A great part of the problem lies in a student's unwillingness to "run the scales." When students view design studies the same way they view courses in traditionally academic subjects—study to pass and not to learn—the process of student development is thwarted. Design programs are lock step, linear, and rise progressively in difficulty. It is the student's responsibility to know that the calisthenics of design study are essential and the responsibility rests in their hands and heads.

Draw Favorite Things from Memory—
Observation is important in the process of design and drawing. Most designers are avid collectors of

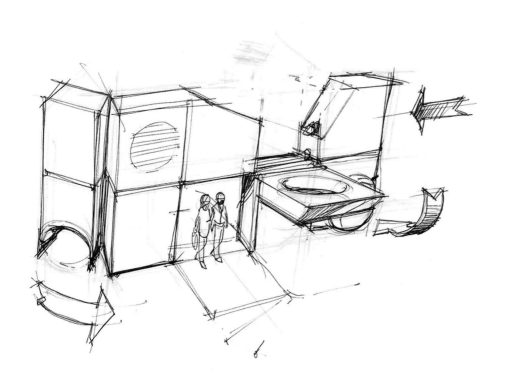

Figure SUPP-5
(Kevin Reeder)
The box is articulated and the scale
is variable. One possible direction is
the development of a display device
that folds and is easily shipped.

images from trade magazines as well as other published sources. Drawing instruction, before the computer arrived on the scene, included drawing the human figure, drawing from nature sources, and product and architectural drawing—from observational study. It is central to the task of designing to build a well of drawing knowledge, as well as a repertoire, of form through observation. Storing such images in memory enhances the ability to produce conceptual drawings.

One of Preston Bruning's favorite sources is aircraft of the world—in ample evidence throughout this text. Pres scours publications and other sources for the most obscure and visually interesting drawings of airplanes. As an automotive designer, he is not alone. Design studios in automotive companies frequently have aircraft pinups covering the walls as inspiration for the design projects in progress. This search for inspiration through "alternative" sources of form giving extends in many directions. The natural world is the bible of sources for form giving. All sources are potentially inspiring, from the sublime resources of nature to the trite content of "what is hot" in design magazines.

Having built a large memory of form from such sources, a process that should be continuous throughout life, it is necessary to interpret those collections regarding how things go together or work into new or novel applications. It does not take much imagination to see a connection between the polyhedral folding wings of a hawk and the swing-wings of the F-14 Tomcat fighter jet. There is a direct connection between the fillets and rounds used in aircraft aerodynamics and the smooth body forms of the contemporary automobile. Going further, the protective padding worn by major league baseball players while batting has great similarity to the armor worn by knights of the Middle Ages and even to the natural armor of the armadillo.

Architects, especially those who are Frank Lloyd Wright devotees, study natural form to integrate their buildings with the natural setting. Birds inspired man's pursuit of flight, the awesome heights of mountains has at least a spiritual connection to our modern skyscrapers, and corporate logotype graphics are derived from ancient heraldry. Connections between the forms of things are products of an individual's creative ability to merge dissimilar ideas and shapes.

Memory and personal interpretation are a mysterious combination as aspects of the capabilities of designers and artists. It really is not possible to

Figure SUPP-6a
Figure SUPP-6b
(Kevin Reeder)
The box with wheels also—and inevitably—is seen as a vehicle, a truck, that is either a toy or an articulated "lorry" having an unspecified purpose.

copy one idea for the solution to a problem of form or function into another solution to a different problem. An arm protector that flexes at the elbow in a similar fashion to that of a medieval knight's armor differs automatically owing to the changes made in materials, connections, and application to function. Design, by its very

nature, is an eclectic process—meaning that all designers "borrow" ideas from other sources. The process of filtering such ideas through any given designer's individual mind will make the solution naturally different. There are no new forms, only new interpretations of the geometries. Seemingly, new responses to design problems are really juxtapositions of form and relationships of three-dimensional objects and spaces.

Manage Time Properly—Design studies are time-consuming. Yet, one of the most difficult issues regarding instructing design studies is the lack of time students have available for practice or project development and completion. Many students work while attending college. Working to cover college expenses in an environment where costs rise steadily is an understandable dilemma for students. Yet, students, especially those from general student populations, must understand the commitment any and all arts and architecture based curricula make upon their lives. Design programs expect total commitment from students. Those who are unprepared for these demands should carefully consider this area of study as a career option and move to some other area of study where their own self-assessed talents match the demands of the program.

Design studies consume time beyond other types of curricula—especially for students who have little to no previous involvement in the arts or design. The expectations of the professional fields and programs of design instruction demand all time available to the student.

Managing time properly means using class time class productively and fully understanding the purpose of external practice and skill development. One hour per day is a minimum target for the expenditure of effort—not just time—to practice drawing. It is wise to establish a routine, and to even plan out that routine on paper to maintain the fit of this commitment with other obligations. It is not possible to change the demands and obligations of design studies to sustain lifestyle attractions of college, employment, and other conflicting commitments. The same yardstick measures everyone and lack of commitment of time to the work of becoming competently skillful can result in missing the opportunity for entry-level professional employment.

Figure SUPP-7
(Kevin Reeder)
There are options in the design progression that need not be so specific as to have an obvious purpose. Frequently, such explorations lead to more purposeful ideas such as the direction conceptualized in Figure SUPP-8.

In *The Spooky Art*, Norman Mailer (2001) discusses the formidable task of writing a novel. He speaks of time management in a way that resonates for any artist or designer. Mailer does not believe in so-called "writer's block." Paraphrasing Mailer, he states that no matter how one feels at any particular moment, time of the day, or day of the week, it is necessary to put words on paper. Further, it is necessary to commit the self to a schedule of time and output. He, personally, writes in the mornings and reviews his writing in the afternoons. He always begins his writing days at 10 A.M. and has specific habits he follows to prepare himself. He always writes a specific amount no matter how uninspired he may feel. Every artist and designer needs this sense of discipline of which Mailer speaks so eloquently in his book. Inspiration is not a lightning bolt from the blue. Among the most productive creative people, inspiration is a continuous process of mental effort releasing possibilities.

Practicing drawing for the benefit of building skill requires that students set aside a time that is always used for a predetermined purpose. Repeating the general rule of thumb, students should practice a minimum of one hour every day, seven days a week. That hour of time should be devoted to drawing practice, and nothing but

that practice should take place. Practicing more than an hour is encouraged. As the late designer and educator Edward Lawing once said, "Students are always invited to exceed minimum specification!"

Focus on the Task at Hand—This simple saying applies to more than learning to draw for the college student. Study habits begin with the ability to focus and the ability to block out external environmental influences. Turn off the hip-hop, rap, and the television. Some studies have noted that a background of music by Mozart, Hayden, or Bach played at a low volume aids intellectual development and that is likely just as true regarding drawing. It makes sense that such music sets a peaceful background to individual concentration and helps isolate the individual from other external environmental sounds. Nevertheless, many students believe that studying while slumped in front of a television, watching the latest reality show on television, and chatting with friends is perfectly appropriate. This is frequently justified as "multi-tasking"—but it is only effective in the most superficial forms of work.

The environment of interference is not a supportive environment for acquiring drawing skills. The full measure of drawing exercises can happen during such an unfocused session, but they will

Figure SUPP-8
(Kevin Reeder)
Now the visualization has transformed into a lift truck that is articulated off the forward end—much like the initial sketches.

have little effective impact on improving drawing skill. Lessons from the practice of yoga and from Tai Chi that apply to focus and concentration can be applied to drawing. In many ways, study habits and the practice of drawing require clearing the mind to prepare for the engagement and mastery of the drawing task.

Seek Out Critical Review—The nature of criticism in the classroom can be found in an earlier section of this text. It is important to *value* critical review of work, not to fear or avoid it. Therefore, this discussion focuses on the critical review of work students should seek out in order to develop their skill sets as well as their capacities for full expression of design.

When young children take their drawings to show to their parents, the reaction they seek and usually get is "good job." The drawing finds its way under a couple of refrigerator magnets and the work remains on display until another drawing replaces it or the child goes off to college. This early encouragement is essential for the child

to continue such self-initiated activities in art and craft and for the child's psychological development. On the other hand, when students of design seek praise for conceptual drawings they have generated—regardless of how proficient—this can be counterproductive to the improvement of skill.

Again, sport analogies work in this situation. Golf and tennis pros, especially those on tour, do not go to teaching professionals to hear how great they are. Their standings among their peers inform them of their relative proficiency and capability. They expect critical review of their swing, body position, ball striking, and form in order to improve their game and maintain their edge in competition. Likewise, the aspiring designer should seek out critical review of their work—not expecting to hear praise—but to elicit comments about how their work can be improved. In the final analysis, and after graduation, students of design are entering a very competitive field where they will need an edge. That "edge" may come in

Figure SUPP-9
(Joseph Koncelik)
Back to the doodle! Preparing for the development of a product that requires drawing the human head form also entails exploring which media will become part of the palette. This doodle has the purpose of examining the use of pen and marker setting up Figure SUPP-10.

various forms not necessarily connected to conceptual drawing. Nevertheless, it is the initial capacity to demonstrate thinking through conceptualization that determines the successful applicant for entry-level design positions in the majority of hiring decisions.

From the standpoint of the teacher, *critical review means having something clear and definitive to say about the work being shown in every instance where students seek them out.* Students will not be helped by grimaces and mumbles. As discussed in the DVD, the critique,

"I don't like it," is not helpful and begs the question "Why?" Such subjective statements are meaningless to students when coming from teachers. The teacher/instructor should be prepared to give specific advice about how the work can be improved. With regard to the initial startup of learning conceptual drawing, comments would include measures to take to improve quality of line, correctness of perspective, level of detail incorporated in the drawing—or the lack thereof—and many other areas of comment.

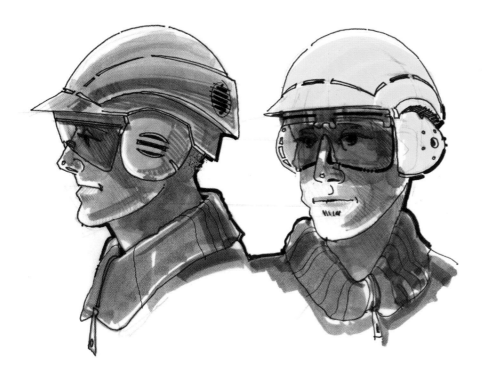

Figure SUPP-10
(Joseph Koncelik)
Practice and warming up produces the feel for the media necessary to develop more detailed sketches. While the color of the helmet is an additional marker experiment, the palette chosen for the face is the result of the doodling in Figure SUPP-9.

Figure SUPP-11
(Joseph Koncelik)
Students should keep in mind that instructors get excited when there is real effort and enthusiastic preparation on the part of the student. That combination will always result in an equally enthusiastic response from instructors.

Falling back on the fundamentals is always a good basis for critical commentary.

From the standpoint of the student, there must be sufficient work and sufficient content in the work for the teacher/instructor to comment. All too frequently, students shyly pull out a single sketch and expect an in-depth review of their abilities, the drawing itself, and how to lift the level of their skills. Ironically, it is always easier to make comments about the work of the more skilled students than it is to comment on the work of less gifted, less-motivated students. It might seem that criticism would be easier when reviewing poor work. This is not the case. When students produce little in the way of content in their drawings, only the most general criticism from teachers is appropriate: practice more, observe the fundamentals, et cetera. When students have produced 25 to 50 drawings for review, it is possible to comment on the differences between drawings, where drawing fundamentals seem to be working, and where they are not. It is possible to discuss composition, the quality of the drawings submitted, and how the content of the drawing either infers or describes the intent of the creative act.

Also, from the standpoint of the student, do not divorce drawing from the intent of the drawing because they are integral. Frequently students will say to instructors, "Don't look at my drawing, look at the design." That is not really possible. Design is always part invention and part quality of that invention. The quality of the drawing is inherently part of the quality of the design. Students should expect to hear comments that are intertwined about both the drawing submitted and what that drawing represents.

It should also be made clear that the "better" students in the design classroom include those who are talented who also have a well-developed work ethic. Since the goal of conceptual drawing is communication of ideas, achieving competent communication is possible for those who are not well endowed with innate drawing gifts. Perspicacity as well as perspiration counts in the striving to improve conceptual drawing skills. No instructor has a magic wand, as much as all who teach might wish to have one. In addition, students should never resent others who are more gifted. Everyone improves faster and to a higher level in design classes that include talented students. Seeing how someone draws well and knowing that there is a standard above one's own work—along with the critical review of instructors—pushes whole classes to do better.

Another form of critical review is that of peer review and criticism. While it is inappropriate for instructors to utter difficult-to-understand subjective and offensive comments about student work, the peer review process differs somewhat. It is useful to hear from a peer that they "like" or "do not like" the drawing of another. This can prompt discussion between classmates about the work in a

meaningful way. Usually, students have to be in a situation with peers for some time before there is sufficient comfort with one another to criticize another's work. It takes time to separate professional criticism from the personal. Hearing these comments is useful because a person must develop the capacity to take criticism to sustain one's sense of worth in the professional world where criticism will be much harsher.

Students should keep in mind that avoiding criticism is not helpful or useful in developing conceptual drawing skills. Students should seek critical review on a continuing basis. Time spent in the design studio and in drawing classes goes by quickly. Criticism of work is rarely praise and is aimed at improvement and attaining a professional level of capability. Since no design curriculum can ever produce a sufficient number of courses to provide complete conceptual development, it is the student's responsibility to continuously seek critical review beyond the classroom.

Index

NOTE to readers: locators ending in "f" indicate figures.

Bibliography

Barber, Barrington, *The Fundamentals of Drawing: A Complete Professional Course for Artists.* New York: Barnes & Noble Books, 2004.

Beal, Nancy, & Gloria Bley Miller, *The Art of Teaching Art to Children: In School and at Home.* New York: Farrar, Straus and Giroux, 2001.

Begleiter, Marcie, *From Word to Image.* Michael Wiese Productions, 2001.

Beitler, Ethel Jane, & Bill C. Lockhart, *Design for You.* New York: John Wiley and Sons, 1961.

Bresman, Jonathan, *The Art of Star Wars, Episode 1: The Phantom Menace.* New York: Ballantine Publishing Group, 1999.

Bridgman, George B., *Bridgman's Complete Guide to Drawing from Life.* New York: Weathervane Books, 1952.

Ching, Francis D. K., *Architectural Graphics.* New York: Van Nostrand Reinhold Company, 1975.

Ching, Francis D. K., & Steven P. Juroszek, *Design Drawing.* New York: John Wiley and Sons, Inc., 1998.

Ching, Francis D. K., *Interior Design Illustrated.* New York: Van Nostrand Reinhold Company, 1987.

Doblin, Jay, *Perspective: A New System for Designers.* New York: Whitney Publications Inc., 1977.

Dreyfuss, Henry, *The Measure of Man.* Cambridge, Massachusetts: MIT Press, 1947.

Edwards, Betty, *Drawing on the Right Side of the Brain.* New York: Penguin/Tarcher, 1979, Revised and Printed 1989.

Edwards, Betty, *The New Drawing on the Right Side of the Brain.* New York: Penguin/Tarcher, 1999.

Elam, Kimberly, *Geometry of Design: Studies in Proportion and Composition.* New York: Princeton Architectural Press, 2001.

Elam, Kimberly, *Grid Systems: Principles of Organizing Type.* New York: Princeton Architectural Press, 2004.

Evans, Joy, & Tanya Skelton, *How to Teach Art to Children.* Monterey, CA: Evan-Moor Corp., 2001.

Fraioli, James, *Storyboarding 101: A Crash Course in Professional Storyboarding*, Los Angeles: Michael Wise Productions, 2000.

Gerds, Donald A., *Markers, Interiors, Product Design*. Red Cliffs, Victoria, Australia: Dag Design, 1983.

Goodwin, Archie, Simonson, W., *Alien, The Illustrated Story*. New York: Heavy Metal Communications, Inc., 1979.

Hanks, Kurt, Larry Belliston, & Dave Edwards, *Design Yourself*. Los Altos, CA: William Kaufmann Inc., 1977.

Hanks, Kurt, *Rapid Viz*. 2d ed. Los Altos, CA: Crisp Learning, 1990.

Hallett, Lisa, Taylor, T., *How to Draw Cars Like a Pro*. Osceola, WI: Motorbooks International Publishers and Wholesalers, 1996.

Johnston, Joe, *The Star Wars Sketchbook*. New York: Ballantine Books, 1977.

Johnston, Joe, & Rodis-Jamero, N., *Star Wars Return of the Jedi Sketchbook*. New York: Ballantine Books, 1983.

Kemnitzer, Ronald B., *Rendering with Markers: Definitive Techniques for Designers, Illustrators and Architects*. New York: Watson-Guptill Publications, 1983.

Koncelik, Joseph A., *Designing the Open Nursing Home*. Stroudsburg, PA: Dowden, Hutchinson and Ross, Inc., 1976.

Landay, James M., Myers, Brad A., *Just Draw it! Programming by Sketching Storyboards*. Pittsburgh, PA: School of Computer Science, Carnegie Mellon University, CMU-CS-95-199, or CMU-HC!!-95-106, 1995.

Lawson, Phillip J., *Perspective Charts*. New York: John Wiley & Sons, Inc., 1940.

Lee, Stan, Buscema, J., *How to Draw Comics the Marvel Way*. New York: Simon and Schuster, 1978.

Lin, Mike W., *Drawing and Designing with Confidence: A Step-By-Step Guide*. New York: John Wiley & Sons, Inc., 2004.

Loomis, Andrew, *Figure Drawing for All It's Worth*. New York: The Viking Press, 1943.

Lockard, Allen K., *Design Drawing*. New York: W. W. Norton, 2000.

Lowenfeld, Viktor, *Creative and Mental Growth*, 7th ed. York, NY: McMillan Publishing, 1947.

Lucasfilm Ltd, *The Art of Return of the Jedi Star Wars*. New York: Ballantine Books, 1983.

MacMinn, Strother, Mead, S., *Steel Couture—Syd Mead—Futurist Sentinel*. Netherlands: Dragon's Dream, 1979.

Mailer, Norman, *The Spooky Art: Some Thoughts on Writing*. New York: Random House, 2003.

Malchiodi, Cathy A., *Understanding Children's Drawings*. New York: The Guilford Press, 1998.

McKim, R., *Experiences in Visual Thinking*. Monterey, CA: Brooks/Cole Publishing Company, 1972.

Mead, Syd, *Oblagon*. Tokyo, Japan: Kodansha Press, 1996.

Montague, John, *Basic Perspective Drawing: A Visual Guide*. New York: John Wiley and Sons, Inc., 2005.

O'Connor, Charles, *Perspective Drawing and Application*. Upper Saddle River, NJ: Prentice Hall, Inc., 1998.

Murphy, Daniel, & Salinas, Andrew. "A Quantitative Business Case Is Not Enough: Document the Qualitative Benefit of Integrated CRM Technology in a Future-State Customer Experience Scenario." Retrieved December 20, 2008 http://www.crm2day.com/library/EpFkyAEEVVoaTleWkF.php.

National Center for Educational Statistics. Retrieved January 15, 2005, from http://nces.ed.gov/

Sakai, Stan, *Usagi Yogimbo Book One*. Seattle, WA: Fantagraphics Books, 1987.

Scroggy, David, Huebner, M., Kaplan, M., Knode, C., Mead, S., Scott, R., (1982) *Blade Runner Sketchbook*, San Diego, CA Blue Dolphin Enterprises, Inc.

Shay, Don, Duncan, J., *The Making of Jurassic Park*. New York: Ballantine Books, 1991.

Stoops, Jack, & Jerry Samuelson, *Design Dialogue*. Worcester, MA: Davis Publications, 1983.

Tilley, Alvin R., *The Measure of Man & Woman: Human Factors in Design*, Rev. ed. New York: John Wiley & Sons, Inc., 2005.

Tumminello, Wendy, *Exploring Storyboarding*. New York: Thomson Delmar Learning, 2003.

Ulrich, Karl T., & Steven D. Eppinger, *Product Design and Development*. New York: McGraw-Hill Inc., 1995.

Wallschlaeger, Charles, & Cynthia Busic Snyder, *Basic Visual Concepts and Principles for Artists, Architects and Designers*. Dubuque, Iowa: William C. Brown, 1992.

Wang, Thomas C., *Pencil Sketching*. New York: Van Nostrand Reinhold Company, 1977.

Zimbert, Jonaton, & Mead, S., *The Official Art of 2010*. New York: Pocket Books, 1984.

IMPORTANT! READ CAREFULLY: This End User License Agreement ("Agreement") sets forth the conditions by which Delmar Cengage Learning will make electronic access to the Delmar Cengage Learning-owned licensed content and associated media, software, documentation, printed materials, and electronic documentation contained in this package and/or made available to you via this product (the "Licensed Content"), available to you (the "End User"). BY CLICKING THE "I ACCEPT" BUTTON AND/OR OPENING THIS PACKAGE, YOU ACKNOWLEDGE THAT YOU HAVE READ ALL OF THE TERMS AND CONDITIONS, AND THAT YOU AGREE TO BE BOUND BY ITS TERMS, CONDITIONS, AND ALL APPLICABLE LAWS AND REGULATIONS GOVERNING THE USE OF THE LICENSED CONTENT.

1.0 SCOPE OF LICENSE

1.1 <u>Licensed Content</u>. The Licensed Content may contain portions of modifiable content ("Modifiable Content") and content which may not be modified or otherwise altered by the End User ("Non-Modifiable Content"). For purposes of this Agreement, Modifiable Content and Non-Modifiable Content may be collectively referred to herein as the "Licensed Content." All Licensed Content shall be considered Non-Modifiable Content, unless such Licensed Content is presented to the End User in a modifiable format and it is clearly indicated that modification of the Licensed Content is permitted.

1.2 Subject to the End User's compliance with the terms and conditions of this Agreement, Delmar Cengage Learning hereby grants the End User, a nontransferable, nonexclusive, limited right to access and view the enclosed software on an unlimited number of computers on one network at one site for noncommercial, internal, personal use only. The End User shall not (i) reproduce, copy, modify (except in the case of Modifiable Content), distribute, display, transfer, sublicense, prepare derivative work(s) based on, sell, exchange, barter or transfer, rent, lease, loan, resell, or in any other manner exploit the Licensed Content; (ii) remove, obscure, or alter any notice of Delmar Cengage Learning's intellectual property rights present on or in the Licensed Content, including, but not limited to, copyright, trademark, and/or patent notices; or (iii) disassemble, decompile, translate, reverse engineer, or otherwise reduce the Licensed Content.

2.0 TERMINATION

2.1 Delmar Cengage Learning may at any time (without prejudice to its other rights or remedies) immediately terminate this Agreement and/or suspend access to some or all of the Licensed Content, in the event that the End User does not comply with any of the terms and conditions of this Agreement. In the event of such termination by Delmar Cengage Learning, the End User shall immediately return any and all copies of the Licensed Content to Delmar Cengage Learning.

3.0 PROPRIETARY RIGHTS

3.1 The End User acknowledges that Delmar Cengage Learning owns all rights, title and interest, including, but not limited to all copyright rights therein, in and to the Licensed Content, and that the End User shall not take any action inconsistent with such ownership. The Licensed Content is protected by U.S., Canadian and other applicable copyright laws and by international treaties, including the Berne Convention and the Universal Copyright Convention. Nothing contained in this Agreement shall be construed as granting the End User any ownership rights in or to the Licensed Content.

3.2 Delmar Cengage Learning reserves the right at any time to withdraw from the Licensed Content any item or part of an item for which it no longer retains the right to publish, or which it has reasonable grounds to believe infringes copyright or is defamatory, unlawful, or otherwise objectionable.

4.0 PROTECTION AND SECURITY

4.1 The End User shall use its best efforts and take all reasonable steps to safeguard its copy of the Licensed Content to ensure that no unauthorized reproduction, publication, disclosure, modification, or distribution of the Licensed Content, in whole or in part, is made. To the extent that the End User becomes aware of any such unauthorized use of the Licensed Content, the End User shall immediately notify Delmar Cengage Learning. Notification of such violations may be made by sending an e-mail to delmarhelp@cengage.com.

5.0 MISUSE OF THE LICENSED PRODUCT

5.1 In the event that the End User uses the Licensed Content in violation of this Agreement, Delmar Cengage Learning shall have the option of electing liquidated damages, which shall include all profits generated by the End User's use of the Licensed Content plus interest computed at the maximum rate permitted by law and all legal fees and other expenses incurred by Delmar Cengage Learning in enforcing its rights, plus penalties.

6.0 FEDERAL GOVERNMENT CLIENTS

6.1 Except as expressly authorized by Delmar Cengage Learning, Federal Government clients obtain only the rights specified in this Agreement and no other rights. The Government acknowledges that (i) all software and related documentation incorporated in the Licensed Content is existing commercial computer software within the meaning of FAR 27.405(b)(2); and (2) all other data delivered in whatever form, is limited rights data within the meaning of FAR 27.401. The restrictions in this section are acceptable as consistent with the Government's need for software and other data under this Agreement.

7.0 DISCLAIMER OF WARRANTIES AND LIABILITIES

7.1 Although Delmar Cengage Learning believes the Licensed Content to be reliable, Delmar Cengage Learning does not guarantee or warrant (i) any information or materials contained in or produced by the Licensed Content, (ii) the accuracy, completeness or reliability of the Licensed Content, or (iii) that the Licensed Content is free from errors or other material defects. THE LICENSED PRODUCT IS PROVIDED "AS IS," WITHOUT ANY WARRANTY OF ANY KIND AND DELMAR CENGAGE LEARNING DISCLAIMS ANY AND ALL WARRANTIES, EXPRESSED OR IMPLIED, INCLUDING, WITHOUT LIMITATION, WARRANTIES OF MERCHANTABILITY OR FITNESS FOR A PARTICULAR PURPOSE. IN NO EVENT SHALL DELMAR CENGAGE LEARNING BE LIABLE FOR: INDIRECT, SPECIAL, PUNITIVE OR CONSEQUENTIAL DAMAGES INCLUDING FOR LOST PROFITS, LOST DATA, OR OTHERWISE. IN NO EVENT SHALL DELMAR CENGAGE LEARNING'S AGGREGATE LIABILITY HEREUNDER, WHETHER ARISING IN CONTRACT, TORT, STRICT LIABILITY OR OTHERWISE, EXCEED THE AMOUNT OF FEES PAID BY THE END USER HEREUNDER FOR THE LICENSE OF THE LICENSED CONTENT.

8.0 GENERAL

8.1 <u>Entire Agreement</u>. This Agreement shall constitute the entire Agreement between the Parties and supercedes all prior Agreements and understandings oral or written relating to the subject matter hereof.

8.2 <u>Enhancements/Modifications of Licensed Content</u>. From time to time, and in Delmar Cengage Learning's sole discretion, Delmar Cengage Learning may advise the End User of updates, upgrades, enhancements and/or improvements to the Licensed Content, and may permit the End User to access and use, subject to the terms and conditions of this Agreement, such modifications, upon payment of prices as may be established by Delmar Cengage Learning.

8.3 <u>No Export</u>. The End User shall use the Licensed Content solely in the United States and shall not transfer or export, directly or indirectly, the Licensed Content outside the United States.

8.4 <u>Severability</u>. If any provision of this Agreement is invalid, illegal, or unenforceable under any applicable statute or rule of law, the provision shall be deemed omitted to the extent that it is invalid, illegal, or unenforceable. In such a case, the remainder of the Agreement shall be construed in a manner as to give greatest effect to the original intention of the parties hereto.

8.5 <u>Waiver</u>. The waiver of any right or failure of either party to exercise in any respect any right provided in this Agreement in any instance shall not be deemed to be a waiver of such right in the future or a waiver of any other right under this Agreement.

8.6 <u>Choice of Law/Venue</u>. This Agreement shall be interpreted, construed, and governed by and in accordance with the laws of the State of New York, applicable to contracts executed and to be wholly preformed therein, without regard to its principles governing conflicts of law. Each party agrees that any proceeding arising out of or relating to this Agreement or the breach or threatened breach of this Agreement may be commenced and prosecuted in a court in the State and County of New York. Each party consents and submits to the nonexclusive personal jurisdiction of any court in the State and County of New York in respect of any such proceeding.

8.7 <u>Acknowledgment</u>. By opening this package and/or by accessing the Licensed Content on this Web site, THE END USER ACKNOWLEDGES THAT IT HAS READ THIS AGREEMENT, UNDERSTANDS IT, AND AGREES TO BE BOUND BY ITS TERMS AND CONDITIONS. IF YOU DO NOT ACCEPT THESE TERMS AND CONDITIONS, YOU MUST NOT ACCESS THE LICENSED CONTENT AND RETURN THE LICENSED PRODUCT TO DELMAR CENGAGE LEARNING (WITHIN 30 CALENDAR DAYS OF THE END USER'S PURCHASE) WITH PROOF OF PAYMENT ACCEPTABLE TO DELMAR CENGAGE LEARNING, FOR A CREDIT OR A REFUND. Should the End User have any questions/comments regarding this Agreement, please contact Delmar Cengage Learning at **delmar.help@cengage.com**.